HISTORY OF AMERICAN THOUGHT AND CULTURE

Paul S. Boyer, *General Editor*

Let Your Life Speak

A STUDY OF POLITICS, RELIGION, AND ANTINUCLEAR WEAPONS ACTIVISM

Robert D. Holsworth

The University of Wisconsin Press

The University of Wisconsin Press
114 North Murray Street
Madison, Wisconsin 53715

The University of Wisconsin Press, Ltd.
1 Gower Street
London WC1E 6HA, England

Library of Congress Cataloging-in-Publication Data

Holsworth, Robert D.
   Let your life speak: a study of politics, religion, and
antinuclear weapons activism/Robert D. Holsworth.
      236 p.   cm.—(History of American thought and culture)
      Bibliography: pp. 217–220.
      Includes index.
      1. Nuclear warfare—Religious aspects—Christianity—Case studies.
   2. Christianity and politics—Case studies.   3. Antinuclear
   movement—Virginia—Richmond Region—History.   4. Richmond (Va.)—
   Church history—20th century.   I. Title.   II. Series.
   BR115.A85H65   1989
   261.8′73—dc19   88-40436
   ISBN 0-299-12090-2 cloth; ISBN 0-299-12094-5 (pbk.)

To the memory of my mother, Katherine Holsworth

Contents

Acknowledgments

I HAVE incurred a number of debts in researching and writing this book. I am grateful to the activists in Richmond for giving generously of their time to answer my questions. Herb Hirsch and Scott Keeter, two of my colleagues in Political Science at Virginia Commonwealth University, read parts of the manuscript and offered helpful comments. I was also aided by constructive criticism of the work by numerous political scientists at various conferences in the last few years, by Paul Boyer and Marlie Wasserman, and by the readers from the University of Wisconsin Press. The staff at the University of Wisconsin Press is an extraordinarily skillful and helpful team. My other colleagues in Political Science and friends here in Richmond have created an atmosphere in which it was enjoyable to work and write. Marianne Graves expertly typed the manuscript. All these people have contributed to what is interesting and valuable in the book. Responsibility for its shortcomings is mine alone.

Chapter Four, "A World Worth Living In," first appeared in significantly altered form in *The Massachusetts Review*.

LET YOUR LIFE SPEAK

Prologue

IN THE fall of 1981, discussion of religiously motivated political participation focused almost exclusively on the Moral Majority and other right-wing religious organizations. The election of Ronald Reagan, the bulging coffers of television ministers, and the confident talk about implementing a conservative social agenda led many to view the religious Right as an emerging political juggernaut. I was impressed by the reports of the remarkable fund-raising accomplishments of the religious Right and the evidently successful electoral campaigns it had waged against liberal politicians. Yet my own experience left me a bit puzzled by the portrait of it as a formidable grassroots machine. Despite living in a generally conservative area located in the Reverend Jerry Falwell's home state, I saw little evidence of the Moral Majority's clout. Indeed, the grassroots activism in Richmond that was religiously motivated had its origins in an outlook quite contrary to that of the evangelical Right. In the spring and summer of 1981, a number of local churches hosted teach-ins critical of official policy in El Salvador and the entire Central American region. Religious adult education classes were offering sessions on "The Church and Nuclear War." And the area's most outspoken religious leader, the Catholic bishop Walter Sullivan, was fast gaining a reputation for his critical stance not only on nuclear weapons policy but also on President Reagan's budgetary priorities and U.S. involvement in Central America.

Moreover, it became clear that there was a fledgling organizational structure framing this local activism. An entity called the Richmond Peace Education Center had been established in 1980 and 1981. The impetus came from people in the local churches who were concerned that the religious community was not giving effective witness to peace when a program of remilitarization was increasing the threat of nuclear confrontation. The

3

center was functioning as a central resource base in the area for peace-related activities. It had a book and film library; it maintained a speakers' bureau of men and women trained to address community groups on the facts of the arms race and the threat of nuclear war; and it published a monthly newsletter containing information about military policy and disarmament, reflections on issues of peace and justice written by members of the local community, and a calendar noting events of possible interest scheduled in the city or the region. Steve Hodges, the coordinator of the center, quickly became the spokesperson for the peace community and an important leader in it.

Since the formation of the Richmond Peace Education Center, other groups had been started or revived in the city. Catholics had formed a local chapter of Pax Christi International. There were peace fellowships begun in other churches. A War Tax Alternatives Group (WARTAG) was meeting to acquaint people with the possibility of tax resistance and to support those already engaged in it. It too was composed almost entirely of religiously motivated activists. A more secular organization, the Women's International League for Peace and Freedom, was experiencing a resurgence. The Richmond Nuclear Freeze campaign was taking root and commencing a petition drive.

The membership of these groups frequently overlapped. I estimated that, taken together, there were about seventy-five to one hundred people working actively on behalf of peace issues. Numerically, this might not appear especially significant. Yet it was probably not much smaller than the number of people in the area who devoted an equivalent amount of energy to the local Democratic party.

At that time, I decided to begin a study of people whose religious beliefs motivated them to become involved with the peace movement. My original intent was to describe and explain the "hidden side" of religious activism in the eighties. I wanted to show the persistence of perfectionist and social gospel traditions of political engagement during a period when American liberalism was in retreat against a conservative assault. Furthermore, I was interested in discovering what led these people to develop this commitment when the drift of the times seemed to be moving against them. What could they possibly think would be the outcome of their efforts? To begin to address these matters, I embarked on an extensive program of participant observation. I attended most of the public programs sponsored by the various groups in the Richmond peace community, ranging from lectures by well-known figures from outside the area, such as William Sloane Coffin, to seminars on tax resistance for people interested in protesting government budgetary policies on their income tax return. I also observed the organizational and strategy sessions of a number of local groups.

To complement these observations, I conducted a series of in-depth interviews with a dozen people in the peace community, a large majority of whom were committed to the issue because of their religious faith. These conversations ranged over a variety of subjects, but they followed a similar format. The interviews began by exploring the genesis of the activists' commitment to the antinuclear weapons movement. This normally resulted in a discussion of family influence ("My parents were totally apolitical" or "My aunt was a political boss in Cleveland"), previous moral and political commitments, and significant events or people that had been important to the person. The next segment of the interviews examined the moral and political values that the activists currently hold. I asked the men and women to whom I spoke what general concepts such as freedom, equality, and democracy meant to them. I probed their feelings about the American economy and culture and how they viewed their own responsibilities as citizens of this nation. Moreover, I asked them to tell me what issues they felt were most important and how they drew the connections between these matters and their work on behalf of peace. Observing their public activities for a significant amount of time, I attempted to see how closely their ideas meshed with the actual practice of the movement. The final interviews, conducted toward the end of the study, concentrated on the participants' assessments of their activities. I questioned them about the changes which they saw in their own lives that were related to their involvement. We also talked about where they thought the movement had succeeded, where it had failed, and what direction they believed it ought to take in the future.

The study was barely four months old when its original intent was, in some ways, transformed by the turn of events within the United States. The policies and rhetoric associated with President Reagan's military buildup generated much discontent in the country. Opposition to American involvement in El Salvador and Central America became a rallying point for the critics of the Reagan administration. More important, the antinuclear weapons movement that had lain dormant for almost twenty years was reinvigorated as people expressed their anxieties about the possibility that the deterioration in superpower relations made a nuclear confrontation more likely. By the spring and summer of 1982, peace activists across the nation had succeeded in mobilizing extensive support.

Politicians who had been silent on defense issues for years now spoke vigorously on behalf of the nuclear freeze. George Kennan, the former diplomat and prominent Soviet historian, claimed that "the public discussion of the problems presented by nuclear weaponry which is now taking place in this country is going to go down in history . . . as the most significant that any democratic society has ever engaged in."[1] And while most conservative supporters of President Reagan worked to discredit the freeze proposal as simplistic and possibly dangerous, there were some notable defections from the ranks. James J. Kilpatrick, for example, looked favorably upon the movement, remarking that since 1945 the world has witnessed "37 years of lunacy, of idiots racing against imbeciles, of civilized nations staggering blindly toward a finish line of unspeakable peril. . . . The prevention of nuclear war is on its way to becoming the most popular cause in the world."[2]

In 1982, Kilpatrick's words appeared to be only slightly hyperbolic. The year saw the largest political demonstration ever held in the United States as between a half million and one million people gathered in New York City to register their discontentment with existing nuclear policies. Freeze resolutions passed 425 New England town meetings, 144 city councils, and 13 state legislatures. The movement was active in more than three hundred congressional districts in at least forty-eight states. Later that year in November, the freeze swept to victory in seven of the eight states that held referenda on the issue. The national councils of most church denominations endorsed the freeze and even stronger disarmament resolutions. What I had begun as an examination of a fringe group was now a case study of people who had helped to introduce a new element into the political debate of the eighties.

Most of the commentary acknowledged that religiously motivated activism on a grassroots level gave the movement its distinctive coloring. But the acknowledgment of the religious and community basis of the movement usually only disguised the lack of attention that was actually paid to it. With some notable exceptions, commentators rarely went beyond mentioning these facts to exploring the activities that took place in localities. How did these participants come to hold their beliefs? What strategies did they follow to influence others? What did they think they could accomplish in areas of the country where peace activism had previously been largely nonexistent? How did they attempt to organize their own lives—in their families and with each other—to embody their ideas about peace and social justice? What difficulties did they face in putting an alternative global vision on a solid local footing? How did they deal with the disappointments that accompany political activism when the freeze movement did not alter the outcome of the 1984 presidential elections and when

President Reagan successfully refocused public attention from the freeze to his own Strategic Defense Initiative?

This book attempts to answer these questions. I try to show how religious faith has been a spur to political commitment among the activists in Richmond. I describe how particular understandings of Christianity prompted people to become involved in the antinuclear movement and how their religious faith motivated them to devote their energies to a cause at a time when a so-called rational analysis of the chances of success may well have vitiated the commitment. I tell how this faith led them to alter their own living routines, how it prompted some to consider civil disobedience, and how it sustained the activists when the movement did not achieve all that they had hoped it might accomplish.

The organizing theme of the work is that the efforts of these religiously motivated activists are rooted in a personalist approach to political change. This orientation can be seen in the participants' ideas about citizenship; it can be viewed in their attempt to build a local community which serves as a model for the society they are trying to build; and it can be observed in the way they strive to relate lifestyle choices and child rearing to their beliefs about peace and justice. I hope that the description and analysis of this perspective is worthwhile, regardless of how one evaluates the success or failure of the freeze movement. Personalism is not a fully developed philosophy with identifiable positions on epistemology, human nature, and the proper role of government. But it is an orientation that combines ideas about the practical and moral shortcomings of modern politics with notions about how these problems can be addressed, and it is becoming, I think, increasingly visible in contemporary reform movements. The principal features of the personalist approach and its application to antinuclear weapons politics are outlined below.

1. PERSONAL OBLIGATION. Individuals must assume responsibility for the problems that they see in the world. This duty is not lessened by the magnitude of the task to be confronted or the difficulty of its successful completion. Apathy and inaction with respect to the nuclear arms race cannot be justified by referring to the odds against disarmament, because the demands of morality are not grounded in arithmetical calculations. The witness furnished by faithful action has a value that is partially independent of its immediate effectiveness.

2. THE HARMONY OF POLITICAL BELIEF AND PERSONAL LIFE. The commitment to creating a peaceful world on a global level should be reflected in the conduct of one's personal life. Individuals should

examine their own character, temperament, and lifestyle to see if these are consistent with their professed support for peace and disarmament. They should look at their interaction with friends, their family relationships, their consumption of resources, and their occupational goals. They should be open to the possibility of making significant changes in their manner of living. While a sense of personal wholeness can never be perfectly achieved, it is a goal toward which individuals should strive.

3. THE SIGNIFICANCE OF LOCAL ACTION. Activists must work locally as well as nationally and internationally on behalf of their cause. Significant and enduring change of national policy will necessarily be related to cultural changes resulting from grassroots organizing. Peace making is a face-to-face activity with neighbors and townspeople and not just a relatively anonymous process conducted by diplomatic exchanges between governments. Only local action will provide the foundational support for the changes in national policy that will reflect a genuine commitment to disarmament.

4. THE IMPERATIVE OF COMMUNITY. Although working for change can be a risky and lonely task, it should be embedded within a communal context. Such a community serves a therapeutic function, as it helps to alleviate the loneliness and disappointment that will inevitably be experienced. It enables individuals to maintain their commitment and provides the emotional resources that can sustain it. More important, communities serve as living examples of the changes that can be made in the larger world. By transforming their own lives, activists show that faithful communities are possible and that there are realistic alternatives for individuals dissatisfied with the quality of contemporary life.

5. THE INTERDEPENDENCE OF POLITICAL AND CULTURAL REFORM. Political issues cannot be examined or adequately addressed in isolation. In American society, some of the obstacles to stopping the arms race include the general direction of the nation's foreign policy, economic priorities, and excessively materialistic culture. Peace activists should build coalitions with groups who share their general assessment of these issues and they should work to illuminate the connections between the threat of nuclear war, intervention in the Third World, and social justice at home. In the 1980s, this entails involvement in efforts to oppose U.S. policy in Central America and an attempt to broaden the movement beyond its traditional white middle-class base.

6. THE RELEVANCE OF HOUSEHOLD VALUES TO THE POLITICAL WORLD. There are many values normally excluded from public life and relegated to the household and private relationships that should be made politically relevant. Politics has become an activity defined by the pursuit of material advantage and the acquisition of power for socially irresponsible purposes. Citizens need to think of how hope, trust, friendship, compassion, reconciliation, love, and faithfulness can be incorporated into public life. Preventing nuclear war and creating a more humane society depend, to a large extent, on the capacity to bring these themes to bear on the conduct of politics. What is called realism in the political world is increasingly becoming a prescription for brutality, injustice, and, perhaps, global annihilation.

In historical terms, personalism is most closely associated with Emmanuel Mounier and the ideas expressed in the French journal *Esprit*. From 1930 to 1950 Mounier labored to demonstrate how a religiously informed political analysis need not endorse the reactionary views that had been so prominent in French Catholicism. Mounier wanted to "bear witness" to what he labeled the established disorder and to discover a path to political reform that would avoid the impoverished individualism of contemporary liberalism and the ruthless collectivism of authoritarian Marxism. In his own words, he desired "to free the sense of the person from individualist errors and the sense of communion from collectivist errors."[3] To accomplish this, he criticized the politics of liberal democracy, the moral and economic consequences of capitalism, and the spiritual effects of a materialistic culture, while calling individuals to a life of religiously informed public engagement. In the United States, Dorothy Day and Peter Maupin's Catholic Worker movement was, in part, an explicit effort to apply Mounier's ideas in an American context.

The features that I have described as characteristic of a contemporary personalist approach are slightly different from those articulated by Mounier and Day. But these are, I think, in keeping with the original spirit of the term and with Mounier's belief that personalism had to be modified according to the circumstances of an era. The decision to refurbish it to describe an ongoing movement comes from a belief that the personalist label helps to draw our attention to aspects of politics that might otherwise be ignored. In particular, it brings into focus the movement's insistence that individuals embody their beliefs in the details of their lives, on its emphasis on the need to build a more communal orientation in American life, and on its endorsement of local action, even with regard to global dilemmas of nuclear security. I believe that personalism captures these emphases more accurately than terms such as liberal reformism, postmaterialism, or new-class politics that could be applied to the activities described here.

A number of features of the personalist approach contributed to the movement's appeal. In the first place, personalism resonates with certain prominent themes in the American political tradition. It calls, for instance, upon widely held beliefs regarding individual responsibility and optimism about the future. Americans have traditionally believed that individuals should take control of their fates, that they should respond to setbacks and defeats with renewed commitment, and that sheer persistence will enable them to overcome the obstacles in their path. Personalism embraces this ethos, but does so with a curious political twist, applying it to the fatalism often present in discussions of contemporary politics. It suggests that individuals are responsible for problems in the world, that apathy is not a morally appropriate response, and that by pooling resources, individuals might be effective in promoting change. Personalism thus draws upon sentiments normally attached to the conditions for achieving material success in contemporary America and utilizes these on behalf of constructing a citizens' movement.

Personalism is also compatible with the distrust of authority and the suspicion of centralized power that have long been part of American political culture and that became even more prevalent in the wake of Vietnam and Watergate. For the most part, conservative political figures have been able to capitalize on this, pointing to government inefficiency as a rationale for reducing social welfare and deregulating business. But the antinuclear movement has demonstrated that these sentiments can serve other purposes as well. Quotations from presidential advisers about the possibility of prevailing in a nuclear war, the stockpiling of arms to the point where the Soviet Union could be destroyed twenty times over, and exposés of indefensible waste in the Defense Department all lend credence to the claim that the public should be skeptical of the policies supposedly designed to protect its security.

A third reason for personalism's attractiveness is that it harmonizes with the ambivalent feelings that many people have about the direction of modern life. Participants in the movement adhere to ideas about self-development and support causes that have typically been associated with a "progressive" approach to life. But they also believe that there is something very troubling and even fundamentally deficient with the direction in which modern societies are moving. Individuals seem to be helpless and at the mercy of decisions taken by large bureaucratic organizations. The potential annihilation of all life by nuclear weapons is the most grievous expression of this tendency, one which they see in other parts of the culture as well. Personalists appeal to this sense of a world gone awry and suggest that others who share this feeling have recognized an important problem of contemporary life. By speaking about possible changes in one's daily life and by working to construct alternative communities, personalists offer an immediate sense of hope and furnish an experience that may help to sustain it.

At the same time, many of the difficulties which the activists faced are themselves related to the personalist approach that they had adopted. To some extent, these problems have to do with the imprecision and vagueness of personalist assumptions. What are the principal features of a peaceful world and how will it be governed? What will be the relationship between local communities, nation-states, and a global world order? How will a nonmaterialistic, nonconsumerist society operate? What precisely is meant by combining peace with economic justice? How would the United States actually proceed from here to there and what would the process entail in other nations? In many instances, the activists themselves were still struggling to answer questions that most people would want resolved before giving full support to the movement. They were especially weak on questions related to the long-term political strategy of the movement.

Some of the problems which confronted the activists were, I think, a consequence of the distance which separated their ideas about American politics and culture from those held by the majority of the people whom they were interested in reaching. Although personalism is consistent with some elements in American political culture, it is not clearly compatible with others. The personalist suggestion that political life can be organized according to the morality that guides interpersonal relationships is a good example. In a highly bureaucratic and impersonal world, such a claim can tap heartfelt sentiments, but it can also appear to be naive in an imperfect and volatile international situation. Indeed, many Americans believe that it is a dangerous stance to take with respect to the Soviet Union, one that will ultimately result in a loss of American freedom. They believe that security is best guaranteed by a steady pursuit of national interest untrammeled by moral considerations.

Personalist arguments about individual responsibility face a different but no less formidable set of obstacles. The personalist assumption that the professed values of individuals ought to be embodied in their lives is a proposition that commands widespread assent. Translated into specific terms, however, people may well find these demands too strenuous to accommodate without a major upheaval in their lives. Parents, for example, may endorse the notion that they should promote a commitment to peace and justice among their children. But they find the suggestion that the family volunteer at the soup kitchen on Wednesday evenings overly demanding. People may agree that the society is excessively materialistic, but they may also find it very difficult to take concrete steps to loosen their connection to the consumerist ethos. The demanding nature of personalist ideals has created serious tensions in the lives of some of the participants.

Finally, personalist ideals are sometimes expressed in ways that are, ultimately, antipolitical and almost guaranteed to preclude dialogue with the very people activists would like to persuade. I do not believe that this is a necessary feature of personalist ideas nor a defining characteristic of the men and women to whom I spoke. Indeed, I take issue in the book with those who have argued that the movement is inherently antipolitical. What I do claim, however, is that the skepticism about political authority that contributes to the movement's strength and appeal also contains an underside that, on certain occasions, leads some activists away from politics and the effort to engage other citizens in political dialogue.

I have organized the book with the intention of showing the roots of the personalist orientation, its actual practice among the activists in Richmond, its strengths and weaknesses as a method of political education, and, finally, its wider implications as an approach to political reform in the United States. Chapter 1 explains the intellectual origins of antinuclear political theology and examines changes within the churches that have contributed to its present relevance. I describe how developments within the Catholic church since Vatican II have meshed, in important ways, with the outlook of religious pacifists and the revival of radical evangelicalism within Protestant denominations to form a relatively consistent position on the nature of the nuclear threat and the responsibility of Christians in the face of it. This convergence can be seen in the pastoral letter of the Catholic bishops on nuclear war, in the editorial outlook of a number of Christian magazines, and in the official pronouncements of many Protestant denominations about nuclear war. The literature of antinuclear political theology routinely voices personalist themes, though it does not always adequately examine the tensions contained in this approach to political change.

Chapter 2 sketches the backgrounds of four of the local activists in Richmond. It shows how faith has been important in animating the political commitments of people from three different religious traditions. It also illustrates how particular forms of religiously motivated political commitment contributed to the origins and growth of peace activism in Richmond. The personal narratives which form the bulk of the chapter also introduce certain representative themes—the necessity of practicing a consistent Christianity, the effort to combine merciful action with political reform, and the equation of good citizenry with religious witnessing—that are vital to the analysis of the succeeding chapters. In addition, these narratives raise issues such as the political inexperience of the activists and the demanding nature of personalist ideals, which have made political success difficult to achieve.

Chapter 3 examines the attitude of the participants in the local movement toward citizenship and politics. I suggest that the personalist orientation of the activists generates ambivalent feelings on these matters. On the one hand, the moralistic criterion used to judge American policy and political figures lends itself to a profound pessimism about politics as it is currently practiced. Activists are acutely aware of the compromises and sellouts that frequently occur and of the difficulty in changing policy through the conventional political process. On the other hand, the need to assume personal responsibility for making these changes impels the participants toward the political arena in a variety of ways. In so doing, the activists are attempting to develop a hopeful and redemptive politics in which citizenship is redefined as a form of moral witness. This endeavor provides an interesting alternative to the contemporary practice of citizenship, though it also possesses its own characteristic problems.

Chapter 4 describes how the activists relate their ideas about nuclear weapons to a more general critique of American culture. It shows how many of them believe that the problems of the arms race are related to the excessive materialism of American society, to social injustice, and to an ethos that is not able to adequately reconcile personal freedom with social responsibility. The attention which the religiously motivated activists pay to building and maintaining their own community is, in large measure, an experiment in creating a new, more preferable society in which materialism is reduced and individualism balanced with a sense of communal responsibility. Yet the present limitations of the personalist approach are also evident in the activists' difficulty in explaining how their local experiments might be related to national policy changes and how they might convince more people to join them in their quest to build alternative communities.

Chapter 5 demonstrates how their ideas about refurbishing American culture are reflected in their notions of family life and childhood education. I suggest that the general controversy about nuclear education curriculums has, to some degree, missed the central point of what the movement has been trying to accomplish in this regard. I argue that programs

such as Parenting for Peace and Justice and religious education curriculums are examples of the personalist desire to combine the pursuit of
individual development with a commitment to the wider community and
to posterity. In this sense, antinuclear education shares the conservative
concern with excessive individualism in the contemporary United States.
But it implies that addressing this problem does not require abandoning
progressive notions about self-development that were incorporated into
educational programs during the past twenty years. The chapter suggests
that the personalist effort to encourage self-development and socially responsible activity in children serves more as an indication of the movement's commitment and future direction than as testimony to its actual
accomplishments.

Chapter 6 examines the forms of unconventional politics that have been
practiced by people in the local movement. I look at an effort by some of
the younger members to create an ecumenical Christian community that
would combine a commitment to structural change in the wider society
with traditional acts of Christian mercy. The chapter also analyzes the
halting yet growing effort of the participants to discover forms of civil
disobedience that are morally justified and politically effective. The preparation given to these activities and the growing interest in them are evidence
of the personalist demand that individuals be willing to take risks for their
beliefs. But the failures of the ecumenical community and the difficulty in
developing mass campaigns of civil disobedience reflect both the internal
dilemmas of building a peace community and the limits of the movement's
present appeal to the wider culture.

Chapter 7 examines the successes and failures of the activists in Richmond, presents their assessment of what participation has meant to their
lives, and analyzes their ideas about future directions for the movement. In
general, the participants point to the endurance of their movement and its
institutionalization as positive accomplishments. They also speak with pride
about the development of their "peace community" and the changes that
have taken place in their own thinking as a result of this experience. The
most frequently mentioned disappointment has been their inability to persuade large numbers of people to support their ideas about the need for arms
reduction and cultural reform in a manner that would make for a political
difference. The experiences of the past four years have largely reinforced the
personalist beliefs of the men and women to whom I spoke. This has led, I
argue, both to creative efforts to overcome the movement's problems and to
a certain hardening of outlook that may well be counterproductive.

The final chapter addresses the issue of representativeness by placing the activists in Richmond, the recent antinuclear movement in general, and the concept of personalist politics within a broader framework.[4] I suggest that elements of a personalist politics described here are important in other predominantly middle-class movements of the past twenty-five years, most notably environmentalism and feminism. In each of these movements, there were variants which protested against the logic that seemed to be inherent in large, bureaucratic states. Participants maintained that there were parts of human experience, most often associated with the caring and nurturing capacities of people, that had been defined as irrelevant by the dominant powers in our society. They called for a general "disarming" of this logic, hoping to restore a sense of wholeness to a fragmented world poised on the brink of self-destruction. They have urged individuals to begin the process of restoration in their own lives and their own communities. The chapter also suggests that some personalist features can be discerned in the activities of Christian conservatives. Although the political outlook of the religious Right is far different from that described in the body of this book, I suggest that its use of personalist themes helps to show why some of the sentiments tapped by the activists in Richmond are likely to have continuing influence on the direction of contemporary society.

Before delving into the body of the work, I would like to comment briefly about the case-study approach taken here. The attempt to examine a local movement and frame it within a larger context is a common practice in historical circles. It is less common, though by no means entirely absent, within mainstream social science. The decision to proceed in this manner was made deliberately. Too often, I think, the quest to develop researchable generalizations prompts scholars to ignore or even to "lose" the movement that is being examined. We might not be sufficiently attentive to the beliefs and stories of the participants or to the courage and foolhardiness that they sometimes exhibit. It would be especially ironic and regrettable if this happened while discussing a "personalist" approach to political change. To adopt this method does not mean that I remain uncritical of the movement or inattentive to some of the broader questions that its ideas and activities raise. It only means that these reflections and criticisms emerge from what I hope is a clear account of the participants' beliefs and practices.

1

Antinuclear Political Theology

THERE ARE many reasons why a peace movement emerged in the United States during the early eighties. The impetus from European antinuclear protests was considerable, as demonstrations in England, the Netherlands, and West Germany sensitized many Americans to the controversy surrounding the proposed modernization of NATO forces. Here at home a small, but relatively influential, group of scientists and physicians lent their prestige and organizational skill to the cause of weapons reductions. Groups such as the Union of Concerned Scientists, the Federation of American Scientists, and the Physicians for Social Responsibility maintain a nationwide communications network, help to fund local programs, and are an invaluable source of information for activists across the nation. At least a score of Nobel laureates can be mobilized to oppose the funding and development of many new weapons systems and to support fairly radical recommendations about disarmament. Finally, it would be difficult to overestimate the influence exercised by Ronald Reagan and members of his administration in prompting Americans to become concerned about the threat of nuclear war. While Reagan's geniality during his first campaign for the presidency was effective in downplaying fears of his potential dangerousness, it did not take long for the rhetoric in Washington to kindle people's anxieties. Loose and irresponsible talk about military superiority, about prevailing in a nuclear exchange and then surviving it by passing out shovels to the population, led many citizens to question the inclinations and policies of the Reagan entourage.

But it is also evident that the movement never would have become as strong as it did or assume the particular shape it has taken if the involvement of the Christian churches had not been central to it. While the most attention has been paid to the preparation and publication of the Catholic bishops' pastoral on nuclear arms, other church communities have not neglected the issue. The synods of various Protestant denominations have endorsed the freeze and condemned further escalation of the arms race. In hundreds of localities across the nation, congregations have started study groups on the relation between faith and nuclear arms and church members have debated the stance that people of faith ought to assume about the defense posture of the United States. Activists from the churches are often the backbone of the movement, organizing, fund raising, licking envelopes, and writing letters to the editor.

Within religious circles, a proliferation of books, articles, pamphlets, and study guides have been published during the past ten years, providing a Christian justification for opposing and taking various kinds of action against the present direction in nuclear weapons policy. Many of these works also relate nuclear weapons policy to other matters, from the economics of capitalism to the dilemmas of raising children in a materialistic culture. Although most of this material has not been principally directed toward an academic audience, some of it is theologically and politically sophisticated. A number of publications have also been composed especially for children and teenagers enrolled in religious education classes. Taken together, these works of antinuclear political theology provide an intellectual foundation and a programmatic orientation for the participation of Christians in the political debate about the arms race.

This chapter examines and analyzes the background and content of antinuclear political theology. It begins by outlining its historical roots in religious pacifism, radical evangelicalism, and the changes in the Catholic church that were the outcome of the Second Vatican Council. The second part of the chapter describes how two principal lines of argument—the just-war theory and Christian pacifism—are used by antinuclear weapons activists today to justify their position. The final section shows how these two approaches share a number of common assumptions about the possibility of fighting a limited nuclear war, the role of the United States in world affairs, and the obligations of a Christian in the modern world. But these approaches also contain unresolved tensions about the relationship between religion and politics that can be discerned in the contemporary antinuclear weapons movement.

Roots

Christian pacifism is one source from which antinuclear political theology draws its ideas. Since the early days of Christianity when many of its converts refused to bear arms for the Roman Empire, pacifism has periodically surfaced as a response to the war-making tendencies of political entities. In modern America, pacifism has been associated most frequently with the so-called historic peace churches—the Quakers, the Mennonites, and the Church of the Brethren—and with the Jehovah's Witnesses. On many occasions, pacifists have not posed a direct challenge to the state insofar as they concentrated primarily on obtaining recognition for their beliefs and eschewed working to change the political order. At times, however, pacifism has become a dissident ideology as its supporters have sought to imbue the political world with its principles. Pacifists have thus been active in numerous antiwar movements and have also seen fit to apply their ideas about human rights and the dignity of all people to related causes. In American society, pacifists were prominent in the abolitionist crusade, in the early days of the civil rights movement, in prison reform, and in agitation against capital punishment.

Religious pacifists have always been part of the antinuclear weapons movement in the United States. During World War II, pacifists who had accepted the option of alternative service were placed in Civilian Public Service camps. Many of those who declined spent the war years in prison. At this time, the magazine *Fellowship* was one of the principal organs of pacifist communication. Edited by A. J. Muste for the Fellowship of Reconciliation, its twin foci during the war were conditions in the CPS camps and the prisons and the imperative of bringing the fighting to a negotiated conclusion. *Fellowship* had opposed the war on the classical pacifist ground that it was immoral to kill other human beings, but it had also maintained that technological advances made it increasingly difficult to legitimate war according to traditional just-war theory. Muste furnished a running commentary on the totalistic and nondiscriminatory nature of modern warfare. He felt that the obliteration bombing conducted by the Allies was a perfect example of how the "just participant" was compelled to match, if not outdo, the evil of the original aggressor. When the fighting was terminated with the bombings of Hiroshima and Nagasaki, *Fellowship* viewed it as devastating proof of its assertions, a cosmic disturbance calling for universal repentance.[1]

In the years immediately following the war, religious pacifists became active in the initial movement to control atomic weaponry, a crusade whose most celebrated participants were the atomic scientists themselves.[2] Arguing against Reinhold Niebuhr's contention that political behavior could not be patterned on the model of individual morality, Muste contended that Christians were called to give witness to their belief in ways that could help to establish the Kingdom of God on earth. He believed that atomic weapons were the culmination of a trend in modern technological societies which had rendered human life increasingly meaningless. Prefiguring some of the arguments that were to be central to the work of social critics such as Jacques Ellul and Herbert Marcuse, Muste wrote that "we live in an age where the individual is in danger of becoming a cipher. He is overwhelmed by the vast and intricate technological machinery around which he is increasingly dependent and by which he is increasingly regimented in peace and war."[3] In the face of this centralized, technological juggernaut, Muste implored individuals to take responsibility for the fate of the world, to reassert the claims of conscience against those who would find such statements naive and idealistic. The assumption of personal responsibility was, for Muste, a paradigmatic act that symbolized the character transformation and moral courage required for genuine disarmament. "It is the individual conscience against the atomic bomb which constitutes our sole safeguard."[4]

Dorothy Day and others in the Catholic Worker movement concurred with the personalist orientation of Muste's pacifism. She felt that it was critical for individuals to learn how to "say no" to the powerful when their dictates violated individual conscience and the message of the gospel. Day insisted that this no-saying be connected to personal humility and a serving demeanor. People in the Catholic Worker movement rejected forms of radicalism in which commitment to structural change was not complemented and tempered by merciful activities. They believed that work on behalf of peace and social justice ought to be rooted in the personal lives of activists who followed the plain but demanding gospel commands not to kill, but to feed the hungry, clothe the naked, and shelter the homeless. The distinctive contribution of Day and the Catholic Worker activists was their attribution of importance to community, underscoring the notion that social change was best undertaken by people who were part of communities of resistance and reconstruction—witnessing to injustice, ministering to the disadvantaged, and embodying a living alternative to mainstream America.[5]

The political implications of the pacifist stance were not always precisely enunciated. In their heart of hearts, pacifists hoped that the United States might see fit to send a letter to the Soviet Union noting that "we are through with war and preparation for war. We hope you are too and that we may have universal disarmament. But whether you join us or not, we are through. War simply does not make sense any more. . . . We shall do the best we can to secure ourselves against attack. Knowing how desperately poor the rest of the world is, we shall be prepared to share with others a good deal of the resources God has given us. . . . Anyway we prefer giving it away to spending it on atom bombs and death rays. What is left for ourselves we shall enjoy in peace and quietness during the few years that remain to us and our children."[6] Barring the realization of this dream, pacifists became involved in the forties and fifties in a number of campaigns against nuclear weapons. They called for international control of atomic energy and were active in pursuing a test ban. They advocated personal and communal resistance to the nuclear arms race. They engaged in tax resistance; they participated in sit-ins during public evacuations; and they entered testing areas to dramatize their opposition to the further refinement of nuclear weaponry. Far outside the political mainstream in the forties and early fifties, their direct influence was slight. But they were to become key participants in the civil rights struggles of the fifties and they had developed tactics of resistance that were to be central elements of the antiwar protests and the antinuclear agitation of later years.[7]

A second source of antinuclear political theology has been evangelical reformism and radicalism. This statement may appear curious because evangelism is today principally associated with personal religion and political conservatism. Historically, however, this has not always been the case, as the quest for personal holiness and the desire to lead a sanctified life were not divorced from an active engagement with the world. Inspired by a burning earnestness, numerous nineteenth-century reformers combined their quest for salvation with campaigns to eliminate evil in the wider society. In the antislavery, labor reform, and temperance campaigns, they often set their hopes quite high, calling for changes more far-reaching than those endorsed by the typical reformer of the twentieth century. While entreating the individual sinner to repent, they also desired to usher in the millennium. As Timothy Smith has pointed out, "The evangelist played a key role in the widespread attack upon slavery, poverty and greed. They thus helped prepare the way in both theory and practice for what later became known as the social gospel."[8]

From the mid-1960s to the beginnings of the 1980s, the United States experienced a revival of evangelicalism. This was evident in the increasing prominence of personal religion, the self-definition of the churchgoing public, and the tremendous sales of evangelical materials in the religious marketplace. The evangelicals were a varied group, but they shared a number of emphases. They stressed the authority of the Bible, the inadequacy of a formalistic Christianity, the imperative of personal repentance and conversion, and the necessity to spread the Word. Religion was to be heartfelt and publicly expressed. For the most part, the new evangelicals were moderate to conservative in their political outlook. Strong defenders of free enterprise, unremitting critics of communism, and indefatigable opponents of the new permissiveness, they offered few explicit challenges to the political leadership of the nation. Yet for all their praise of American society and for all the prayer breakfasts at the White House and the Pentagon, there was more than a hint of ambivalence in their attitude. In many respects, America was a fallen nation—awash in an orgy of pornography, materialism, and selfishness that could only hasten the country's downfall and the advance of its enemies.[9]

By the start of the seventies, however, a reformist element and a genuine left wing had again become present within American evangelicalism. This latter development was most visible in the magazines *The Other Side* and *The Post-American*. The left-wing evangelicals, or radical Christians as they were fond of calling themselves, professed to be theologically conservative but socially radical. Along with their politically conservative colleagues, they spoke of the need for personal repentance and conversion. They denigrated a "spongy" liberal theology which was insufficiently attentive to the pervasiveness of sin in the world. And they claimed that their ideas were biblically grounded and based in the lessons embodied by the life of Jesus. But they also maintained that mainstream evangelicalism was conveniently ignoring the challenge which the Bible posed to the lifestyle of most Americans and to the content of the government's policies. They suggested that most well-known evangelicals were too comfortable with contemporary America and that, consequently, they had permitted the church to become captured by the princes of the secular world. From the perspective of the left-wing evangelicals, the Bible's injunctions against war were pointed criticisms of the national security state and its denunciations of materialism raised serious questions about the legitimacy of capitalism. Believers were called not to prayer breakfasts with generals and presidents who had ordered the bombing of Southeast Asia but to basic Christian communities that identified with the poor and the outcasts of society while experimenting with alternative values and lifestyles.

Besides offering a theological justification for social activism, left-wing evangelicalism utilized biblical imagery to evaluate the country's political direction. They echoed their more conservative counterparts by employing the image of a fallen nation to characterize the United States, but reached a very different conclusion about its causes and implications. Calling mainstream evangelicalism's interpretation of the Fall "naive, narrow, trivial and misinformed," the radical Christians saw an America with few redeeming qualities.[10] Crass materialism, an unholy war in Vietnam, an unconscionable gulf between rich and poor, and a smug disregard for the rest of suffering humanity indicated how far the nation had strayed from its biblical heritage. "The chaos, the insanity, the brutality that is America can only be adequately explained by the biblical doctrine of the fall; the alienation of the whole of creation from God. The biblical doctrine describes the fall as pervasive, not only affecting persons, but also relationships, institutions, nations, corporations, movements, ideologies—all the principalities and powers."[11]

The political leanings of the radical evangelicals were similar to those of many Christian pacifists, especially those involved in the Catholic Worker movement. They stressed the importance of a personalist orientation toward social change, beginning with individual repentance and the initiation of a new life on the model of Jesus. They also experimented with the formation of Christian communities grounded in biblical faith that would combine interest in the spiritual growth of their participants with merciful action and a commitment to structural change in the wider society. Perhaps the best example of this was the formation and development of the Sojourners community in Washington, D.C. Formed in 1975 by men and women who had been part of the *Post-American* when it had been located in Chicago, the community moved to an inner-city neighborhood in Washington, D.C., to highlight its identification with the poor. The membership developed a variety of ministries to the residents of the surrounding area—hospitality, day care, food cooperatives—while they strove to simplify their lives and loosen their connection to the consumer society. The community also published a magazine, *Sojourners,* that related its call for a biblical lifestyle to a highly critical analysis of the "princes and principalities" of American life. By the end of its first decade of existence in 1984, *Sojourners* had become, in some religious circles, a well-known voice of protest against American foreign policy as well as a practical guidebook to the joys and tribulations of radical Christian living.

The United States Catholic Church's gradual working out of the implications of the Second Vatican Council has been a third source of antinuclear political theology. In the early sixties, Vatican II contributed to a reorientation of the Church's teachings on social issues, a body of thought known since Leo XIII's *Rerum Novarum* encyclical of 1891 as Catholic Social Doctrine. Until the Second Vatican Council, Catholic Social Doctrine was in large measure characterized by its hierarchical formation, abstract tone, and lack of direct challenge to the policies of Western capitalist democracies. It was defined almost exclusively by the pope's pronouncements on social and political issues, rather than by the outcome of a process of discussion and debate among the members of the Church community. Moreover, while the popes did side with the laboring masses and the poor in opposition to the most heartless capitalist practices, their statements were as often intended to combat the appeal of socialism as they were to criticize the the inequities of capitalism.[12] In the United States, the modest critical thrust of Catholic Social Doctrine was further blunted by the hierarchy's interest in assimilating the Church into the culture as a way of avoiding nativist attacks on its alien nature.

Vatican II supplied a way of looking at the world that altered the traditional emphases. John XXIII had spoken of the need for the Church to discern what he called the spirit of the times, a spirit he observed in the demands for freedom and dignity being raised by the poor, by women, and by the colonized peoples of the globe. As Peter Hebblethwaite has written, "No longer does Catholic Social Doctrine simply parachute principles down from great height. Instead, it takes the hopes and aspirations that people really have and reads in them a message from the Holy Spirit."[13] Furthermore, while the Second Vatican Council reserved a special place for pastors and theologians in the interpretation of these signs, it acknowledged that it was the task of the entire people of God, not just the pope, to contribute to the response which the age demanded.

With respect to issues of war and peace, the Second Vatican Council reiterated the condemnations of total war which had been issued by recent popes. The council noted first that "any act of war aimed indiscriminately at the destruction of entire cities or of extensive areas along with their population is a crime against God and man himself. It merits unequivocal and unhesitating condemnation."[14] The council then proceeded to criticize the arms race as a deceitful method for keeping the peace which, in the short term, robbed the poor and, in the long run, undermined the possibility of genuine peace. "The arms race is a treacherous trap for humanity, and one which injures the poor to an intolerable degree. It is much to be feared that if this race persists, it will eventually spawn all the lethal ruin whose path it is now making ready."[15] Finally, it urged both nations and individual Christians to "strain every muscle" to prevent nuclear war and to bring a new cooperativeness and civility to international politics.

In this country, Vatican II ushered in a period of experimentation, examination, and controversy. For many Catholics, its initial effects were experienced in liturgical changes and the abandonment of certain traditional regulations. People debated whether it was better to hear the Mass in English, whether it was preferable to have the priest face the congregation, and whether it was good that Catholics could now eat meat on Friday. But as time passed, the council's broader implications became apparent. The American bishops agonized over their stance toward the U.S. involvement in Vietnam, moving as a body from qualified approval in 1966 to an oppositional posture by the early seventies. During the seventies, the turmoil in Latin America and the controversies in which the Church was embroiled there led numerous American Catholics to become more interested in international affairs at precisely the moment when many cultural observers were lamenting the inward, narcissistic turn of the American population.[16]

The encouragement that Vatican II offered to Catholics desirous of contributing to the formation of the Church's position on the spirit of the times also lent greater legitimacy to previously dissident positions. As David O'Brien has written, "The torrents of self-criticism unleashed by the Council passed the bounds clearly present in the minds of the council fathers, creating a situation of doubt and uncertainty amid wholly new styles of religious thought and action."[17] The opening provided by Vatican II was taken in its most radical direction by the liberation theologians of Latin America who gave a literal reading to the theme of the poor inheriting the earth by wedding the message of the gospel to the revolutionary struggles of the oppressed. But it also called many Catholics within the United States to witness to the ferment of the gospel by exploring the connections between their faith and the pressing social issues of the day. One consequence of this process was a greater willingness to take seriously the manner of thinking and style of activism represented by people like Dorothy Day and Daniel Berrigan. With his embrace of pacifism, his call for a more faithful Church, and his willingess to engage in civil disobedience, Berrigan was mustering a challenge to the just-war tradition. Widely criticized as an outlaw, Berrigan was also found by surprisingly many others to be prophetic, bringing Catholics back to their true calling. To be sure, the disorder in American society may well have been enough to gain an audience for Dan Berrigan even without the existence of the Second Vatican Council. But it is equally certain that the council helped to create the atmosphere which obtained a serious hearing for him among the Catholic hierarchy and the activist minority.

Two Approaches

By the end of the seventies, the changes in the Catholic church, the revival of the evangelical Left, and the renewed attention given to pacifist ideas had begun to generate the first stirrings of opposition to the remilitarization plans of Jimmy Carter and the increased American presence in Central America. With the election of Ronald Reagan in 1980, these concerns were intensified as activists in the churches were joined by other Americans worried that the president's foreign policy would involve the nation in a senseless war in Central America and might be the trigger for a nuclear confrontation that would bring global destruction. The churches themselves became a principal arena of political debate as the Catholic bishops commenced hearings on their pastoral, as Protestant denominations debated the freeze at their yearly councils, and as activist organizations and discussion groups were started in local communities.

The sheer amount of discussion about nuclear weapons that occurred makes it difficult to characterize the arguments without a measure of simplification. Nonetheless, I think it is accurate to suggest that two broad orientations are evident. One line of argument uses traditional just-war theory as its starting point. It then proceeds to suggest that most imaginable nuclear conflicts could not be justified according to its criteria, and raises criticisms about the current policies of the United States, exhorting both elected officials and individuals to work more diligently on behalf of arms reduction. A second approach relies more heavily on the traditions of religious pacifism and radical evangelicalism. It begins with a literal interpretation of the biblical injunction to love one's enemies and pray for one's persecutors. It describes the policies of the superpowers as idolatry which, if continued, could result in the extermination of life as we currently know it. This line of argument concludes with an urging that individuals and groups resist the potentially murderous policies of idolatrous states.

The first approach is, I think, best exemplified in the Catholic bishops' pastoral "The Challenge of Peace: God's Promise and Our Response." The work relates the question of nuclear arms to an interpretation of Scripture, to the documents of the Second Vatican Council, and to the statements of recent popes. The pastoral begins by speaking of a warrior God in the Old Testament who was gradually transformed in the New Testament as the conception of peace grew more highly developed. In the absence of this warrior God, Jesus furnishes the gift of peace to his followers, a gift "so intense . . . that the remembrance of it becomes the hallmark of the community of faith."[18] But though this gift remains active and ever-present in the world, the Kingdom of God is never fully realized historically. Bad men obtain power and wield it to oppress their subjects and harm the innocent. Hence the urgings of numerous popes for Catholics to understand that while "peace is possible, . . . a totally and permanently peaceful human society is unfortunately a utopia, and that ideologies that hold up that prospect as easily attainable are based on hopes that cannot be realized, whatever the reason behind them."[19]

The just-war theory is viewed as the principal means by which Catholicism acknowledges this tension. It provides criteria sufficiently rigorous to disapprove of wars that have been conducted or are being planned, while legitimating certain kinds of defense by violence against specified kinds of provocations. Applying the theory to contemporary circumstances, the bishops maintained that "we do not perceive any situation in which the deliberate initiation of nuclear weapons, on however restricted a scale, can be morally justified."[20] In making this assertion, the bishops explicitly condemned attacks against civilian populations. "Under no circumstances may nuclear weapons or other instruments of mass slaughter be used for the purpose of destroying population centers or other predominantly civilian targets."[21] The bishops also rejected a nuclear response to a conventional attack by repeating their contention that the "danger of escalation is so great that it would be morally unjustifiable to initiate nuclear war in any form."

Despite these unequivocal statements, the bishops left what J. Bryan Hehir, one of the principal drafters of the pastoral, has called a "centimeter of ambiguity" about whether it would conceivably be possible to justify a limited nuclear exchange. While the bishops argue that the burden of proof lies squarely on those who believe it to be justifiable, they do not entirely foreclose the possibility that it could be permissible.[22] The bishops' position on deterrence reflects a similar line of reasoning. They reject strategies of deterrence that would call for counterpopulation attacks and a nuclear response to a conventional provocation. At the same time, they give what they call a strictly conditioned approval to deterrence as a temporary measure so long as it is combined with genuine efforts to move toward disarmament. Yet although the START talks and the INF negotiations are positively mentioned in this regard, the bishops leave no doubt that American policy has been woefully inadequate as they endorse a halt to the building and further deployment of nuclear weapons.[23]

The debate leading up to the bishops' pastoral had demonstrated the growing influence of the pacifist position within the Catholic hierarchy in the United States. Archbishop Hunthausen of Washington had encouraged tax resistance as a principled response to the use of public revenues for purchasing nuclear weapons. Bishop Leroy Mathiesson had urged workers at the Pantex plant in Amarillo to examine their consciences about the propriety of continuing to work for a company whose products held such dire implications, and he volunteered the offices of the Church to help people who sought alternative employment. Many of the bishops who had joined Pax Christi were interested in reopening the question of whether wars could ever be considered just. Although the pastoral itself was clear in stating that "even when speaking of individuals, the council is careful to preserve the fundamental right of self-defense," the influence of the pacifists was manifest.[24] Pacifists were praised as "deeply sincere individuals . . . far from indifferent. . . . to world evils" and nonpacifists were enjoined not to "simply assume that such individuals are mere pawns of conspiratorial forces or guilty of cowardice."[25] The pastoral went so far as to claim that the just-war theory and pacifism were not incompatible, that "both find their roots in the Christian theological tradition; each contributes to the full moral vision we need in pursuit of human peace. We believe that the two perspectives support and complement one another, each preserving the other from distortion."[26]

The bishops' suggestions about how ordinary citizens ought to respond to the dilemmas posed by nuclear weapons also reflected the pacifists' personalist orientation, albeit couched in carefully guarded language. "To have peace in the world, we must first have peace within ourselves and that . . . interior peace becomes possible only with a conversion of the spirit."[27] The bishops maintained that it was important not to see peace solely as a state brought about by government action, but as an eschatological vision which relates the personal level of existence to that of community life and international affairs. The final section in the pastoral enjoins individuals located in the military, the media, the sciences, and the political world to reflect on the meaning of their faith for their public activities. It asks educators and parents to bring their anxieties and hopes to the education and upbringing of children. And it suggests that Christians truly concerned about the issue form their own communities for the purpose of generating a model of a pilgrim people exploring the implications of their faith.

The second approach to antinuclear political theology has developed directly out of the pacifist and radical evangelical positions. Its principal adherents today are the people centered on the Sojourners community, the Berrigans and the various Plowshares groups, activists in the historic peace churches, and authors such as John Yoder, Dale Aukerman, and Donald Dayton. Men and women from this background tend to reject the validity of just-war theory. Their repudiation is occasionally made on the historical ground that the theory has been used more frequently to legitimize wars than to limit or prevent them. More typically, however, they claim that just-war theory waffles and compromises about a matter explicitly condemned in the Bible. From their perspective, the life of Jesus teaches that war is wrong, that the mentality which undergirds warfare is personally harmful and socially destructive, and that Christians are compelled to seek alternative ways of resolving disputes and living in this world.[28]

The rejection by the pacifists and radical evangelicals of just-war theory is manifested in their animus toward the nation-state, the very unit of analysis at the center of contemporary just-war thinking. In the minds of these critics, the nation-state has frequently replaced Jesus as the true lord and object of worship. They argue that citizens have looked to the nation and its military preparations for security instead of to the message of Jesus. The state thus represents the secularization of the concept of security and, by implication, the nuclear threat symbolizes all the dangers attendant upon secularization. "There is in the nation and its weapons something like a gravitational field which draws itself to devotees and absorbs them into senselessness whose ultimate fulfillment would come in nuclear obliteration. . . . The chief negation of the gospel in our time and thus the central provocations of God's judgment lies in the attitudes which impel the nations toward nuclear war."[29] The most commonly used word to describe this attitude and the worship of the nation-state is "idolatry."

Radical Christians frequently apply the theme of idolatry to the United States. As a *Sojourners* editorial explained, "Today America is bound by sin. As a people we have become captivated by greed, power, selfishness and pride. We have become poisoned by years of unrepentant racism, materialism, violence and oppression. We have ignored the cries of the victims of our many sins—the poor, people of color and women. . . . We no longer trust in God, but in our wealth and military might and the fruit of our idolatry is a nuclear arms race that threatens the world with extinction."[30] A similar line of argument is evident in the justifications for their actions offered by the various Plowshares groups. Tim Lietzke, convicted on charges of depredation of government property for entering the Martin Marietta plant and beating on a missile launcher with a kitchen hammer, writes in *Resistance in Hope* that "idolatry has far too long pervaded the psyche and mentality of the American public, including its so-called leadership."[31] Dan Berrigan suggests in his public speeches that the American polity resembles Nazi Germany in its preparations for massive extermination and its definition of those who would oppose such horrors as outlaws.

According to the radical Christians, the worship of the nation-state is complemented by a corresponding denigration of people outside its borders. Americans, it is said, dehumanize the citizens of other countries, viewing millions as incorrigibly immoral, unable to behave as civilized peoples should. Instead of acting upon the teachings in the Bible which urge people to recognize their own imperfections as the first step in a process of forgiveness, mutual understanding, and reconciliation—"for if you forgive men their trespasses, your Heavenly Father will forgive you"— nations reinforce prejudices that make mutual accommodation and the reduction of tension unlikely. Pacifists and radical evangelicals suggest that recognizing the solidarity of all peoples is essential to the creation of a more peaceful world. "Only if there is a turn to some rough collective approximation of forgiveness and blessing of each side by the other . . . can the Heavenly Father extend to us the forgiveness and blessing that averts doom."[32]

How might all this be brought about? Radical Christians resemble their predecessors by insisting that the connection must first be forged at the personal level, reiterating A. J. Muste's assertion that it is the individual conscience against the atomic bomb. The notion is that individuals ought to give witness to their beliefs by learning how to live consistently with what they profess and by searching for opportunities to give testimony to others. Too often, it is argued, individual Christians desire what Dietrich Bonhoeffer called "cheap grace." They want to consider themselves followers of Jesus without acknowledging the costs that accompany genuine discipleship. It thus becomes imperative for people who profess to be true Christians to make the difficult choices their faith may entail and to participate in activities that offer living witness to this choice.[33]

Pacifists and radical evangelicals frequently endorse civil disobedience as an appropriate form of witnessing. Since they believe that the laws of the state can transgress higher moral dictates, they argue that these laws must occasionally be violated. In the more recent antinuclear activism, this defiance has taken a variety of forms. A number of people have refused to pay a portion of their federal income tax or the federal tax on their phone bill as a protest against war taxes. There have been organized efforts by Christian groups to connect acts of resistance to the liturgical calendar. In late December, for instance, the feast of the Holy Innocents supplies the organizing metaphor for statements of protest against the potential slaughter of a nuclear holocaust. The Lenten desert experience connects the seasonal

themes of repentance and hope to the actions of resisters who enter the
Nevada testing grounds in order to stop the weapons tests. Perhaps the
most dramatic steps have been taken by the various Plowshares groups that
have gone to plants involved in the manufacture of nuclear weapons to
engage in acts of "symbolic disarmament."[34]

Besides recommending individual acts of conscience, radical Christians
have encouraged the formation of communities which give visible witness
to the teachings of Jesus. There is a pragmatic justification for this emphasis insofar as the activists believe that resistance can be maintained only if
individuals are supported and nurtured by others with similar values. "It is
doubtful whether God calls any Christian to be a lone prophet. His intent
is that faithful, cohesive, shalom communities echo his call, resist the
nationalist-militarist negation in all its breadth and live as beachheads of
his shalom in the midst of encircling chaos. . . . A fellowship of two or
three, if it is the primary one for those in it, can provide the sustaining
context for being strong in the Lord and in the strength of His might."[35]

Yet the therapeutic value of these communities is not the primary reason
for their formation, for they are to serve not only as the locus of resistance
to the nuclear juggernaut, but are themselves models of what a new life can
be. These communities are places where goods are shared, where members
attempt to have nurturance replace mutual manipulation, and where individualism is reconciled with a receptivity to the common good. Moreover,
as with Sojourners, these communities are not self-contained but reach out
to the world in very practical ways. Members work with the poor on
community reconstruction; they staff soup kitchens and shelters; and they
agitate for a more general reconstruction of American society. The community thus becomes not only an activity directed toward bringing the Kingdom of God to earth, but a moment in its creation shared by all who
participate.[36]

If the Catholic bishops' pastoral can be said to have made some conces-
sions to the pacifist viewpoint, radical Christians have acknowledged certain pragmatic considerations. This is rarely evident in their theoretical
arguments, but is visible in the movement's actual practices, in which, as
activists labor to persuade others of the validity of their arguments, the
stridency that characterizes their analysis is occasionally muted. They support the nuclear freeze and have worked determinedly on its behalf in
localities across the country. Instead of simply dispensing with just-war
theory, they are frequently willing to speak about it in order to convince
their audiences about the difficulty of justifying preparations for nuclear

war. And they try to understand that most people are unlikely to give away their possessions tomorrow and join a radical Christian community.

The pragmatic strain sometimes evident in radical Christianity is related to two features of its belief system and actual practice. The first is the importance given to developing a merciful disposition. While this urging is most often applied to caring for the homeless, the hungry, and the unemployed, it can also be relevant to how activists relate to the people who do not share their vision of peace. It leads at least some of them to believe that that is important to "accept people as they are" and to work within the framework of their beliefs, while still posing a challenge to the conventional wisdom.

The other moderating tendency in radical Christianity comes from the role that autobiography occupies among the activists. People spend a good deal of time writing and talking about their "personal journey to peace." These reflections serve several purposes. One important function is to show that although conversion is sometimes a dramatic experience, as it was with Saul on the road to Damascus, it is just as often the result of a slow accumulation of doubts, anxieties, and hopes that percolate within the individual for some time before they become outwardly manifest. These stories, in conjunction with a merciful disposition, serve as a reminder that there can be a certain arrogance as well as a counterproductivity in condemning the rest of the population as hopeless sinners.[37]

Convergence and Tensions

The two approaches to antinuclear political theology have converged during the past decade to produce an analysis of American nuclear weapons policy and a prescription for changing it that can be supported, at least in broad outline, by people from a variety of religious traditions.

First, both just-war theories and radical Christians agree that the likely uses of nuclear weapons are morally unjustifiable. Radical Christians have absolutely no doubt about this, given their belief in the fundamental immorality of all wars. The Catholic bishops have been less definite in their statements, attempting to maintain a "centimeter of ambiguity" here. Yet even this needs to be placed in the context of the general thrust of their argument and their insistence, in language very reminiscent of that of Dorothy Day and A. J. Muste, that Catholics "say no" to nuclear war. The attention and interpretation given to the bishops' statement by the national media have surely served to reinforce this element of its content.

Second, both lines of argument are unequivocally critical of national defense policy as it is currently shaped in the United States, noting explicitly that the nation's political leadership has not acted with sufficient dispatch or adequate commitment to reverse the arms race and pursue genuine disarmament. There is a general dissatisfaction with the behavior of the country's political elite and this is not confined to a critical outlook on the Reagan administration. The assessment of the radical Christians is more severe because of their regular references to the Fall and sinful compromises, but the discontent is certainly present in just-war approaches also. The rapidity with which the Catholic bishops acted to prevent the Reagan administration from co-opting their critique was ample evidence of this.

Third, a personalist orientation is evident throughout antinuclear political ideology, one that asks individual Christians to make the commitment to peace a part of their own existence, which calls for incorporating this commitment into family life and which often applauds those whose conscience leads them to break the laws of the state. Both approaches encourage individuals and groups to discover ways of becoming involved in resistance. Despite the critical orientation toward politicians, Christians are urged to remain hopeful that faithful action will lead Americans to reassess their attitudes and patterns of behavior. While radical Christians tend to place greater emphasis on the "costly" nature of the commitment to stop the arms race, it is significant that a group such as the Catholic bishops has spoken so positively about Christian pacifists.

Opposition to the further development and deployment of atomic weapons first surfaced publicly in the United States during the mid-forties in the wake of Hiroshima and Nagasaki. Since that time, numerous spokespersons for the cause have maintained that its success was dependent on developing a concerned citizenry in localities across the nation in order to pressure elected officials to make decisions that would preclude the nation's reliance on these weapons for its security. They hoped that Americans could be persuaded to see that an arms race was suicidal and that future survival was best guaranteed through a political commitment to arms reductions. This is why Albert Einstein insisted that it was "to the village square that we must take the message of atomic energy." Yet the movement never really developed its local base outside of the major urban areas on the East and the West Coasts. It certainly never penetrated to the village squares of Main Street America as Einstein had fervently hoped. Indeed, the movement tended to be isolated from the local institutions that could help it gain access to the hearts and minds of ordinary Americans.

Perhaps the signal importance of the Christian churches' extensive involvement in the recent activism is that it contributed to altering the political geography of opposition to nuclear weapons. The churches have provided, one might say, the political space which has nurtured examination, debate, and controvery about the wisdom of American nuclear policy. The statements of the clergy, the formation of peace-making caucuses, and the response to these developments by more conservative members of various denominations have often resulted in the kind of discussion associated with the practice of democracy in its more elevated form. At a minimum, there has been a significant democratization of the debate about missiles in Europe, the MX, and antisatellite weapons systems across the nation. Ideally, such debate should take place through the party system and local channels that are established for the purpose of nurturing citizen participation. Since the American party system is not, however, especially dedicated to promoting citizen involvement in issue formulation, it is not surprising that the antinuclear weapons movement originated in extraparty locations. Having churches become a central forum for political debate carries certain problems with it in a society grounded in a separation of Church and state. Yet it is also undeniable that the involvement of the churches has enabled the movement to obtain greater breadth than it has previously possessed.

There are numerous indications of the geographical expansion of antinuclear activities, but perhaps the most vivid illustration is the resistance to the passage of the White Train. The protest is conducted by people offering witness against the fourteen-car cargo train that carries nuclear weapons across the country. As the train leaves Bangor, Washington, or the Pantex plant in Amarillo, Texas, citizens are notified by train watchers of the route that it appears to be taking. Most of the Catholic bishops whose dioceses are traversed by the train have supported direct action as a legitimate response to it. Vigilers and protesters gather along the tracks in song, prayer, and sometimes silent meditation. At times, civil disobedience is committed as the watchers stand on the tracks as a sign of disapproval and wait to be removed by the police. What is particularly interesting about the White Train protests is that they have occurred across the heartland of the country. A list of locations includes Shoshone, Idaho; Hastings, Nebraska; Cheyenne, Wyoming; and Norfolk, Virginia. Arrests have been made in Portland, Oregon; Nampa, Idaho; and Elma, Washington. Some of the people incarcerated have been grandmothers and grandfathers committing civil disobedience for the first time in their lives. In 1983, the government attempted to avoid the protests by rerouting the train. The result was only a more extensive game of cat and mouse. In time, those keeping the lookout discovered the alternative routes and notified friends and fellow resisters, thus widening the circle of protest.

Noting how various religious traditions have converged to help produce and legitimate the recent antinuclear weapons movement does not mean that the dilemmas commonly arising when religion becomes politicized have been eliminated. Nor does it imply that the tensions between these perspectives are no longer evident. Scholars familiar with previous attempts to guide political action with religious values will be acquainted with the difficulties that confront religiously motivated activists today. I would like to mention three of these dilemmas that are, I think, especially relevant to the personalist approach adopted by many of the participants in the antinuclear weapons movement.

The first problem that activists have to address is the widespread belief that religion should not instruct people about their political commitments. Although statistical measures normally indicate that the United States remains more religious than the other industrial democracies, Americans are also committed to the separation of Church and state. At times, the desire to keep religion out of the political arena stems from the fear that religiously guided policy will be socially intolerant. This seems to be the case, for instance, with the public's anxiety about the religious Right. On other occasions, the desire to segregate religion and politics is linked to a belief that politics demands a much more hardheaded and less mushy view of how relationships ought to be arranged than is recommended by religious ethics. This seems to be the problem for antinuclear weapons activists insofar as they have to persuade citizens that their policy inclinations are practicable as well as morally desirable.

A second issue for antinuclear weapons activists concerns the manner in which they frame their criticism of the American government. Radical Christians tend to condemn the very idea of nationalism as antithetical to biblical teachings. They point to idolatry and sinfulness as the distinguishing features of nationalism and rarely speak out about the morally worthwhile acts that might be inspired by love of one's country. Just-war theory, however, largely accepts the existence of nations as legitimate and even approves of wars undertaken in self-defense. By implication, it assumes that it is appropriate to love one's nation, to take pride in its accomplishments, and to act according to what is best in its traditions. In practice, personalists have to deal with a tension between those who condemn all manifestations of nationalism as idolatry and those who find within the American political tradition the moral and political resources that could rectify a mistaken nuclear weapons policy.

Finally, efforts to politicize religion invariably face problems related to the difficulty of maintaining the commitment of the participants. Morally inspired religious movements often recruit people who have previously been inactive politically or who have participated in only a nominal fashion. This political inexperience can sometimes promote an unfounded optimism. Participants may believe that they are fundamentally changing the political order when leaders enlist their support and give rhetorical support to their goals. Newcomers to the political arena may become co-opted and not recognize how politicians use their support to promote their own interests while relegating the goals of the movement to the back burner. Perhaps more frequently, participants in morally inspired political movements become disillusioned with the prospects for change and withdraw from the battle altogether. Confronted with evidence of devious political maneuvering and the difficulty of changing national policy, religious activists may retreat from public engagement to more morally satisfying private or charitable pursuits. Movement leaders continually face the task of sustaining commitment to the cause in the face of defeats or politically unpleasant experiences.

Whether the men and women who are participating in the effort will successfully hurdle these obstacles cannot yet be fully determined. Their arguments that Christians ought not to be captivated by the state, that they ought to be skeptical of official rhetoric, and that they have a personal obligation to work for change makes sense to many citizens. But they also have much more to do to convince a majority of Americans that there are more workable alternatives for Soviet-American relations than the one presently grounded in theories of deterrence. I want to turn now to a few of these people and take a closer look at how they came to embrace these commitments.

2

Portraits of Commitment

ON THE last day of February in 1982, Daniel Berrigan was speaking in Richmond. The crowd in attendance was surprisingly large, as four to five hundred people made their way into the auditorium at Virginia Commonwealth University. Only about fifty of those present were students; the vast majority were people from the local churches who had recently become interested in peace issues. Berrigan was plainly attired in corduroys and a red flannel shirt. His only concession to vanity was that he combed his hair forward over a balding head. He addressed the audience in a soft-spoken, reticent, sometimes even inaudible manner and occasionally appeared almost to vanish from view as he slumped behind the podium. Yet the content of his message was in marked contrast to the meekness of his appearance and the softness of his voice.

Berrigan began by mentioning that he had just arrived from Norfolk, the city which houses Virginia's largest naval installation. Calling the area a "gateway to hell," he went on to say that visiting the city brought him to think that "the whole world is being mined and turned into a no-person's land." Berrigan told the audience that the "nukes demand a fascistic atmosphere, the approval of multinational crime, an effort to make genocide legal and an impregnable wall of indecency and injustice." He described his own commitments and actions during the past fifteen years as an attempt to "make it a little less easy for them to plan our death." Speaking specifically about his use of civil disobedience, Berrigan noted that he had come to realize that the "massive cultural and social fallout of Hiroshima required an equally massive conversion and that there would be a next generation only if there is courage in this generation." Berrigan remarked wryly that after having reached the decision in the sixties to practice civil disobedience, he "really got a taste for crime and became thoroughly unrehabilitable."

It is an indicator of how much some of the mainstream churches have changed in the last fifteen years that so many people were in agreement with Berrigan's diagnosis of the American condition. His remarks were greeted with generous applause and from the questions which followed, it was obvious that many people saw Dan Berrigan as a path breaker who had enabled the churchgoing public in 1982 to express its revulsion at the nuclear arms race and the seeming unwillingness of politicians to adopt measures for ending it. No longer an outlaw in their minds, Berrigan was now a living representative of the prophetic church, following the path which Dorothy Day and Thomas Merton had opened up.

While few people were explicitly critical of Berrigan, a number of questions were directed to him which probed his feelings about what could be done to increase the effectiveness of the antinuclear movement. People asked how to influence public officials and opinion leaders; they wanted to discuss the relative merits of various strategies that peace activists could follow; and they wanted to hear Berrigan's opinion about how they could mobilize the moral outrage that burned inside them. These were questions that did not hold the interest of Dan Berrigan all that intently, for he suggested that people be more concerned with determining the proper expression of conscience for themselves than with worrying about the strategic effects of their choice. To one query which asked what the movement could do to become more effective, Berrigan responded that he did not worry about effectiveness and that, if he did, he would join the FBI or the CIA because they were organizations which knew how to get things done.

Almost all of the activists to whom I spoke in the peace community have enormous respect for Dan Berrigan. Many share his belief that action needs to be guided by considerations that are not purely pragmatic. This understanding has been a great source of consolation and encouragement for them. At the same time, they are not entirely comfortable with the notion that pragmatic effects should be disregarded. They are more willing and eager to discuss strategies for persuading other people than Dan Berrigan is, and their activities represent a blend of utopian thinking and practical deeds. Most peace activists are interested in the dismantling of nuclear weapons throughout the world, but they have also devoted time and energy to promoting the nuclear freeze. Many resist at least a token amount of what they call war taxes and a handful of people in Richmond have been arrested and incarcerated for their antinuclear activism. Yet they are also perfectly willing to sit down and discuss the best way of approaching public officials to gain their endorsement for the freeze. They spend time thinking of imaginative ways of reaching others who have not previously supported arms-control initiatives. And they devote energy to the mundane tasks of selling T-shirts, distributing literature, and developing a reliable group of financial supporters.

Perhaps a good way to describe these personalists who share Dan Berrigan's outlook on contemporary life but are more concerned with discovering practical steps that can reverse national priorities is to call them pragmatic utopians. Their understanding of faithful action does not prompt them to dismiss completely the advantages that can be gained from working within the system and making compromises. But neither are they so attached to compromise and conventional politics that they permit the existing culture to shape their goals and muzzle their voices. Their commitment to getting things done exists side by side with a determination to live honorably and morally in a world which they believe often does not reward such character traits. They attempt to remain relevant while focusing people's attention on a vision of the world in which a number of its more intractable problems have been resolved.

This chapter examines how four of the local activists to whom I spoke became involved in peace activities. For two of these people, Steve Hodges and Katherine Smith, their personal commitment to the cause emerged rather early in their lives. Steve Hodges had barely graduated from college when he became convinced that giving witness to the threat of nuclear war was one of the primary obligations of a Christian in the contemporary world. Katherine Smith attended her first demonstration in the fifties when her high-school classmates were interested in banning the bomb. For Wendy Northup and John Gallini, commitment to the antinuclear weapons movement emerged later in life, at a point after the political beliefs of most people have been formed. In the seventies, their own understanding of what needed to be accomplished in the world was shaped, at least in part, by the ideas concerning social responsibility that were becoming more prominent as the generation of priests who had been energized by the changes of Vatican II moved into positions of authority and influence within the local churches.

In these sketches, I try to be attentive to how involvement in peace activism, like participation in most reform movements, often meets the particular personlity needs of the individual man or woman. But this should not be viewed as an effort to disparage either the individuals or the movement. I agree with the historian David Brion Davis' observation that the "debate on the pathology of reform . . . misses the point that virtually all significant moral change springs from people who are in some sense deviant, at least insofar as they are willing to suffer the risks of continuing unpopularity."[1] Indeed, involvement generates its own set of tensions among the participants (more for some people than for others), compelling them to confront issues than can be personally discomforting.

A Consistent Christianity

Steve Hodges was the first coordinator of the Richmond Peace Education Center and held that position until November of 1984. His dress, his manner of living, and his way of relating to others embody the precepts set forth by the religious pacifists years ago. He is most often attired in a tan khaki shirt, pants of similar material, and work boots. Although he sometimes puts on a sport jacket for his appearances before the public, it is one that was probably purchased when he was in college or recently picked up at a thrift shop. While coordinator of the peace center, he lived in an ecumenical community that rented inexpensive housing in Oregon Hill, a poor and working-class neighborhood in the city. He accepted a salary of only six thousand dollars a year for his labors. Steve speaks about his beliefs in a direct and straightforward manner and it appears only fitting that he engages in war tax resistance as a means of demonstrating his personal opposition to nuclear weapons.

Steve was born in 1954. His parents were Methodist missionaries in Korea for all but one year from 1959 till 1970 when he returned to the United States to attend college. As a child, Steve can remember "appropriating a sense of deeply founded faith" which has remained the driving force in his life. When he speaks about his convictions regarding disarmament, race relations, or raising children in a materialistic culture, he is very careful to explain the religious roots of his beliefs. In fact, some of his terminology will be a bit unfamiliar to people who have examined these issues only from a more secular bent. Steve will talk about the lessons he has drawn from the history of the Christian churches; he will use biblical writings as reference points in elaborating on questions; and his discussions of protest and civil disobedience are sprinkled with terms such as prophecy and witnessing.

Steve developed his social consciousness as a child and teenager in the missionary community in Korea. "I recall noticing at a very early age the vast discrepancy between the wealthy and the poor in Korea. I vividly remember the contrast between the people walking down the road carrying 'honey buckets' and those who drove cars, owned homes, and then built walls outside the homes to shield themselves from the unseemly sights on the road outside." One of the first memories Steve has of talking to his parents about their work is telling them after seeing the living conditions of the poor that "they needed a horse and not a car to perform their mission properly." By the time he was a teenager, Steve concluded that the missionaries themselves had made the unfortunate choice to live in relative wealth. In the high school he attended with the sons and daughters of American missionaries and businessmen, the faculty spoke regularly about the obligation of witnessing to one's beliefs. "I wondered about how you could provide effective witness when you lived so differently from the people with whom you were working. I was also concerned about the inconsistency of caring about people's souls and not their physical needs. This made me less certain that you can really love people when you don't acknowledge such a central part of their lives."

Steve returned to the United States in 1970 to attend Earlham College, a Quaker school in Richmond, Indiana. At Earlham Steve established a pattern that was to characterize his process of self-discovery for the next fifteen years. He would choose a particular area of interest, one that he hoped would contribute to the well-being of others and bring personal fulfillment. Yet he would eventually decide that this choice was not precisely what he wanted and discover that his energies were best utilized in another area. He never wavered from his original purpose of finding an appropriate manner to embody his faith in his daily life, but he never found a fully satisfying way of achieving this.

He enrolled initially as a biology major, intending to acquire the skills that would enable him to serve more effectively the kind of people that had been neglected by the missionary community in Tad Jung. "I was originally interested in becoming a public health worker because I thought that it would be a good way of meeting the needs which people really had." He completed the biology curriculum at Earlham, but realized in the middle of it that his heart had not been as fully engaged as he had hoped. Instead, Steve was more engrossed with the theology classes which had a direct bearing on his faith and his courses in Greek and Hebrew. He eventually recognized that he wanted his religious convictions to be more visible in his career and not function only as a backdrop to his labors. His principal dilemma was that he could not yet pinpoint the calling that would allow him to do this most appropriately.

Steve graduated from Earlham in 1974 and he and his new wife, Diantha, started to look for short-term volunteer work. "We both had a commitment to serving God through serving other people and this seemed like a good point in our lives to get some practical experience." They obtained it through the Christian Service ministry and moved to Floyd County, Kentucky, where they worked in a community center. Drift, the town in which they were located, was a hamlet of about five hundred people, most of whom worked for the Beaver-Alcorn coal company, the largest employer in the area. Their principal task was to function as general social workers for the populace. They established recreation programs for children; they helped the poor and the elderly maneuver through the labyrinth of public assistance; and they worked on programs sponsored by the local Presbyterian church. The Hodges found their two years in Drift enjoyable and rewarding. But Steve experienced feelings similar to those he had had as a biology major at Earlham. "I recognized that social work was not my calling and that my heart was not completely in it. I concluded that I would be more fulfilled in the ministry."

The Hodges therefore moved to Dallas in 1976, where Diantha trained as an occupational therapist and Steve enrolled in the Perkins Theological Seminary at Southern Methodist University. Steve became involved with the Social Action Committee at Perkins, quickly rising to the position of chairperson. "I was active planning human rights and hunger workshops. I brought in guest speakers and I became connected to groups outside the university. One semester I was an intern helping CROP [Christian Rural Overseas Program] organize in the Dallas-Fort Worth-Garland area. I helped to organize the CROP walk and I was reaching out into the community, calling pastors up and helping them plan their social ministry. I really enjoyed this and my education as an organizer was one of the most important parts of my seminary education."

In the summer of 1978, Steve and Diantha returned to Drift, where Steve worked this time as a summer pastor. On arriving, he passed out a questionnaire in order to obtain some information about the congregation's expectations of a summer minister. One of the items which Steve included was a request for suggestions regarding possible themes about which he might preach. Among the responses was a request that he offer a sermon on the Church's position with respect to the threat of nuclear war. Given Steve's own interest in social issues, he eagerly grasped the opportunity and immediately threw himself into preparing for the sermon. He checked Sidney Lens's book, *The Day Before Doomsday,* out of the local library—the only volume it had on the subject—and he studied the Sojourners packet on faith and the arms race that was being made available at that time. Preparing the sermon exercised a strong influence on Steve's thinking. He began to believe that the "threat of a nuclear war was the critical issue of our time and the churches were remaining silent with millions of lives at stake."

That summer Steve eventually preached several sermons about the threat of nuclear war and the faithfulness (or lack of it) of the churches. He titled his first homily "Elijah, Hiroshima and a Job Left to Do." In it, he compared God's insistence that Elijah turn the Israelites away from the false prophets of Baal to the task which confronts the churches so long as nations rely on nuclear weapons for their security. "The sermon suggested that Christians who shirk their responsibility for creating a peaceful world are actually repudiating the tasks which God set before the human race." Although he never discovered the precise reactions of the congregation in Drift to his sermons, the themes contained in Steve's original homilies— the importance of social activism, the overweening threat of nuclear war, and the reproach of a casual Christianity—animated his life and work for the next several years.

The summer in Drift also resulted in a sharper clarification of Steve's vocation. Once again, he realized that he was not entirely comfortable with the path he was traveling. On the one hand, he learned that he did not relish the life of a parish minister who presents a Sunday sermon and performs a variety of counseling and administrative duties during the week. "While I did enjoy working twenty hours a week on a sermon, I didn't want to spend the rest of my life doing it. Nor was I sure that I would have enough patience with people who see religion as a Sunday morning affair, but then are offended if their ministers 'meddle in politics.'" On the other hand, the fulfillment Steve obtained from working on the homilies buttressed his conviction that the ministry was his proper calling, provided that he dedicated himself to tracing the connections between his faith and social responsibility.

In 1978, Steve and Diantha moved to Richmond so that Steve could complete his training at Union Theological Seminary. By this time, Steve had become somewhat disillusioned with the growing professionalization of the ministry. The reservations he felt about his summer in Drift were reflected in his growing disenchantment with seminary training. "I felt that there was so much emphasis on the skills of the ministry that it reached the point where the ministers were learning management by objective. There was too much stress on it as a job and not enough emphasis on the ministry as a vocation." To make matters worse, Steve listened to a few of his classmates express a desire not to be called to certain churches because of the low salary that was being offered, rekindling the disturbing memories of life within the missionary community in Korea. Enrolled in a course on the church's mission in the contemporary world, Steve looked for ways to combine his strong interest in social ministry with his conception of what faithful people ought to be doing in contemporary society.

The Hodges had become involved with the small group of peace activists who were visible in Richmond during the late seventies, both on the seminary campus and in the wider community. Steve and a friend at Union constructed a study guide about faith and nuclear arms which listed relevant books, articles, and films that were available in the city or could easily be procured. They then took the guide to the staff at the school library and discussed how the materials could be made available to interested students. Simultaneously, Steve began to meet the men and women in the larger community who shared his concerns. "Having bridged the distance between seminary and community in Dallas, I tried to duplicate this in Richmond. I attended the Quaker meeting. I became involved in the local response to the New Call for Peacemaking. And I utilized the organizational skills that I had developed at Perkins in helping to plan the Richmond Conference on the Arms Race."

In the spring of 1980, Steve was coming to a final decision about the precise nature of his vocation. He knew for certain that he wanted to be involved with social ministry, placing special emphasis on peace issues. Historically, social ministers operated out of a church's regional office. Atlanta, for instance, functions as the home base for social ministers in the Southeast who develop programs for local ministers and then encouraging neighborhood pastors to utilize the materials which they provide. Steve calls this "the trickle-down notion of social ministry," one which he "did not find especially appealing." In the late 1970s, however, there was an alternative idea about the purpose and function of the vocation circulating that Steve found more attractive. "I began to be a believer in grassroots social ministry, one in which people develop programs themselves based on local conditions and implement these programs themselves. This made good sense to me because it allows you to follow up on the programs that you develop and it is much easier to work ecumenically. I preferred this to working in a national office and I sincerely believed in the concept."

So when John Gallini, a Catholic peace activist, suggested that Richmond really needed a peace education center and that it could be a permanent, ongoing concern only if a person like Steve performed the task as a ministerial commitment, Steve gave the idea serious consideration. The more he thought about it, the more he saw how perfectly it fit his ideas about both the role of the Church in the contemporary world and the vocation that was personally appropriate. Steve spoke to a number of people and ministers in the Richmond area and they were almost uniformly encouraging. He did so, not quite knowing what the chances for success were, but well aware that he could now be faithful in a manner consistent with his beliefs.

Many people in the antinuclear community in Richmond who were interviewed credit Steve Hodges with making the peace education center a viable entity in the city. Once previously, in 1971, enthusiasm had been generated for creating a similar office. But the idea foundered in a sea of good intentions, primarily because no one could promise to devote the necessary energy to developing the center's activities. Even people who committed a significant amount of time to working in the peace movement felt that assuming the director's responsibilities would be too burdensome. Since Steve conceived of his work as a ministry and held to a version of Christianity that sees worldly riches as potentially corrupting, the interest of people in the peace community meshed with what was financially possible.

As coordinator of the Richmond Peace Education Center, Steve was continually active. When the center was established in 1981, he initiated contact with a variety of local groups and promoted its programs throughout the community, especially in local churches. By the beginning of 1982, however, the center was being called upon by numerous churches to help prepare programs dealing with the relationship between faith and war and peace issues. Steve sometimes served as a resource person who provided guidance and references. On other occasions, he personally spoke before church groups and helped other groups organize around antinuclear sentiment. He also used these latter contacts as occasions for promoting the center's newsletter and expanding its mailing list. The center grew so rapidly that it soon hired two full-time workers who were funded by grants from various church organizations and employed a number of volunteers on both a regular and a periodic basis.

Steve Hodges' actual efforts, however, went far beyond his official responsibilities at the Richmond Peace Education Center. He participated in numerous ecumenical peace groups; he continually sent information to pastors in the Richmond area who might be at all sympathetic to peace concerns; and he regularly spoke at churches, schools, and Christian education programs. Furthermore, he maintained a rigorous schedule of political activities, testifying before committees at the state assembly, starting peace groups at local universities, and sitting on the state board of the Virginia Nuclear Freeze campaign.

Erik Erikson has written that one of the tasks which an exceptional leader performs is to deal with personal conflicts in such a way as to help people in the culture at large confront difficulties which are characteristic of the era. Great leaders, in Erikson's mind, permit all of us to lead better lives. Erikson's work is obviously concerned with what Hegel called world historical figures, but his ideas also have relevance to the more mundane tasks of leadership on a local level. In Steve Hodges' case, his own search for a calling—what Erikson labels an identity—was entirely consistent with the desire of other people to establish an active peace-making presence in Richmond. Responding to his own needs, he also responded to the wishes and needs of others, thus creating the possibility of an enduring community.[2]

Steve Hodges' effort to embody a consistent Christianity makes him unusually scrupulous about the details of his personal life. It it not surprising that he lived in a community where the members vowed to forswear income above the poverty level. His own example challenged other activists to reconsider certain personal habits of their own in light of their potential social and political implications. But there is also a sense in which his intense scrupulousness may appear excessively demanding. What Steve views as components of a holistic outlook may be viewed differently by others. They may believe that some of his concerns are petty and trivial and likely to deflect energy from more important causes.

In 1983, for example, Steve was one of the two coordinators of the local mobilization for the twentieth anniversary of Martin Luther King's March on Washington. To ensure that everyone who wanted to attend would have a seat on the bus, a benefit concert was held at a local park. The event went well and afterward the organizers carried the tables that were used as a bandstand to a church across the street. Sweating from laboring in almost ninety-degree heat, one of the organizers remarked that he would like nothing better than a cold beer. Since Steve's own abstinence is based on notions that drinking is morally and socially harmful, he felt compelled to respond not only that he preferred an ice cream soda but that he could not understand why alcohol was viewed as a reward for hard work. A few years later, he brought up the issue of alcohol once again, this time in the more formal setting of the meeting of peace education center's board of directors. He argued that alcohol should not be permitted at the center's annual dinner and that he was even more adamantly opposed to having the center itself supply wine for those who wished to drink with their meal. For Steve Hodges, airing this issue is part of his effort to live consistently. For others, it may be evidence that what radical Christians call "costly grace" may require illiberal and puritanical restrictions on personal choice.

From Mercy to Politics

When Wendy Bauers Northup was growing up in Kansas City, Missouri, during the late forties and early fifties, her parents rarely talked about politics. The emerging Cold War, the American involvement in Korea, the rise and fall of Joseph McCarthy, the beginnings of civil rights agitation, and the debate over radioactive fallout were subjects a bit too distant for a family that thrived on personal relationships. Conversation in the Bauers household was more likely to focus on schoolwork, the upcoming visits of relatives, and the immediate obligations of each member of the family than on the broader issues of American politics and culture. Matters which allowed individuals in the household to exercise some influence always seemed more interesting and worthwhile than the distant affairs that politicians addressed.

The lack of interest in the political world manifested in the daily life of the Bauers family did not mean that its members shunned social responsibility altogether. It was just that one's obligations were primarily limited to the people that could be directly touched through one's efforts. For instance, Wendy recalls that her mother "was always bringing people home. She would just meet them on the street and if they needed a meal or a place to stay, she would invite them to the house. She volunteered in a home for unwed mothers and was always trying to do what she could for the immigrants who arrived in Kansas City without the means to support themselves. I can't remember a Christmas without all the widows in the neighborhood at our place for dinner." Reared in this environment, it is understandable that Wendy developed what she describes as a "strong sense of obligation, a belief that you're supposed to do things for people, sometimes whether you like to or not."

Animated by this sense of obligation, Wendy entered the convent after high school and attended Fontbonne College, a small Catholic school in St. Louis. She pursued a degree in education and after graduation began teaching at a private girls' high school. Involvement in a charitable activity at a public housing project was her first exposure to the broader problems of the American political economy. Characteristically, Wendy was most affected by the connection between the structural condition of poverty and the everyday life of the project's inhabitants. What struck her most forcefully was the residents' absolute lack of privacy. "The apartments were tiny and the walls were paper thin. I spoke to someone who told me that necessary repairs were rarely made without long and inconvenient delays. I realized that if the residents did hold jobs, they were hardly the kind that would allow them to save money and to escape the conditions of the projects. Yet I had no idea how the conditions could be improved and, to tell the truth, I didn't spend that much time thinking about it."

Wendy left the convent in 1967 to attend graduate school at the University of Illinois. Here most of her acquaintances were liberal Democrats who were becoming part of the growing opposition to Lyndon Johnson's foreign policy. While Wendy generally shared their perspective, she was not charged by the same enthusiasm. As with the rest of her family, political involvement was simply not a constituent element of her self-identity. "I can remember opposing the war in Vietnam in a mushy kind of way, but not in a manner that made it into a pressing moral and ethical issue." Although Wendy did quite well in her courses during her first semester in graduate school, she was disappointed in the experience and was not especially contented with what she felt was a gossipy cliquishness and narrow professionalism in the department. When the man she was dating, her future husband Steve Northup, was drafted, Wendy quit school, moved to Atlanta after Steve was stationed in Columbus, Georgia, and again took up teaching, this time not in a Catholic high school, but in a predominantly black, inner-city elementary school.

The experience in Atlanta left an enduring impression on Wendy because of the alteration it wrought in her social consciousness. She candidly admits, "My teaching experience was a disaster. I was a high-school teacher working in an elementary school and while I was qualified on paper, I discovered that I was really not prepared to teach fourth grade. I had never taught outside of a Catholic school and I was simply unable to respond to the challenges presented by the new environment. I was tentative and uncertain about how to relate to children from low-income backgrounds. I was unsure of the best way to respond to the 'testing' which the students administered to me. At times, I was so befuddled and out of place that a few of the children would bring sticks to class and give them to me to help with discipline."

Although Wendy suffered from her inability to reach the children in the manner she felt befitted a competent teacher, her year in Atlanta provided her with a valuable education. "I learned that the pupil-teacher ratio had been deliberately altered to imply that there was one teacher per twenty-five students when the reality was one instructor for every thirty-five children. I saw that Atlanta in the late sixties was still busing to avoid integration. I even heard from my colleagues that the physical improvements in the facilities— painting, window repair, and a general cleanup—were probably the result of hiring a white teacher in a school where the faculty had been uniformly black. Atlanta had a long-term effect in raising my consciousness. I felt a lot of anger there and I developed a sense of structure to my thinking to a much greater extent than I had previously."

Steve and Wendy were married later in the year and they moved to Washington, D.C., while Steve was stationed in nearby Virginia. Wendy continued teaching, but returned to a private high school in Laurel, Maryland. Steve was soon shipped off to Vietnam and served as a payroll officer away from the combat zone. Wendy's anger about racial discrimination did not spill over into an indictment of American war aims and policy. "I still kind of opposed the war and even attended a demonstration or two wearing a black armband. But I wasn't strongly political and, if anything, the women's movement had become much more important to me. I started laying the groundwork and thinking about how we could pursue the relationship with the changes that my ideas about the women's movement led me to believe were necessary. I started to write letters to Steve in which I would mention, 'Hey, by the way, we're going to change some things in this relationship and do things differently when you return."

When Steve returned from the service in 1971, the Northups moved to Boston. Wendy taught at a public high school in Melrose and enrolled in the graduate program at Northeastern during the evening. Steve attended law school at Harvard. From Boston, the Northups moved to Scranton, Pennsylvania, where Steve took his first job as an attorney and Wendy devoted herself to the growing family responsibilities. Toward the end of their stay in Boston, the Northups had adopted a boy, their first child. In Scranton, they adopted a girl and Wendy bore a daughter of her own. On Wendy's initiative, the family moved to a farm and made an effort to live a more self-sufficient and simple lifestyle, a commitment she pushed at the time more for health purposes than for any ideological reasons. Wendy learned how to garden organically, how to make maple syrup, and other country skills. Moreover, the family made dramatic reductions in its consumption of meat, giving it up entirely during the Lenten season one year and donating the money saved to a relief agency. Yet the Northups were not especially happy in Scranton. "We met a lot of nice people in a short period of time, but our friendships weren't as substantial as I had wanted them to be. There was a lot of blatant sexism which was difficult to take and I had the feeling that few people were concerned with anything outside their own immediate interests." In retrospect, one might suggest that Wendy was struggling to discover how a woman influenced by feminist ideas could, in the 1970s, raise a family and embrace the ethos of social responsibility that her mother had exemplified.

This discontent in Scranton eventually prompted the family to return to Steve's hometown of Richmond in 1976. Steve accepted a job with a prominent downtown law firm for which he still works today. Wendy managed the household and taught freshman English on a part-time basis at Virginia Commonwealth University. But while the Northups knew that they wanted to raise their children in the city, they also realized how much they wanted to seek out other people and form a more sustaining community than they had experienced in the previous five years. The principal obstacle was that they did not quite know where to find this community. Wendy was not comfortable in the social circles to which lawyers in prestigious firms have access and, more important, "wanted to be part of a community in which the children are regularly involved in the activities of the adults."

Searching for this community led Wendy and Steve to participate actively in their church. They decided to attend, for instance, a Marriage Encounter group that was sponsored by their parish. Marriage Encounter was a weekend retreat that focused on communication and the potential for improving it. The Northups found the experience helpful, and later many of the couples who attended formed a community of their own and became close friends. But Wendy still desired a slightly different sense of community, one grounded in values broader than her commitment to communicate with her husband. "I wanted to find a group that wasn't so inward-looking." While the Marriage Encounter weekend reinforced her belief in the importance of community to their lives, it also demonstrated that they would have to take the initiative in helping to form and establish one.

Wendy and Steve ultimately decided to ground one element of this communal orientation in the religious education of their children. Because they wanted their sons and daughters to receive a multiracial education and because they felt it was important for middle-class parents not to remove their children from the Richmond public school system, they had enrolled them in the city schools. At the same time, Wendy and Steve felt that the religious education classes which their children were attending once a week were not providing the training which they felt was necessary, especially a religious education connected to family values. The Northups therefore got together with four other families and initiated their own program on a monthly basis. This self-run program became an important educational experience for Steve and Wendy as well as for the children. "Most of the couples did not share our social and intellectual orientation and I found it important to understand that community means something more than just a bunch of like-minded people getting together to socialize."

Ultimately, it was through this search for community and their friends in the Catholic church that Wendy and Steve became involved in the peace movement. In August of 1980, John Gallini, who taught a youth group along with Steve and Wendy, asked Wendy to help put together a program relating the Catholic faith to war and peace issues. Given her long-standing sense of obligation to friends, Wendy naturally consented. "I spent the next two months poring over factual material on the arms race, theological perspectives on national security issues, and political arguments that had appeared in various magazines. It seemed a terribly immense chore at first, but as I became familiar with the material, it proved also to be very interesting. I would sit around home at night and ask Steve, 'Do you know what this weapon can do?' Or I might just express my amazement at the direction in which we were heading. I became convinced that the just-war tradition could not support a nuclear exchange under any conditions." And while Wendy considers herself to be "basically an apolitical person," her faith and friends prompted her to become one of the most active members of the Richmond peace community.

It is sometimes argued by radical activists and scholars that charitable and merciful actions are politically inadequate and poor substitutes for genuine reform when conditions demand structural change. Yet what Wendy Northup makes apparent is that the relationship between a merciful disposition and a commitment to political change is more complex than is commonly thought. In all of Wendy's political commitments today, the influence of her apolitical yet merciful mother can be seen, along with glimpses of the enduring effects of her years as a teaching nun. It can be seen very clearly in her insistence in connecting global and national issues to the conduct of everyday life. As a speaker for the peace community, Wendy always makes an effort to define issues in terms which her audience can understand and which make possible a concrete response on the part of individuals, however small it might be. Her interest in the freeze stemmed, in part, from the intentions of the originators to help loosen the popular paralysis about the threat of nuclear war. She was fond of emphasizing that the freeze is a concrete step which individuals and groups can take to register their disapproval of military strategy. "I think it is terribly frustrating to go listen to a speaker talk about an issue and come home feeling that there is absolutely nothing you can do about it."

Perhaps the most vivid example of Wendy's efforts to connect structural issues to the warp and woof of daily life is her emphasis on the family. She has not rejected the ethos of the Bauers household, but rather has related her concern about family life to her more recent interests in peace and social justice. Concerned, for instance, that her children would grow up without being sufficiently attentive to the condition of less advantaged people, she and Steve placed their home on a list as a "safe house" for battered women. Twice a month the family goes to a local soup kitchen and laundry facility, Freedom House, to serve meals to the homeless and the hungry. Wendy views these works not only as acts of mercy, but as a way of educating her children to be responsible toward those who are less fortunate. Steve and Wendy have also initiated and organized the Parenting for Peace and Justice program, which offers parents a host of tips for incorporating social values into family life and encourages children to view their family life as the core of a peaceful world. And through her membership in the Pax Christi group, Wendy is attempting to connect the elements of her faith to both daily activities and to her desire to create a more communal form of life within middle-class existence.

Wendy Northup does not regret that she has become an activist who works for peace and justice as well as being a merciful person. This activism has given a meaning to her life that she finds important: she has made good friends and can raise her children in what she considers a nurturing environment. But while the peace community has fulfilled her needs in many ways, it has also introduced some tensions and discomfort. There are a few elements of her newfound activism that she cannot bring herself to relish. She finds, for example, some of the political work in which she participates to be extremely boring. "I can understand why people like Reagan. He sounds like he knows what is going on and he appears confident that he can handle it. People like myself want to hear that. We want to know that somebody else can take care of things so we can spend our time elsewhere."

Unlike Steve Hodges, Wendy Northup exhibits little of the intensity that is quickly felt in his presence. With her blond hair, easy smile, and a Volkswagen van often filled with kids, she looks more like the women who sell household products on television commercials than a local leader of an opposition movement. One could never imagine her echoing the sentiments of Angelina Grimke, the nineteenth-century abolitionist, who wrote in her diary, "I cannot be too zealous."[3] Indeed, she sometimes finds it hard to understand that she may not be viewed as a helpful and decent person, but as a political figure whose performance is to be assessed and criticized. She does not enjoy rancorous debate and although she recognizes that her motives will be impugned, she remains taken aback by it. Certain people who share her positions worry that she may be insufficiently radical; those who are upset with her positions on nuclear weapons and U.S. involvement in Central America dismiss her as part of the leftist cadre in the churches. Says Wendy (perhaps echoing other personalists who have never relished political debate), "One of the hardest things that I have to learn to accept is that not everyone is going to like me."

A Midlife Odyssey

When you speak to members of an activist group which is relatively small, people continually refer you to other members of the community. For instance, if the topic of childhood education is raised, a person might note that "you should speak to Makanah Morris because she is very interested in the issue." If tax resistance was mentioned, people regularly told me to "get in touch with Father Bob Quirin because he knows the history of it in the city." In the course of these referrals, John Gallini's name was mentioned several times. Invariably, the person mentioning his name followed up with a brief but extremely laudatory description of him. People told me that he was "really fantastic" and had "been a big influence" on them. As Steve Hodges put it, "John Gallini was the person who persuaded me to pursue a ministry through the peace education center."

By the time I had arranged my first meeting with John, I had already etched a picture of him in my mind. I imagined that his two most dominant traits would be enthusiasm and persuasiveness. I envisioned a person who was never at a loss for an idea, who influenced people by the infectiousness of his personality—a local version of the Reverend William Sloane Coffin. Thus I was more than a bit surprised by the first impression that John Gallini actually makes. He is cautious, soft-spoken, and even slightly deferential. Outside of work (he is a chemical engineer at DuPont), he wears an open-necked shirt, brown slacks, and tan walking shoes probably purchased from the budget racks of discount stores. He routinely apologizes for answering your questions in too much detail. He asks if you are aware of any material that he should be reading. And he offers generous praise for other members of the peace community while downplaying his own contributions. In coming to understand why other people praise him so highly, one learns much about the attributes which the members of the local peace community hold in esteem.

John was raised in Detroit, Michigan, during the late thirties and forties. His father was a mechanical engineer and his mother was employed as a lieutenant for the city police, basically functioning as a social worker for teenagers gone bad. Like Wendy Northup, John cannot recall politics being a frequent subject of discussion in the Gallini household. He did, however, learn from his parents the values of Catholic welfarism. Applied to politics, this meant supporting liberal Democrats and the programs which they had initiated. This belief was reinforced by the Jesuits who taught him in high school and repeatedly emphasized the responsibility which individuals have for one another. Yet throughout childhood and early adulthood, this "belief was not a motivating force in my life, but one element in the package of ideas to which I subscribed." Interested in science and its technical applications, John attended college at the University of Detroit, graduating in 1955. He then pursued advanced studies at the University of Michigan, where he received a Ph.D. in chemical engineering. John remembers being almost entirely consumed by his work and today recalls, "Except for the fact that I got married, which means that I cared for at least one other person, I didn't seem to care about anything else."

After leaving graduate school, John moved to Delaware, where he had received a job offer from DuPont. His political interest was somewhat piqued because he and his wife Nancy became involved in arguments with some acquaintances who held white supremacist views about race relations. The Kennedy-Nixon race was the first campaign in which he took an active interest and like many Americans he stayed up most of the evening on election night awaiting the final outcome. Despite this heightening of interest in national politics, John was not prompted to become involved on the local level. The spare time he had from work and his responsibilities as father of a family that was eventually to number eight children was spent as a religious education teacher, instructing classes once a week for Catholic high-school children who attended public schools.

When he was transferred to Buffalo in 1967, John continued his involvement in religious education classes. At the time, he was unaffected by the opposition to the war in Vietnam. In fact, most of his political views were still held rather unreflectively. "I was a strong proponent of racial equality. I was sympathetic to the extension of social welfare programs. In foreign policy, I was supportive of whatever the President defined as our national security interest. With respect to Vietnam, I just assumed that we were defending an embattled democracy and this was the proper course for the United States to be pursuing." What happened in Buffalo, however, was that because of his work as a religious educator John came into contact with a priest, Father Chris, who introduced him to an alternative conception of morality, one which influenced John to see a more direct connection between his faith and his obligations to be socially responsible.

Father Chris was the curriculum director of a local seminary in Buffalo.

By disposition, he "was strongly committed to the Catholic church. But he also had an explorer's bent, a natural intellectual curiosity which led him to investigate wherever his intellect took him." For priests such as Father Chris, Vatican II was a profoundly liberating event because it gave official sanction to personal leanings that might have been stifled or repressed in the older Church. Filtered through Father Chris, Vatican II encouraged Catholics like John Gallini to reevaluate their assumptions about morality and theology. As John describes it, "Morality had been a branch of practical mathematics in which individuals merely applied existing principles to particular cases. Under the guidance of Father Chris, I had what could be called a 'conversion experience' that resulted in a shift in my understanding of moral reasoning. I came to believe that reflective individuals held a much greater responsibility for the creation of moral truths. I also began to think that an exemplary life was not so much dependent on dutifully following rules, but on examining what your faith meant for the conduct of your entire life."

This altered conception of morality encouraged John to pay more attention to the social and political issues of the day. While he did not renounce his earlier perspective on the Vietnam War and join the ranks of the demonstrators marching in the streets, he did examine his previous views more carefully as he was less disposed simply to accept the claims of the authorities. The group of teachers in his religious education program themselves reflected the divergence in outlook that was polarizing American society in the late sixties. "The staff included a couple of FBI agents, a retired naval officer, and two students from the state university in Buffalo who were active participants in the local chapter of the Students for a Democratic Society. At one time, the students were holed up in a local Unitarian church evading the police while the FBI was outside peering through binoculars trying to discover where they were hiding." The teachers in the religious education programs held a number of meetings and discussions about the war. None of these led John to reverse the opinions he had formed about Vietnam. The debates did, however, implant a sense of doubt in his mind about the wisdom of American policy that was to become more deeply rooted in the ensuing decade.

In the early 1970s, DuPont closed its laboratories in Buffalo and the Gallini family moved to Richmond, where the company had another plant. The powerful nature of the experience with Father Chris was reflected in the fact that when the Gallinis were looking for a home to purchase in Richmond, their criteria included that it be located near a church with a progressive religious education program. They ultimately settled on a house in Bon Air, an upper-middle-class suburb in which the Catholic church was staffed by a number of relatively liberal priests. The Gallinis immediately volunteered for the religious education programs at St. Edwards, John as a teacher and Nancy as an administrator. The experience proved rewarding in more than one way. Given the inclination to innovate among the Catholic hierarchy in Richmond, local churches granted religious educators wide latitude in formulating their programs. This permitted John to examine further in his teaching some of the questions in which he had become interested in Buffalo.

Moreover, the teachers in the religious education programs themselves formed a small community of inquiry. John feels today that it was almost an ideal group. "There were people who came from different backgrounds and held divergent ideas about the ties that should be established between faith and social responsibility. At the same time, the trust and respect among the five couples who formed the groups was sufficiently deep so that we could overcome many of the natural barriers to an honest investigation of our differences." As in Buffalo, the religious education group constituted a miniature example of how democracy is supposed to work, with responsible people exchanging their views candidly within an atmosphere of tolerance. "We did a lot of struggling with important matters. We spent a lot of time talking about what community meant. We addressed race issues and talked about the propriety of living in predominantly white neighborhoods. None of these questions were ever resolved but we realized that some level of ostentation was unacceptable, that some level of luxury was sinful, and that some measure of social responsibility was required of people."

As a sign of his growing interest in the meaning which his faith held for his responsibilities as a citizen, John became involved with the Social Ministry Commission of the Catholic diocese. The commission is an amorphous group of laypeople and clergy who are concerned about social issues. It is divided into subcommittees on refugee resettlement, peace and justice, and social welfare, which engage in both outreach work and self-education. Typically, some of the members of each subcommittee have clearly formulated ideas about what problems are significant and how these should be addressed, whereas others have less definite views and are primarily intent on learning about possible alternatives. At the behest of a priest with whom he was acquainted, John joined the Peace and Justice Subcommittee of the Social Ministry Commission.

For John, the subcommittee was an extension of the discussion that had begun in Buffalo and was continued among the group of religious education instructors at St. Edwards. A few of the people on the subcommittee had been active for a number of years in the small antiwar community in the area. Father Mike Schmeid was a pastor in a black church in a poor section of the city. Walt Grazer, a layman employed by the diocese, had been influential in bringing peace issues to the attention of the present bishop, Walter Sullivan. Father Bob Quirin was involved with tax resistance as well as the more traditional forms of antiwar protest. By now, however, John had become convinced that his faith required a strong stand against issues which he had previously supported. "The subcommittee addressed questions such as militarism in the schools. We drafted a latter to the bishop asking him to ban draft registration in the diocesan high schools and we spoke with him about the possibility of influencing Benedictine Academy, a Catholic military school that was not under diocesan control. We opposed the B–1 bomber and worked to develop a disarmament perspective that was grounded in the Catholic faith. We also organized a Hiroshima day event as a small-scale protest against what we perceived as the erosion of life values to the norms of militarism."

The members of the Peace and Justice Subcommittee, John included, decided that the teachings and values of the Catholic faith do not permit nations to use or threaten to use nuclear weapons. Moreover, the group believed that "nations and individual Catholics should work on behalf of disarmament objectives. Most of the people on the subcommittee felt that one of our major shortcomings was our inability to reach more of the Catholics in Richmond with the ideas and studies we had authored. In particular, we felt that not enough Catholics were thinking about the nuclear arsenals of the superpowers and the threat of a nuclear war. So we reached a decision in the late seventies to promote education about the relationship between national security issues and foreign policy in a much more vigorous way." The consequence of this decision was the formation of the local Pax Christi chapter in 1980.

These days, John Gallini devotes much of his energy to Pax Christi. He works on its disarmament committee, helps to organize its educational and political efforts, and devotes a substantial amount of money to supporting the group financially. John has also worked on a twinning program with the congregation of a black church in an effort to build interracial understanding, and is on the board of directors of the Richmond Peace Education Center. It is because of people like him that the Catholic peace community has obtained a degree of visibility in the area. By quietly encouraging others to persist in and increase their efforts while being a responsible activist himself, he has become highly respected. He spends much of the little spare time that he does have continuing to read and study, not only about nuclear arms but about the relationship between his beliefs and a wide range of social issues, including matters of economic justice.

When John reflects on the time, effort, and money he has given to the Church and to social causes over the past ten years, he does so with satisfaction, albeit tinged with humor and irony. He thinks about sitting in a room with six other people in Richmond in 1978 and engaging in a serious discussion about how they might persuade others that American foreign policy was heading down a dangerous path. "I sometimes thought that we were crazy. Indeed, I still continue to get involved with issues about which some people would say, 'You're crazy to spend your time on that.' " I once asked John what he thought would have happened if he had channeled his energies into party politics instead of these efforts for justice and disarmament. He responded, "I do get involved in the political process and I feel that it is important. But if I had put all the effort into the Democratic party that I put into the Church, it is not inconceivable that I would have a position of considerable importance in the state party apparatus instead of having to see myself occasionally as an honest-to-God weirdo."

It is, of course, more than a bit ironic that the efforts of people such as John Gallini in their churches had an impact on the conduct of American political debate in the early eighties. John remains interested in learning how he might bring more people into the discussion that has so greatly affected his life. Yet he is equally concerned about continuing to explore his own beliefs and what they should mean for his own actions. He wonders, for example, how far he should go in resisting American military policy. "I sometimes think that I should do much more to give witness to my beliefs." He has even debated whether his faith is such that he "should be in prison for commiting acts of civil disobedience." At the same time, he is not in jail, and will avoid going so that he can keep his commitment to put his children through college. He will also continue to use his organizational skills to pursue utopian goals on a daily basis. But that he considers questions such as economic justice and war tax resistance seriously is evidence that the recent history of the Catholic church is written across the concerns of his daily life. It may also be evidence, at least on a small scale, of how personalist ideals can deepen and modify the commitments of a traditional liberal.

The Other Social Darwinism

Katherine Smith works as a science librarian at the University of Richmond. When she speaks about her involvement in peace issues, she frequently alludes to scientific theories and discoveries. For her, science is not a demon to be excoriated for bringing us to the verge of extinction or even a neutral activity devoid of humanistic merit. She believes that science, if viewed properly, can tell us something important about the way we ought to lead our lives. Katherine is especially interested in some biological research which might lead us to revise how we look at human social relations. Most notably, she refers to findings that appear to demonstrate that human beings are not merely competitive creatures, but may also possess an innate potential for cooperation. Katherine particularly concerns herself with what this means for our capacity to work together and create a world in which war becomes obsolete. She notes that "it has taken a long time for human beings to evolve culturally" and that "if we survive the threat of nuclear war, we will have reached a new understanding of the purposes of government." In believing that science teaches a very different lesson from that proposed by the cruder social Darwinists, Katherine is in the tradition of nineteenth-century reformers like William Allen and Peter Kropotkin, who thought that the social implications of science were quite different from those which Herbert Spencer was to draw.[+]

Katherine Smith arrived at this new understanding of the purposes of government long before she became committed to understanding the lessons of science. As a teenager, her parents sent her out of Richmond and enrolled her in a Quaker high school in Philadelphia by the name of Westtown. Here she was confronted by a major lifestyle change, for many of her classmates were precociously political, having already drawn the connections between their religious convictions and the wider world. Not only did her fellow students find it more enjoyable and worthwhile to talk about politics instead of fashions, sports, and movies, but "one half of my classmates were already ardent socialists. They held earnest discussions on the meaning of the Supreme Court's decisions in *Brown* v. *Board of Education*. They discussed Eisenhower's positions on the offshore islands of Quemoy and Matsu and they debated whether Red China should be admitted to the United Nations." More than a few students were planning to picket Nike missile sites. For someone who had barely given any consideration to political affairs, it all constituted an intense and exciting experience.

Katherine left the politically charged atmosphere of the Philadelphia Quakers when she returned to Richmond to attend Westhampton College, a private women's school that was affiliated with the Baptist church. Westhampton was not known as a breeding ground for social activists. This was certainly the case in the late fifties, as the suburban campus was unaffected by the political ferment that was beginning to brew in many of the neighboring southern states. Few of Katherine's classmates engaged in sophisticated analysis of political affairs and even fewer could be labeled ardent socialists. Katherine majored in the sciences and devoted most of her time to her studies and to the social life that revolved around the college. She did, however, begin to attend the Friends meeting in Richmond. While the local Quakers were not the seasoned political activists of Philadelphia, they did maintain an interest in the issues which Martin Luther King, Jr., and the burgeoning civil rights movement had placed at the top of the American political agenda.

After graduating from college in the early sixties, Katherine became very active in the local meeting. The fifty or so people who attended regularly were becoming progressively disenchanted with the Vietnam War, and Quakers as individuals and as an organized group became part of the tiny, local opposition that was in its gestation period. The meeting's peace committee brought speakers to Richmond, helped with draft counseling, and gave serious thought to how effective witness for peace might be offered in the city. Katherine's husband, William, a Baptist "who fell in love with the ethic of Quakerism," became an active dissenter who "regularly marched around the Federal Building protesting the war." Katherine herself "had absolutely no quarrel with the belief that the war was an improper use of the nation's energies. I just never had any questions about it." In 1967, the Quakers were instrumental in organizing the local activity on behalf of the nationwide educational campaign called Vietnam Summer. By this time, Katherine was also marching around the Federal Building and participating in the local peace vigil organized by members of the Women's International League for Peace and Freedom.

As the years progressed, Katherine remained committed to the weekly witness and today proudly remembers it as "one of the most long-standing peace vigils in the country." When the war wound down in the seventies, Katherine retained her interest in social issues. Along with other Quakers, she participated in an unsuccessful effort to develop a school-integration plan that might help to avert a white flight from the city's classrooms. "I was also involved in local campaigns against world hunger and for the promotion of human rights." In the late seventies, Katherine's membership in the Quaker Meeting also prompted her to take seriously the New Call for Peacemaking's local initiative. Like other people in the small but growing peace community, Katherine became convinced that "survival in the nuclear age was rapidly becoming the paramount issue of our time and one to which concerned individuals needed to devote a considerable amount of energy." She immediately put this belief into operation, becoming active in the formation of the Richmond Peace Education Center, educating herself so that she could speak intelligently about science and national security issues and donating a portion of her discretionary income to the peace movement.

As a Quaker, Katherine Smith draws upon a long tradition of emphasizing personal responsibility for ameliorating social problems. Quakers have always placed a significant emphasis on the importance of letting one's life speak. American Quakers may no longer send out teams of visitors to remonstrate with backsliders, but they continue to stress the concept of giving witness to one's beliefs. "We use the concept of witnessing in a very personal way. For many of us, it is a fundamental part of how you lead your life. Your witness is how you follow through on your beliefs." Moreover, witnessing includes the actions which members take collectively on behalf of their principles. Politically, "we recognize that the government is not always right and that we should do what we can to correct it. This is where a lot of our protest comes in, from our desire to correct the government and have it change policies. This witnessing is also what distinguishes us from a group such as the Mennonites who tend to pursue a more quietistic pacifism. Many early Friends spent a long time in jail because they were willing to act upon their beliefs."

Describing her own attempts to be consistent with her professed commitment, Katherine attempts to give the impression that she is merely taking small steps which ought to be pursued. The only information that she volunteers is that she has "devoted some time and money to the center." On further probing, she expands somewhat on this description. "I have pledged money to the center and I have also cut back some of my other activities so that I can make an effective contribution. I have discovered that being up-to-date requires an awful lot of self-education so that I have had to limit my pleasure reading so that I can keep abreast of peace issues and the various controversies." The actual depth of her commitment might best be explained by noting that when the movement was just getting started in Richmond, Katherine also took a week off from her job so that she could staff the nuclear freeze campaign booth at the state fair. Today, she is resisting a token amount of her taxes by withholding the federal tax on her telephone bill as "one way of turning my attention to that side of the issue," though she maintains, "I am not brave enough to resist all war taxes."

One feature of Katherine's religious outlook which promotes active social involvement is her belief that "if there is anything in which all Quakers believe it is that people have an inner light, a capacity for good which can be potentially drawn out." In political terms, this is normally taken to mean that people are capable of listening to reasoned arguments about the importance of living nonviolently and capable of changing their habits accordingly. This understanding imbues Katherine and other Quakers with a democratic optimism that imparts a rationality to social activism. Fellow citizens are not viewed as hopeless militarists or as rednecks who relish violence, but as people willing to listen to reason and to engage in discussion. Democracy is possible because of the inner capacities of human beings. Thus it is perfectly sensible for Katherine to take off work and staff a booth at the state fair because it provides her with an opportunity to talk to her fellow citizens and tell you that she was "pleasantly surprised at how much support we received." It is this same understanding that leads her to think that a combination of diligence, imaginative strategy, and good fortune can make some decisive inroads into the way the population views war and peace questions.

Another element of Katherine's religious tradition which contributes positively to her social efficacy comes from the Quaker practice of reaching decisions by consensus. On the most basic level, this mode of decision making reinforces the prevalent belief in the peace community that there are possible alternatives to violent conflict because it provides an experiential base, albeit not a large one, for the belief. Having seen this procedure work in a small group that shares similar values, there is some confidence among Friends that the procedure can be modified so that it is appropriate in settings of larger scale where interests apparently diverge. Whether this confidence is warranted on an international level is yet to be adequately illustrated. But it is certainly critically important to the capacity of local groups to function effectively and efficiently. One of the perennial dilemmas of local organizations is the simple task of trying to run meetings so that goals are set, plans are accomplished, and people leave with the feeling that they have not wasted their time. Katherine takes pride in this knowledge and believes that it is a "skill which can be developed through training and experience." Consequently, meetings which she chairs often tend to move more smoothly and have a sharper definition than is common in many organizational settings.

While Katherine recognizes that her efforts may ultimately be futile, she exhibits a substantial degree of confidence about the possibilities of success. She talks about the historical roots of her optimism; she refers once again to evolution; and she mentions the initial success of efforts like the opening of the Richmond Peace Education Center. "Anyone who remembers the Vietnam protests knows how small these were at first and how long it took to build the momentum up. We've evolved law, we've evolved religion, and we can evolve to a higher form of government. In Richmond, there will be a long-term payoff to our activities in the freeze campaign and the peace education center. We've now become a recognized resource for schoolteachers, churches, and other groups. The freeze and moving beyond it toward disarmament are ideas whose time is coming in this country. There is a great deal of learning and a great deal of study and sophistication about nuclear weapons that we never had before."

Katherine's confidence in the possibility of a cultural evolution that will lead people to realize the counterproductivity of nuclear weapons is paralleled by her belief that people, if given the opportunity, would prefer not to fight one another. She is fond of telling the story of two Quaker dissidents in the revolutionary period which indicates, she thinks, "where men's hearts really are." It seems that these two young men from Virginia refused to bear arms, maintaining that killing was against their religious principles. There was much discussion about what to do with these objectors and the prevailing sentiment among the authorities was to punish them severely and publicly chastise them as an example to others. George Washington, however, demurred, suggesting that the best policy was to treat the matter lightly and shield it from the public eye, saying, "I fear to make an example of them, lest it become the predominant religion in the commonwealth."

Not everyone in the Richmond movement shares Katherine Smith's Quaker ideals or belief in the likely direction of cultural evolution. But many have found some reason to remain optimistic about potential changes. This is obviously vital for any social movement that wants to endure. But there are also dangers here: hope for the future might replace the kind of political analysis that will be necessary to develop workable strategies, and a commitment to consensus may obscure the abiding divisions that inevitably characterize political debate. The personalists in Richmond are more concerned than Dan Berrigan with the practical effects of their activities. But, as will be seen in the next chapter, they are ambivalent about politics, perhaps the principal activity for effecting their goals.

At the beginning of this chapter, I described the personalists active in the peace community as pragmatic utopians. To some, this label might appear not only strange, but self-contradictory as well. In reality, however, it represents an important strain in American reformism. Historically, it was practiced by those abolitionists who not only called for an immediate end to slavery, but resisted unjust laws themselves and developed pamphlet campaigns in the South. It can also be seen in many populists at the end of the nineteenth century who labored to establish what they called the co-operative commonwealth while they toured the nation teaching farmers how to organize around their immediate objectives. In our time, this blend of vision and pragmatism can be seen in the efforts of someone like Martin Luther King, who was not only a dreamer with a religious vision, but one of the shrewdest political tacticians of mid-century America, capable of combining social prophecy with political dramaturgy.

The attempt to balance vision with pragmatism is always plagued with difficulties. Within reform movements, there are always different points of view on how to get things done without diminishing the moral vision that generated the impulse in the first place. Some movements may fail because they refuse to take the steps necessary to influence others and achieve their objectives. Other efforts, of course, may gain success, but only at the expense of their initial purposes. The next chapters try to describe how people in the local peace movement have dealt with this dilemma, adhering to their own standards of faithfulness while attempting to convince other Americans to become more critical of government policy.

3

Fear and Loving in the Nuclear Age: Political Education and Citizenship in the Local Peace Movement

PROFESSOR Sheldon Wolin criticized the emergent peace movement in 1982 for what he maintained were its apolitical tendencies. Using the events which took place during Ground Zero week that year as an example, Wolin argued in his magazine *democracy* that the "antinuclear movement provides a glimpse into what is quickly becoming the future of American politics. It poses as great a threat to democracy as the invention of thermonuclear weapons does to the future of mankind, for it depoliticizes both the problem of nuclear war and the civic activity that is supposed to prevent it." It accomplishes this through its insistence that education be nonpartisan and that it not encourage mass political action.[1]

Wolin went on to suggest that two negative consequences typically follow from this outlook. First, the movement itself is likely to be ineffective because it can easily be co-opted by the powers that be. "By striking the pose of being above politics the antinuclear movement set itself up to be victimized. It took but a few weeks for Ronald Reagan to accommodate them. By the simple stroke of his 9 May 1982 speech at Eureka College he was able to show how easy it is to regain the initiative and to convince the media of his good intentions while serving up a disarmament proposal that the Soviets can scarcely take seriously." Second, Wolin maintained that such a strategy merely reinforces the existing malpractice of democracy in which "politics is reduced to education conducted within a framework devised beforehand by the authorities qualified to define the choices and the limits of the problem. Discussion then takes place within the terms and on the terrain set by experts. The new politics has special conceptions of membership, participation and civic virtue: a member is anyone on a computerized mailing list; participation consists of signing a pledge to contribute money; civic virtue is actually writing the check. The culminating moment, the functional equivalent to storming the Bastille, is when the paid advertisement appears in the Sunday New York Times."[2]

Professor Wolin's commentary on the peace movement was partially true, but only partially. He was correct to note that political argument is sometimes avoided through reliance on the testimony of experts such as scientists and physicians about the danger of nuclear war and the risks contained in current policy directions. Moreover, there are participants who view politics as hopelessly corrupt and see no possibility of changing the public world through organized, collective action. And there are others who think that whatever activity is undertaken should be resolutely nonpartisan. But the actual situation is considerably more complex. Wolin specifically ignored the local initiatives that encouraged citizens to assume a sense of responsibility for global issues and the efforts by many activists to move the nuclear debate out of the hands of the arms-control experts and into the streets, the churches, and the voting booths. Wolin's omissions precluded him from examining the political education actually conducted by the movement and how at least some of the religiously oriented activists were attempting to loosen the paralysis of cynicism that afflicts the idea of citizen action. An equally important consequence is that he evaded confronting the actual difficulties that people such as the Richmond activists encounter when they try to further their goals. What are workable strategies for convincing the majority of your fellow citizens that the cause is important and that they should provide active support? How are others persuaded that your views are not so far out that it is not worth their time to listen? How are people motivated to believe that their actions can make a difference?

This chapter examines the feelings expressed about politics, the methods of political education, and the conceptions of civic virtue that were found among the people I observed in Richmond. The first part notes that while participants sometimes do eschew political action in favor of nonpartisan rational education about the threat of nuclear war and its attendant dangers, there are also numerous indications that local activists are experimenting with political action on a number of levels. Personalists are ambivalent about politics, combining skepticism about its current practice with a commitment to developing alternative forms of public action. The next section demonstrates how the themes of fear and love are utilized in the political education offered by the peace community. In their public presentations, activists emphasized the dangers of a nuclear holocaust and their belief that current policies are exacerbating the threat. But they also tried to suggest that fear can be alleviated by developing a hopeful politics that builds on the human capacities of empathy, cooperation, and love, qualities embodied in the life of Jesus. The final part of the chapter describes how this redemptive politics is grounded in an atypical conception of citizenship, one in which public action is related to the notion of witnessing. I suggest that this conception of faithful action represents an alternative to what Wolin calls the new politics, but that it is one whose successful implementation is problematic in Richmond and elsewhere.

Nonpartisanship and Politics

Many observers of our society have been struck by the way Americans claim that social problems can be resolved by education and improved communication. Participants in the recent antinuclear agitation are no exception. Reading the literature that the movement produces, observing the programs that it sponsors, and talking to the activists, one notices a reliance on the transforming power of what is labeled education. Phyllis Conklin, for instance, has been involved in peace and social justice campaigns for nearly thirty years. She wrote her first letter to the editor of the conservative Richmond newspapers in 1963, criticizing American policy toward Cuba, and has since maintained that the American media "feeds the public a diet of pablum." Asked what gives her hope and the determination to remain active under these conditions, she responds, "I've often started out in left field only to see the whole country come join me. If people only understand the truth about the arms race, it might well be reversed." John Gallini, the chemical engineer who has been instrumental in the formation and growth of the Richmond Pax Christi chapter, notes that "education is very important, . . . for if people reflected on their faith and had the understanding of the gospel, they might view American politics differently."

The antinuclear weapons movement in Richmond organized a number of programs based on this assumption. The peace education center's speakers bureau offered presentations called "The Facts of the Arms Race." A number of laypeople and clergy addressed religious education classes on the relationship between faith, the message of the Bible, and the threat of nuclear war. These programs in the churches were complemented by similar sessions for children. A chapter of the Physicians for Social Responsibility screened *The Last Epidemic* to community groups and sponsored forums on the medical consequences of nuclear war. This perspective was reinforced by the attention that members of the community paid to self-education. The peace education center's newsletter regularly printed information on national budgetary matters as well as practical suggestions on how to translate peace concerns into daily living practices. Pax Christi invited a guest speaker to lecture about an issue of contemporary concern at its monthly meetings. Many individuals subscribed to magazines of general political commentary along with more specialized periodicals about national security issues.

As Professor Wolin has noted, the movement has a tendency to deemphasize the political elements of its quest to implement a freeze and other steps toward disarmament. This has been particularly true of some self-appointed national spokespersons like Roger Molander and a few people in professional organizations. But it is also the case in Richmond. A majority of participants in the local peace community were not active opponents of the Vietnam War and were not previously involved in politics. For many of them, participation in the peace movement was an outgrowth of their involvement in church activities that were not politically controversial. They may have been volunteers, as John Gallini and Wendy Northup were, in religious education classes. Some have helped to settle refugees from Southeast Asia in the city. Others were part of local campaigns against world hunger. Since their participation in antinuclear activities is related to their religious beliefs, their self-perception is frequently not expressed in political terms. Many of the activists prefer to define themselves as "peace makers" and call what they do "peace making" by referring to passages in the Bible where God instructs his followers to make peace.

The reluctance to define oneself as a political activist can even be noticed among some of the people who were previously connected to partisan organizations and acknowledge the significance of politics to their current efforts. They want to claim that the movement possesses a moral dimension not ordinarily found in partisan activity, that it is not "merely political." Jerry Gorman, for example, is a medical doctor who in the early 1960s was a Republican county committeeman in northern Florida. Comparing his past activism with his present commitments, Jerry is careful to emphasize the moral component of what he is doing today. "No one then really had a commitment to social justice or acting for the good of most people. It was simply a question of trying to get Republicans into office and putting Democrats out. No one seemed to think twice about lying or cheating if it served our purposes. You couldn't really go home and feel proud about what you were doing. I feel much better about what I'm doing today. I am trying to build a better world and I think that I am performing God's work."

The disposition to avoid partisan controversy is also evident in some of the movement's rhetoric. One strategy common in peace circles is to claim that reversing the arms race is not a political issue because nuclear war "threatens all of us equally." Arguing that conventional political distinctions are meaningless when set beside the possibility of a nuclear holocaust, freeze advocates suggest that political affiliation ought not to prevent anyone from being concerned about the arms race and from giving their ideas a serious hearing. Activists were thus quick to direct their audiences' attention to well-known conservatives like James J. Kilpatrick and Cardinal Krol, who have spoken positively of the movement, and to former high-ranking government officials like William Colby, who endorsed the freeze.

Another example of the movement's apolitical rhetoric can be found in the vocabulary used to describe current governmental practices. It was not uncommon for speakers talking on behalf of the freeze to characterize politicians in unflattering psychological terms, specifically as patients in need of treatment. In 1982, "irrational" and "insane" were probably the words most frequently used to characterize the policies of our elected officials. These were catchwords—probably overused—designed to suggest that international relations have become a kind of madness. This strategy of persuasion was justified by pointed references to statements of Reagan administration officials about the survivability of a nuclear war and the government's intention to prevail if one occurs. The apolitical feature of the argument was the implication that nuclear war can be averted primarily by sanity and rationality, and that reasonable people will not have difficulty agreeing on its appropriate political manifestations.

The reticence to grapple with sticky political questions was frequently evident in presentations about the medical consequences of nuclear war. The film *The Last Epidemic* and the lecture often given along with its screening both stress the magnitude of destruction that would result from a nuclear exchange among the superpowers. The program appears to be premised on the assumption that psychic numbing, a concept originally applied by R. J. Lifton to survivors of Hiroshima, now accurately describes the reluctance of Americans to acknowledge the destructive capability of nuclear weapons. The method chosen to resensitize people is a detailed exposition of the likely outcomes of a nuclear attack. This is presented in depressingly graphic yet unemotional terms, with descriptions of buildings collapsing, cities enveloped by firestorms, and millions rendered helpless by radiation poisoning. It is a fire-and-brimstone sermon in which the pictures do the talking. Although the audience was often asked to oppose nuclear war and perhaps to support the freeze, the political context was frequently left unexamined. In the sessions I attended, there was little explanation of the historical trends and political forces both inside and outside the nation which have brought the threat before us.

If these apolitical tendencies were characteristic of the entire range of activity in the local movement, there would be no purpose in dissenting from Professor Wolin's analysis. But there are many other features of recent peace activism that should be considered in any assessment of it. The movement's political nature can be discerned most vividly in its emphasis on grassroots activism and encouragement of mass participation. It can also be seen in the efforts of the Richmond participants to relate the arms race to social justice concerns, build coalitions with other progressive organizations in the city, and organize on a precinct basis for the Democratic party's state convention. Far from being unconcerned about politics, local activists in Richmond have exhibited interest in as great a variety of political forms as do most people who consider themselves highly partisan.

A striking feature of the new peace activism was the determination with which people involved in it sought to bring their message to others. In Richmond, the peace community experimented with a number of methods for influencing the general public, especially people who may not have initially shared the activists' leanings. Members of the various peace groups did not immediately form an insular subculture or identify themselves more closely with regional and national organizations than with their work in the local area. At meetings of the local organizations, the general membership was invariably urged to make their voices heard and "to get out and talk with people." There was discussion about how this might be effectively accomplished and a genuine effort was made to put this commitment into practice. Outdoor concerts were leafletted, contacts made with other political groups in the city, and "freeze parties" held in the neighborhoods to discuss with people the rationale behind the movement. For two years, the peace community staffed an information booth at the state fair

which had a free "Knock a Nuke" game to keep children occupied while
parents discussed the arms race, nuclear proliferation, and the freeze with a
volunteer worker.

Many of the persuasive tactics that can be described as apolitical have
their roots in the activists' efforts to think of ways of reaching more people.
Members of the peace community have struggled to discover ways of
bringing their ideas to others and involving them in their movement. A
strategy which, in the abstract, can be criticized as being apolitical, may
actually be an imaginative method of publicizing the cause. For example, it
might be argued that referring to conservative supporters of the freeze
only disguises the extent of the political changes that would actually have
to occur if leaders were to commit the nation to genuine disarmament. But
the context in which this is done in Richmond has obvious political implications. James J. Kilpatrick, former editor of the *Richmond News Leader,*
originally gained a national reputation for his stand opposing school integration in the fifties. In 1982, he published an essay praising the impulse
behind the freeze and condemning elected officials for not being serious
about arms control. His former paper decided not to run it, claiming that
it had too much local commentary to print that week. When Phyllis
Conklin photocopied the column from the *Atlanta Constitution* and stood
outside the *News Leader* handing it to employees and passersby, she was
not only indicating that the freeze had a broad base of support, but was
issuing an imaginative political challenge to the operation of the local
media.

What is eminently clear about the style of outreach developed by the
peace community is that it differs considerably, in both form and substance, from the new politics that Professor Wolin lampoons in his commentary. Instead of relying heavily on the media, employing sophisticated
techniques of direct-mail solicitation, and concentrating a significant portion of its energy on fund raising, peace activists in Richmond operate very
differently. They are concerned about raising enough money to fund their
programs, but they also work to minimize the role which money plays in
their efforts. They rely on face-to-face meetings with potential supporters,
have developed local organs of communication, and are concerned with
building a permanent culture on a grassroots level. To be sure, some of
these emphases may be attributed in part to the movement's inability to
raise large sums of money or to attract significant media attention. But the
decision is also ethical and ideological. It is rooted in a belief that, in the
long run, the movement's success is dependent on the creation of an
enduring peace culture in the city and that this cannot be constructed

merely by adept fund raising and adroit use of media. Rather, it is a slow and patient process that requires face-to-face work, encouraging active involvement, and developing a personal commitment to work for peace. In this respect, the movement has more in common with the abolitionist and populist crusades of the nineteenth century than it does with contemporary movements which apply the techniques of public relations to politics.[3]

Another element of the political outlook of the local peace movement is the positive light in which most activists view political participation. The members of the peace community are involved in a broad range of political activities, organizing letter-writing campaigns to the local newspaper, visiting their representatives at both their area and Washington offices, and working in campaigns for candidates supportive of the freeze. In 1984, the Richmond Nuclear Freeze campaign used the signatures on the petitions they had gathered to develop a fledgling political organization. Directing their efforts toward the Democratic party's precinct meetings in the city, the campaign solicited delegates and organized support for those who ran under its banner. The immediate goal was to elect delegates to the party's state convention who would support a liberal Democratic candidate for senator. The more significant, long-term objective was to plant the seed for an enduring presence within the local political order. The campaign was quite successful: nearly one quarter of the delegates from the city came out of the freeze campaign and inroads were even made into the normally conservative delegations from the surrounding counties which compose the congressional district.[4]

It would be inaccurate, then, to rely on the Ground Zero organization's disapproval of mass politics as an indicator of the position held by local activists in Richmond. Members of the peace community are cynical about politicians, one reason why they often claim not to be engaged in politics. They are convinced that most elected officials would not, of their own accord, support the freeze or more vigorous steps toward disarmament. But they do operate on the assumption that political leaders act when pressured by the activity bubbling beneath them. In Richmond, Pax Christi rented the buses and worked with the Quakers to organize the logistics for people attending the demonstration held on 12 June 1982 in New York City. The prevailing sentiment among the people I observed was probably best captured by Jerry Gorman, who maintains that "politicians are like surfboard riders. They wait and look for the biggest wave and then they ride it home. What we are trying to do is make the wave so large that they'll eventually have to get on. Demonstrations are a part of this process." At the same time, Jerry and other peace activists believe that protest alone cannot accomplish their aims, so that "while it's important and fun to demonstrate in Washington or march in New York, the real change has to occur in the local culture and this is what we are patiently trying to bring about. We have to work where we can be effective."

The peace community's support of unconventional politics extends to the use of civil disobedience as an instrument of political education. Although it is by no means the predominant mode of collective action in the Richmond community, civil disobedience is practiced by a number of people and taken seriously by many more. Approximately two dozen people are refusing to pay what they label war taxes. Most are simply refusing to pay the federal tax on their phone bill, since it was enacted to help defray the costs of the Vietnam War and remains committed to the military. Each month they include a letter to this effect when they send their check to the telephone company. A few people have taken tax resistance much further and have refused to pay about 40 percent of their income tax during the past two years and have instead placed their monies in a world peace tax fund escrow account not recognized by the government. Steve Hodges, coordinator of the Richmond Peace Education Center, has not only resisted payment, but has transformed his stand into a vehicle of public education, granting interviews to local print and broadcast reporters about his decision. Two other members of the peace community have been arrested for engaging in civil disobedience, one who interrupted President Reagan during a speech in the city and another who participated in the destruction of a Pershing launcher at the Martin Marietta plant in Orlando, Florida. In each instance, the person involved was careful to explain his rationale for the action, his fears, and his hopes to the wider community.[5]

A further indication of the political leanings of the new peace activism is its ongoing attempt to connect peace issues to social justice concerns. Much of the local agitation about American involvement in El Salvador and Nicaragua had its origins in programs conducted by the Protestant and Catholic churches in the spring of 1981. Ministers throughout the area have been insistent in maintaining that there can "be no peace without justice." Continuing concern has been exhibited about U.S. involvement in Central America. In 1983 and 1984, five participants in the local movement became involved in the Witness for Peace in Nicaragua. They returned with the usual collection of memories, slides, and reflections, offering these at the meetings of various local groups. When Wendy Northup decided to travel as part of the Witness for Peace in 1984, she held meetings and parties beforehand as a way of involving others from the community in her journey. In 1985, Pax Christi and other people in the peace community were instrumental in circulating the Pledge of Resistance and making plans to implement it if U.S. military involvement in Central America was escalated.

A final element in the political makeup of the new peace movement is the effort that several activists have made to build bridges with the minority community. It is a commonplace to note that peace activism tends to be a white middle-class affair. For the most part, this remains true in Richmond. Yet it should be mentioned that people in the peace community have begun, in some small ways, to widen their base. They have not only broadened their movement to include other global issues such as Central America, but have attempted to build a progressive coalition in the city. Steve Hodges became involved with black ministers who organized and planned an annual Community Learning Week commemorating the memory of Martin Luther King, Jr. Black and white clergy worked together in designing a program to highlight the connections King was trying to illuminate toward the end of his life between peace issues, civil rights, and economic justice. A number of ministers built on this foundation to establish the Virginia Interfaith Peace Coalition, an ecumenical and integrated group that was the major force behind the first statewide peace conference in Virginia in 1983, which featured Shirley Chisholm as the guest speaker.

Peace activists also worked along with the minority community on the local mobilization effort for the Twentieth Anniversary March on Washington in the summer of 1983. The mobilization involved raising funds so that anyone who wanted to attend could be transported, renting and scheduling buses, and heightening consciousness throughout the city of the day's significance. Planning for the event was time-consuming, as meetings were held regularly over a two-month period. It was also challenging because most of the people involved had not previously worked together. Matters such as routing a bus or deciding how to allocate costs could generate heated controversy insofar as some participants might view the position taken by a person of another race as an example of white insensitivity or black intransigence. On a couple of occasions, it appeared that the coalition would imminently disintegrate into warring camps. Yet the commitment of the people involved eventually overcame the tendencies making for suspicion and disunion, and a successful mobilization occurred. The initial hope of some of the organizers that a "permanent coalition of conscience" would be formed was not realized, but they felt that the mobilization was an important start toward dissipating the fear and distrust that contribute to the difficulty of forming interracial coalitions. It was also an important building block for local agitation against apartheid that emerged a few years later.

The ambivalence about politics expressed by the Richmond activists is almost inherent in the personalist approach. Its depiction of recent American history, its emphasis on the opportunism of political figures, and its concern for developing a morally consistent foreign policy require that adherents be skeptical about political activity. It is not surprising that "expert knowledge," "education," and "peace making" are put forward as alternatives to "politics." Yet the activists' desire to change national policies and the culture of the wider society draws them inescapably into the political realm—regardless of how they might characterize what they are doing. And even if, like Wendy Northup, they do not originally see themselves as political activists, the controversies in which they become involved highlight the political nature of their efforts.

Fear, Cynicism, and Commitment

The outreach efforts of the Richmond peace community repeatedly emphasized certain themes. Most discussions of the arms race averred that there is a "rough parity" between the United States and the Soviet Union with respect to nuclear capabilities. While this balance was acknowledged not to be perfectly symmetrical, activists claimed that it is inaccurate to speak in terms of either side possessing overall superiority. Relations between the United States and the Soviet Union were said to be increasingly unstable because harsh rhetoric and new weapons reduced the level of trust, increased the danger of accidental war, and made verification procedures more difficult. Speakers argued that the magnitude of destruction that would inevitably occur during a nuclear confrontation could not possibly be approved by the just-war tradition. To punctuate this point, films or simply a recitation of statistics about the probable number of deaths and injuries were offered. Activists claimed that a common interest between the United States and the Soviet Union makes it possible to reach agreements diminishing the reliance on nuclear weapons. Speakers suggested that it is up to the population to pressure elected officials to support the freeze and other steps making for a more peaceful world.

Almost all of the activists to whom I spoke were originally pleasantly surprised at how rapidly their audiences came to share their fear about the threat of nuclear war. A common response of people listening to "The Facts of the Arms Race" or watching a screening of *The Last Epidemic* was to express their anxieties about a potential nuclear confrontation to the rest of the gathering. Middle-aged men spoke of waking in the dark of night from a dream about the holocaust unleashed by a nuclear confrontation. A young married couple told about their hesitancy to bring children into a world for which they had little hope. Mothers and fathers related the tragicomic remarks of their children about the end of the world. On occasion, the discussion following the program actually took the form of a collective confessional, with an almost palpable sense of relief passing over the audience as people became aware that others had experienced similar feelings.

The favorable response which the presentations about the danger of nuclear war received was, in some senses, not as stunning as it may have seemed to many people in 1982. Admittedly, the public appeared unconcerned about the prospect of thermonuclear annihilation prior to the inception of the freeze campaign. Yet the educational programs of the activists appealed to sentiments that a sizeable portion of the public already held. Americans have historically been skeptical of the notion that a nuclear war could be won or even survived. In the mid-1950s and for a few years after, many politicians and journalists lamented the failure of the public to embrace Nelson Rockefeller's ideas about civil defense with sufficient enthusiasm. When activists today suggest that a nuclear exchange would be a "war without winners" or "the last epidemic," they are putting on a more sophisticated footing the popular belief that if a war occurs between the United States and the Soviet Union "we'll all be blown to smithereens." It is not inconsistent for those fearful of Soviet intentions to be equally distressed by the prospect of increasing tensions between the two superpowers. Indeed, the statements by Reagan administration officials that nuclear war is survivable were more distant from mainstream opinion than the assessment of nuclear war furnished by the peace activists.

The movement's assertion that politicians cannot always be trusted to make sensible judgments about national security matters and may occasionally deliberately mislead the public about their intentions is another area where peace activists appealed to sentiments that have become widely held. Public opinion surveys consistently reported a decline from 1960 to 1980 in the respect and trust that Americans have in their authority figures. Observers from all vantage points on the political spectrum have commented on the cynicism that has become one of the most distinctive features of contemporary political life. To suggest that politicians are ambitious and self-centered, or even immoral, irrational, and insane is no longer a radical assertion because it has been woven into the very fabric of American political culture. Indeed, it has become so prevalent that it is now a ritual task of a candidate for office to tell us why he or she is not just another politician.[6]

There is another sense in which peace activism was reflective of trends ascendant in the culture. For the past twenty years, it has become evident that many Americans have been influenced by the intimation of a coming catastrophe and that this sentiment is not confined to those of liberal inclinations. It can be seen in survivalists who are certain that a holocaust will occur, but are more intent on remaining alive in its aftermath than in preventing it. It is also evident in numerous conservative religious sects. Billy Graham has lectured for many years about biblical references to a nuclear conflagration, though it is only recently that he has joined the disarmament lobby and proposed that the country skip SALT II and SALT III and go directly to SALT X. Besides Graham, there are other writers and lecturers, such as Hal Lindsey, who have garnered a following for their books and lecture tours by informing the public that the day of judgment is imminent. One of Lindsey's books, *The Late Great Planet Earth,* was outsold only by the Bible among nonfiction titles during the seventies.[7] The threat of oblivion is also marketed by the entertainment industry in the endless production of horror movies and the infinite variations on "Invader" and "Destroyer" games found in video arcades across the nation.

This point can be reinforced by noting that imagining the ultimate disaster has even been a part of mainstream American politics for about twenty years. In 1962, the nation watched as John F. Kennedy went "eyeball to eyeball" with the Soviet Union in the "hour of maximum danger." Then it witnessed Lyndon Johnson's 1964 campaign when a now infamous advertisement made reference to Goldwater's presumed instability by juxtaposing a mushroom cloud with a little girl plucking a daisy. Jimmy Carter tried to rescue a flagging presidential campaign in 1980 by reviving this fear with respect to Ronald Reagan in the waning days of October. Walter Mondale's red phone was only one more effort in what had become by 1984 a routine maneuver to gain electoral advantage by using the threat of ultimate catastrophe to disparage one's opponent.[8]

The success of local activists in 1982 and 1983 in raising public consciousness about the threat of nuclear war thus rested not so much on their challenge to the dominant trends in the culture as on their ability to maneuver skillfully within the dimensions of existing sentiment. But many of the people who are involved in the movement also wanted to challenge other citizens to think more deeply about the substance of American politics and to persuade them to commit time and energy to promoting these alternatives in Richmond. They did not desire simply to reinforce the feeling that nuclear war would be terrible and to confirm people's suspicions about elected officials. They wanted to overcome the notion that there is nothing that an individual, a group, or even an organized movement can do to influence the policies of the megastates that dominate world politics.

The predicament that they faced was perhaps best stated by Jean-Baptiste Clamence, the principal character in Camus's novel *The Fall*. He observes that "there are really efforts and convictions I have never been able to understand. . . . I could better understand that friend who made up his mind to stop smoking and through sheer will power had succeeded. One morning he opened up the paper, read that the first H-bomb had been exploded, learned about its wonderful effects and hastened to a tobacco shop." Having argued that the United States and the Soviet Union pursue a course that makes conflict more likely and then having shown the disastrous consequences of this conflict, activists had to demonstrate that the most appropriate response was not to head for the tobacco shop. In essence, skepticism about the intentions and policies of elected leaders had to be separated from cynicism about organized collective action.

The men and women in Richmond did not shy away from the challenge. They gave consideration to the manner in which, on a local level, the connection between a belief that a policy is misguided and a commitment to change that policy might be restored. In a negative sense, they encouraged action by suggesting that a posture of hopelessness becomes a self-fulfilling prophecy because it allows current trends to proceed unabated without even an effort to reverse them. More positively, there was an emphasis throughout the movement on taking small, personal steps that can give witness to a commitment to peace. People are urged to change the world by first demilitarizing their own lives and taking exemplary actions that reflect this determination. So Steve and Wendy Northup, regional coordinators of the Parenting for Peace and Justice program, opened their house to battered women; John Gallini initiated a twinning relationship between his white suburban church and a more urban, predominantly black church; and Steve and Diantha Hodges pursued "downward mobility" so that they could be without the burdens that they believe wealth imposes. Peace activists were not as demanding with their audiences as they were with themselves. But they invariably encouraged individuals to take positive action, however mundane and trivial it might be. People were asked to sign a freeze petition, speak to their children about peace issues, or serve as volunteers at a movement event. They were invited to become involved in the activities sponsored by the peace community.

Here again, some of the more imaginative ways of attempting to restore the connection between belief and action could be traced to religious conviction. Consider, for example, the programs which Steve Hodges organized in local religious education classes. Steve frequently began his talk, "Religious Perspectives and the Arms Race," by referring to the Old Testament prophets. He suggested that these were people who examined their society with a critical eye and were outspoken in their opposition to the social and economic injustices of their era. The prophets taught people that "God wants a vision of justice and they articulated this vision with images that are beautiful. They told of places where there would be no poverty, where there would be peace under the vine and the fig tree and where social discord would be healed as well as the discord within individual personalities. The images of healing evoked by the prophets foretold a condition in which contradictions would be resolved through a wholesome synthesis of opposites and in the reconciliation of all creation through the life work of a Messiah." Steve went on to say that the New Testament represents a fulfillment of the Old Testament prophecies, albeit in a provocative and unexpected manner. Jesus arrives as the living embodiment of the vision. He is a king who comes as a suffering servant. He heals the lepers and consorts with the unsavory, all the while instructing his disciples to do the same.

To the pragmatists who respect the vision, but think it impossible to pursue in an ethically imperfect and sometimes abhorrent world, Steve offered two responses. First, he maintained that the Bible does not ask us to act as if we are oblivious to the real conditions of the world. He urged people to be both faithful and realistic, to be as "innocent as doves" but also as "wise as serpents." Suggesting that faithfulness is not equivalent to ineffectiveness, he spoke about the importance of approaching people on a level at which they are comfortable and, at least initially, finding an opening for a peace argument within the framework of their professed beliefs. Second, Steve contended that pragmatic calculations are notoriously unreliable. He asks the students in his classes to reflect on their experiences with personal disarmament: "What happens when you lay down some of your defenses so that a relationship might improve?" Inevitably, he maintains, people are compelled by the force of experience to acknowledge that life is not measured in terms of cost-benefit analyses and that "small actions can unlock a greater power of reconciliation and love." This is the case, Steve thinks, in political life as well as in personal relationships. At a minimum, he believes that relations between the United States and the Soviet Union can be unfrozen. He envisions the possibility of redirecting American defense policy and perhaps the culture in general by the cumulation of small, faithful actions which thousands of Americans take in their cities, towns, and neighborhoods.

What is especially noteworthy about Steve's perspective and that adopted by other religiously oriented peace activists is the manner in which faith and faithfulness work to dissolve the cynicism about collective action so prevalent in the secular culture. Katherine Smith's commitment as a Quaker motivated her to take time off from work so that she could go to the state fair and bring the message of the peace community to the visitors. A similar viewpoint is evident in the attitude which accompanies Wendy Northup's efforts. She does not speak of an inner light and admits that it can be very discouraging attempting to involve people in the movement, but she remarks, "I try to appeal to the best in people, to that side of them which wants peace even if it is not fully consistent with their political outlook." Makanah Morris, a Unitarian minister who is director of religious education at her church, reflects a similar outlook when she tells of not being discouraged by knowing that people do not hold her viewpoint. "I know that everyone will not agree with me, but I look for an opening in what they are actually saying to show them that we do share some common values."

Ironically, the traditional claim of some people on the Left that religion is only an opiate of the masses is undermined by this recognition. When commitments are undertaken at times when presumably rational and calculating people would remain cynical and inactive, it is difficult to maintain that religion is a political depressant. The peace community in Richmond operates on assumptions that are altogether different from those prevalent in an era when worries about "wasting time" and a belief that "time is money" are common sentiments. Activists met in church basements many years ago in groups of five to ten to speak about educating the public for peace and disarmament. They helped to plan a freeze campaign when to most people the word signified cold weather or a popsicle. They went to the River Road Baptist Church, the state fair, and Patriotism Day in order to talk with men and women whom many people on the Left had given up as hopeless. It may well be that the real opiate of the people is no longer religion but the general consumer orientation of the secular culture that encourages a retreat from public engagement and organizes time according to a cult of the moment which ridicules long-term commitment.

Personalist efforts to generate commitment and participation may well be overly optimistic and not entirely "rational," if what is reasonable is gauged according to whether the desired outcome will actually occur. For this reason, the kind of appeal that Steve Hodges makes in religious education classes may have only limited success. One can easily understand why people (or nations, for that matter) will want better guarantees of outcomes before they change behavior in a significant way. Nonetheless, personalists are correct to note that social movements cannot succeed if people are not willing to assume risks and to become committed to goals whose success cannot be predicted with a large degree of certainty. In this sense, observers who emphasize the rationality of social movements may inadvertently condescend to the participants by ignoring how different their calculations may be from those of ordinary people.

Citizenship as Witness

When local activists were asked what the concept of citizenship meant to them, it was not uncommon for them to reply, "I hold very old-fashioned values on that topic." Wendy Northup observed, "I think that our country's ideals are really sound. When I think about them or hear them in a speech, I feel deeply patriotic and genuinely moved. I do believe that people should vote, that they should participate in their society, and that they should not complain if they are unwilling to make the effort to change it." Even among some of the more skeptical activists, one can find admiration for American political ideals. John Gallini notes, "Although I'm often cynical about it, I have a great belief in and a strong commitment to the democratic process. I spend much of my time trying to make it work." Phyllis Conklin, who thinks that Friendly Fascism may be coming to America, still admits that she probably doesn't "value enough the freedoms which we do have" and that she is "an old-fashioned conservative with respect to citizen responsibility."

All these comments are perfectly compatible with traditional notions of civic responsibility in a democracy and could as well be voiced by the supporters of Ronald Reagan. The potential subversiveness of the remarks lies in how far removed these ideas are from the dominant perceptions of citizenship and its actual practice. If one looks, for example, at how citizenship is viewed in much of American social science, it is easy to see this distinctiveness. Citizen activity is most often modeled on the pattern of consumer behavior. Citizens are conceived of as rational actors primarily concerned with maximizing self-interest, just as consumers of products are mainly interested in acquiring high-quality goods at the lowest possible costs. Voting behavior is thus explained largely in terms of perceived self-interest and voter apathy is seen as a rational response to the logic of collective action.

Ironically, a person who exhibits an enduring commitment to a cause comes off, at best, as having a peculiar notion of self-interest and, at worst, as being totally irrational. As Jean Baptiste Clamence says, it is commitment and not apathy which really needs explaining.

This idea about what citizenship means is not merely an abstract notion held by academics but one visible to other observers of American politics and well understood by candidates for elected office, irrespective of political affiliation. The noted conservative commentator George Will, for instance, has characterized the actual practice of citizenship today by asserting that the "average American voter has looked into his heart of hearts, prayed long and hard, and come to the conclusion that it is high time the government cut his neighbor's benefits."[9] Ronald Reagan, who professes to be restoring traditional morality, told the public in his final debate with Jimmy Carter in 1980 that they should base their vote on whether "things" were more expensive in 1980 when they went shopping than they were when Carter took office in 1976.

The notion of citizenship to which many of the religiously oriented peace activists subscribe is different in at least three ways from the outlook described above. In the first place, personalists often describe their activism as giving moral witness. This is, of course, a form of self-interest, but not one in which material benefits are the prime motivation. Standing up for one's beliefs, maintaining consistency, and acting when success is not guaranteed are prominent themes in the lives of these activists. Faithful action and public involvement are not just seen as instruments to obtain material benefits to be used or set aside according to the likely return, but are integral features of one's self-definition. Developing the capacity to act faithfully becomes an important element of one's spiritual well-being. This is one reason why activists spend time at meetings assessing planned actions and evaluating completed endeavors in terms of what these activities meant to them personally as well as how they contributed to the movement's goals.

A second notable feature of the activists' outlook on citizenship is their belief that public action should serve as an example to others, both inside and outside the movement. Men and women give witness not only as a means of self-definition, but to provide hope for people who might share their views and to catch the attention of those who have not yet reflected on the issues. This is, I think, most visible in the participants' arguments in controversial civil disobedience actions. They are motivated by strong personal concerns, but also by a desire to offer symbolic hope to their communities, inform the government of the intensity of their commitment, and bring a message to the wider public. Yet this attitude is also present in more mundane forms of political engagement. Participating in the precinct meetings of the Democratic party, aiding a candidate running for city council who has supported the freeze, or merely setting up an information table at a local event can also be exemplary action. As Jerry Gorman remarks, "It is very important for people to recognize that we exist and are working to change the local culture."

Peace activists would not, however, be comfortable with the idea that their involvement is solely a means of obtaining personal fulfillment and providing a good example to others. They have formulated explicit goals which they intend to pursue. In 1982, they wanted names on the freeze petition. In 1984, they wanted to elect delegates to the state convention of the Democratic party. They hope to exercise continuing influence on the local church community. But they have also developed a broad array of goals so that any individual setback is not perceived as fatal to the move-ment. In fact, they have even been able to interpret certain ostensible failures in a positive light. In 1984, for instance, the Richmond Nuclear Freeze campaign was interested in raising money so that a statewide direc-tor could be employed to coordinate its electoral efforts in November. One method used to raise funds was to gather a group of thirty to forty activists together on a Saturday morning to conduct a door-to-door canvass. By most accounts, the canvass was a failure since it brought in considerably less money than its organizers had anticipated. But a number of the partici-pants found the experience to be positive. Wendy Northup, for instance, felt that it was important because "a lot of people who had never been to a freeze meeting and may have just read the newspapers learned that we are decent human beings who aren't waving communist flags." Steve Hodges echoed her opinion, noting that "it permitted us to distribute literature, learn where our strength is when we need to get out the vote and find some new recruits. There are a variety of methods for raising money, but there are some things that need to be done which can be performed most effectively on a door-to-door basis."

The constellation of attitudes about citizenship expressed and exhibited by the activists is not, of course, exclusive to religiously oriented peace communities. Throughout history, men and women have seen political action as a means of self-expression and public education. Moreover, the ability to put a pleasant face on an obvious failure is a trait possessed by even the most conventional of politicians. Indeed, it could be argued that the attitudes exhibited by the people in the peace community are precisely the same as those held by both the most notorious and the most ineffective, self-deluded movements in history. A good case could be made that we should be wary of men and women who use the political arena as a stage on which to act out their own life dramas. Haven't we seen enough murderers and torturers who refer to some presumed higher destiny and proclaim they are doing God's work as they go about killing and maiming? It is also true that groups which have absolutely no influence frequently maintain a sense of purpose by redefining obvious failures so they do not have to face the public rebuke that has been administered to their position. How else could the various Marxist splinter organizations keep active in late twentieth-century America except by a firm commitment to self-delusion?

These charges are frequently true. Yet many of the figures who have brought pivotal change of a positive nature to the world have shared these attitudes. In politics, there is a fine line separating delusion from legitimate hope, infantile fantasies of personal grandeur from a sustaining sense of personal destiny. Commentators sometimes fail to recognize that fostering significant political change requires not only propitious objective conditions, but also a psychic mobilization of faith and hope against the forces of cynicism and despair.[10] Successful political movements need to translate feelings of resignation into purposeful action, pushing anxieties and grievances that were only background murmurings into the forefront of political discussion. The civil rights movement, which is today generally regarded as a righteous protest against deplorable conditions, was once seen as a dangerous threat to the peace of American society by many politicians, and a number of black people saw it as a delusionary quest that would make life more difficult.

In fact, I would suggest that cynicism became so prevalent in the last decade that offering a sense of hope has become a leitmotif in American politics. For the most part, this need has been better understood by conservative activists than anyone else. People critical of the powers that be and interested in promoting progressive change in American society have not been especially attentive to it. Ensnared by a sophisticated despair, they had either acceded to what they felt was the tenor of the times or concentrated on cutting the losses from conservative assaults. It devolved to Ronald Reagan to rekindle the hopeful spirit of Americans by rallying them around a program of budget cuts and the prospect of restoring respect for the nation by exercising military strength. To some extent, activists in the peace movement present not only a challenge to the specific policies of the Reagan administration but also an alternative vision of hopefulness to the one that underlies his appeal. They speak of a future grounded in a vision of a more cooperative world in which power is used in a transformative manner to improve human life and not merely to control or distance ourselves from its nastier elements.

This is not to suggest that the difficulties involved in doing this are not formidable and perhaps forbidding. On the national level, obstacles to the freeze and further steps toward disarmament seem immovable. These are no less problematic in localities, especially places like Richmond where conservative leaders have held sway for most of the century. The controversy over whether the churches should be involved in politics rages more fiercely and has more practical consequences locally than it does nationally. Since Bishop Walter Sullivan is an outspoken opponent of nuclear weapons policy who encourages his priests to speak about peace issues in their homilies and adult education programs, conservative Catholics have taken offense at what they consider to be the politicization of the Church. There has been a running controversy in the letters-to-the-editor pages of the local newspapers and the *Catholic Virginian* about the stands which Bishop Sullivan has taken. One group of conservative Catholics have started a "Bishop Sullivan Watch" in which they regularly report to the Vatican on what they believe are his excessively liberal pronouncements and actions. While Pax Christi is less troubling to many people because it is not an official part of the Church hierarchy, its emphases have disturbed many Catholics who view the Church as an agent more of personal consolation than of personal and social transformation. The division has also affected some of the Protestant churches in town as influential members of the congregation have sometimes objected to the direction in which the Church is moving.

Outside the churches, the problems are even more extensive. In Richmond, the peace community confronts a conservative business establishment and a political culture that has traditionally supported the belief that peace is the result of superior military strength. The power of this culture has been diluted somewhat as the influence of black citizens has increased in the past twenty years, but it still forms the dominant ethos in the area. For this reason, the task of promoting the freeze and opposing the continual modernization of weaponry is much more difficult than it would be in Madison (Wisconsin), Chapel Hill (North Carolina), New York City, or even in some of the northeastern states where a conservative political culture is not necessarily a militaristic one. These problems are compounded by the conservative monopoly on the daily print media. According to the local editorial line, the advocates of the freeze are either "appeasers," "antediluvians," or "naive idealists" led by a "bishop who bombs out." The press has dusted off the arguments used with anti-Vietnam protesters in the sixties and applied them to the antinuclear activists of the eighties. The Women's International League for Peace and Freedom has been labeled pro-Soviet and the readership has been warned that idealists in the movement may be unwittingly fronting for communists desirous of controlling American life. When the Federal Bureau of Investigation concluded that communists apparently exercised very little influence over the direction and policy of the freeze movement, the *Richmond News Leader* saw fit to emphasize the "apparently," remarking that communist deviousness can sometimes escape detection by even the most zealous guardians of freedom.

For people in the local movement, these particular problems are manifestations of a more general dilemma. When the movement stresses themes about which almost everyone can agree—the danger of nuclear war, the immorality of exposing human beings to high levels of radiation, and the irresponsibility of official rhetoric about survivability—its message makes sense to people, though it also risks becoming politically innocuous. Yet when the movement stresses its ultimate goals, it becomes more difficult to elicit widespread public approval. Visions of disarmament are countered by sobering assessments of the "real world" in which the intentions of the Soviet Union necessitate the posture of peace through strength. Relating peace to social justice concerns can turn off an audience in a very conservative political environment, and personal statements of conscientious objection sit uncomfortably amid people who have reconciled themselves to the daily compromises which life appears to require.

The difficulties that the activists confront can serve to reinforce their skepticism about politics. When this happens, one of the principal dangers of viewing citizenship as a form of moral witness becomes evident. Personalists may become so disgusted with what is achievable that they retreat from political involvement. This is not precisely the kind of withdrawal of which Professor Wolin has spoken. Activists can remain publicly engaged, but they may empty citizenship of its social content by relying almost entirely on individual moral statements and ignoring the possibility of changing political attitudes through conversation and compromise.

This is a continual temptation of the personalist approach and the men and women to whom I spoke are grappling with it. Members of the peace community are struggling to create the conditions that will enable them to cope with their self-doubts, weather the attacks of those who dislike them, and still remain dedicated to reaching a wider public with their message and bringing greater pressure to bear on political leaders. They have spent a good deal of time thinking about the inner life of the groups they have formed and of ways to develop a sense of community that can relieve both the general anomie of modern life and the loneliness that can afflict people with dissident views. Moreover, many of them adhere to religious beliefs which instruct them on the importance of patience and the likelihood that those who undertake to change the hearts and minds of people will undergo trials and maybe persecution. These beliefs about the difficulty and long-term nature of a political success hold, of course, no guarantees, but it is hard to believe that anyone seriously interested in promoting fundamental change could accomplish this in contemporary America without possessing them.

4

A World Worth Living In: Building Culture and Community in the Local Movement

DWIGHT EISENHOWER once remarked that someday people are going to want peace so badly that governments will be required to stand out of their way and let them have it. He also maintained that "every gun that is made, every warship launched, every rocket fired signifies, in the final sense, a theft from those who hunger and are not fed, those who are cold and not clothed."[1] There can be little doubt that Eisenhower left the presidency with grave reservations about the military-industrial complex and with genuine worry about the malevolent influence it might come to exercise on the quality of American life. In all likelihood, however, Eisenhower did not anticipate that twenty years hence his statements would become part of the folk wisdom of a movement challenging the policies of a Republican administration. It is hard to believe that the man who selected John Foster Dulles as secretary of state, who offered tactical nuclear weapons to the French in Indochina, and who threatened to use them to stop a Chinese takeover of Quemoy and Matsu would approve of a Baptist minister such as the Reverend David Bailey, who quotes his words while urging his congregation in Varina, Virginia, to oppose the "insanity" of the current policy. Nor is it probable that he wished to give rhetorical ammunition to priests like Mike Schmeid, who refers to the "great General Eisenhower" in a homily accusing the United States of acting sacrilegiously for christening an atomic submarine the *Corpus Christi.*

Although it is doubtful that someone who never befriended the popular movements of his day would support all that has been recently advocated and done in his name, it is, in one way, perfectly appropriate that the peace activists speak favorably about President Eisenhower. While the people involved in the movement speak critically of the militarization of American life and publicize the threat it poses to the nation's liberty, they frequently do so on the basis of defending values which they believe have historically given vitality to American life, sustenance to much of the population, and a measure of hope to those who have been unfairly excluded from its benefits. Despite being a president notorious for his lack of clarity and his inability to communicate, Dwight Eisenhower could occasionally articulate these homespun values with eloquence and conviction. Curiously, he could summon his rhetorical powers most convincingly when he criticized the policy of the government he led for being unfaithful to the values that the country supposedly embodied.[2]

This chapter attempts to explain the range of criticisms that the peace activists in Richmond make of American society and their efforts to create an alternative culture based on conceptions of fairness, nonviolence, community, and simple living. The first section describes how their thoughts concerning the threat of nuclear war are related to a critical outlook on the American economy and to their unease with a culture that too frequently equates selfishness with freedom. I try to show how these criticisms combine a point of view which upholds some of the traditional virtues of American life with support for a variety of progressive causes. The second part of the chapter describes how the peace activists whom I observed attempt to balance a commitment to practical tasks with an effort to create a sustaining community of their own. The final section examines some of the principal dilemmas which confront these men and women as they struggle with the meaning of community and its practical implementation.

The chapter demonstrates that the personalist commitment of the activists extends beyond legislative goals to include an economic and cultural reorientation of American life. Many of them view the changes that they are making in their own lives and the organizations to which they belong as small experiments in the wider process of reconstructing American culture. But the participants have, at the moment, a clearer idea of what their religious orientation entails for individual action than for social and economic policy. This vagueness is indicative, I think, of the intellectual challenges that the personalist approach has yet to address fully. But I suggest that their efforts to build communal elements into middle-class life are important, and take issue with the sociologist Richard Sennett, who has argued that focusing on community inevitably deflects attention from the more significant goal of promoting political change.

Liberalism and Responsibility

The peace activists to whom I spoke in Richmond frequently describe themselves as an "establishment group of people." In many respects, this is an accurate assessment. They are, for the most part, white middle-class men and women who are more highly educated than the general population and who work as doctors, lawyers, homemakers, school teachers, librarians, and engineers. A number of those who have not achieved middle-class economic status could have done so but have deliberately avoided this by choosing occupations and pursuits in which the monetary compensation is minimal. Most are devoted churchgoers who dress modestly and speak politely. If a minor misunderstanding arises in casual conversation, you note that they are quick to blame themselves for not making their ideas sufficiently clear. It does not take long for an observer to realize that they are unusually generous with their time and that they go out of their way to act responsibly toward others. Few people would be unhappy to have these men and women for neighbors and most of us would feel comfortable asking them to look after our homes while we are out of town or to take care of the children when we are called away on emergencies. In fact, if you were unfamiliar with the rest of their beliefs on American society, you might wonder if these are not the people to whom Ronald Reagan refers when he speaks about traditional Americans who care about home, family, neighborhood, and peace.

Yet it is clear that old-fashioned decency, neighborliness, and an abiding respect for American political ideals are not incompatible with a highly adverse appraisal of existing institutions and conditions. Many of the activists to whom I spoke maintained that there was great disparity between the promise of American society and its actual performance in recent years. Almost all suggested that the nation's ideals had been twisted and the promise of American society betrayed over the course of its history. They believe that official policies are not consistent with the expressed values of American life and they uniformly maintain that the priorities of American society are presently misdirected.[3]

Such an indictment is, of course, most obviously reflected in the outlook they hold about American defense policy and the posture that the nation has assumed in the global arena. Members of the peace community think that the threat of nuclear war is real and increasing, that its effects would be catastrophic, and that it is unlikely that a nuclear war could be limited to a "theater" chosen by the superpowers. Recently, people in the peace movement have increasingly turned their attention to Central America. They believe that American actions in this region have been misdirected and that the Sandinista government in Nicaragua is not the totalitarian regime that the Reagan administration labels it. For some, discontent with American military policy had its origins in the bombings of Hiroshima and Nagasaki. For most others, it began later in life as they came to believe that the practices involved in defending the country were morally indefensible as well as practically short-sighted.

While the opposition to American military policy is the most visible sign of the activists' discontent, it is by no means the only one. Whether it be in reference to politics, the economy, or the manner of living promoted by corporate advertising in the media, members of the peace community find the organization of life in the United States to be deeply troubling. Most of them favor not only initiatives on behalf of disarmament but a significant redirection of American culture. As Wendy Northup explains, nuclear weapons are only the most egregious and most threatening symptom of a society and a world in disarray. "I don't quite see how we have got where we are and how we have reached a condition where we hardly see and care for one another. There is something terribly wrong with a society that uses land to maximize profits, that considers food to be a weapon and where middle-class people live in fear and deal with their fear by purchasing burglar alarms. The real question is not only nuclear weapons, but how we can create a world worth living in."

What disturbs them so much about America today is their belief that it has developed into a mean-spirited society. They suggest that people are much too quick to resort to violence as a means of settling interpersonal and group disputes. They are troubled by what they perceive as an excessively materialistic culture that encourages acquisition to the detriment of individual rights and communal respect, both here and abroad. They think that our reigning ideas about self-fulfillment neither promote social responsibility nor provide an adequate foundation for a mature and rewarding individualism. In a moment, I will discuss how these ideas were reflected in their answers to specific questions that were raised about the nature of the economy and the meaning of freedom. But it should be mentioned that these ideas were not manifested only in the interview setting. The activists' critical outlook on American culture was evident in conversations they had with each other, in the programs they sponsored in the community relating peacemaking to lifestyle concerns, and in their practical expression of their professed interest in the long-term cultural renovation of American life.

This concern was frequently voiced in their thoughts about the American economy. As would be expected, peace activists who believe that American economic priorities are misplaced devote a portion of their political education to defending the claim that military spending is wasteful as well as destructive. The newsletter of the Richmond Peace Education Center regularly prints information on and analysis of trends within the military budget and a discussion of military items housed in nonmilitary categories. It has also disputed Caspar Weinberger's assertion that military spending is beneficial to job creation in the civilian arena. Marii Hasegawa, past president of the U.S. branch of the Women's International League for Peace and Freedom and an activist for the past thirty-five years, sums up the prevailing sentiment in the peace community well when she says, "I think that the military is a bad thing economically. Manufacture of military goods is not producing use for people and the costs and pricing have made it impossible for it to be anything but a boondoggle. We could use this money much more fruitfully than we are."

Complaints about wastefulness and misplaced priorities are voiced in reference not only to the military budget, but to the entire operation of the economy. Marii amplifies her commentary. "I get really angry when I hear someone with a yearly income of $100,000 talk about the difficulty of making ends meet or of the special diets they have for their dogs and cats. I think it would do a lot of people some good to live for just one month on a U.S. Department of Agriculture's thrifty food budget." Although Wendy Northup does not believe that wealth and income should be perfectly equalized across the population, she does feel that "the vast disparity in income is inappropriate. How can you justify some people making $400,000 a year when others are on food stamps?" Jerry Gorman maintains that certain government programs should be expanded. "We don't have enough social welfare plans and the ones that we have aren't organized adequately. I think that most people would rather not be dependent on the government, but with the economy the way it is, the government has to take up the slack. My father worked for the WPA and it didn't corrupt him or me."

Despite a general consensus that the American economy ought to work better for those who are presently poor, the peace community's support of social welfare programs is not unmixed. Martha Osborne, a religious educator who has designed peace curriculums for children, speculates that "the last years haven't been tremendously helpful and we have created, to some extent, a society that is dependent on welfare." John Gallini echoes her sentiments, saying, "I'm a little disenchanted with our ability to help people, although I do not want the federal government to be entirely relieved of that role." Says Steve Hodges, "Many of my friends who are social workers and whose hearts are in the right place believe that too many government programs do not provide an adequate incentive to work." Yet none of the activists draw from their misgivings about social welfare programs the conclusions that have been made the centerpiece of Republican economic policy. The peace activists do not argue that social welfare programs should be eliminated so that the poor can experience, in George Gilder's phrase, the spur of poverty. Nor are they likely to blame these programs for the economic problems that the nation has recently experienced. They argue instead that new ways have to be discovered to bring the poor into the economic and political process so that the dependency of the traditional liberal approach and the perceived viciousness of unfettered capitalism can be avoided.

Perhaps the most striking and distinctive element of the peace community's outlook on the economy is the omnipresent criticism of a materialistic culture. Besides wanting to introduce more equity into an expanding industrial order, activists also wish to raise some basic objections to the cultural norms of a modern consumer society. Speaking in her large yet modestly appointed suburban home, Phyllis Conklin maintained, "We have an outrageous standard of having—not living, mind you—in this country and that includes this house. I think that there is a lot of inequity in the way that wealth is distributed in this country and the Conklins have too much. We could live much more simply than this." Jerry Gorman takes Phyllis' assertion one step further to claim, "I don't think that we have fully understood the costs associated with modernity. I think that we're producing a lot of unnecessary, wasteful and harmful products. Moreover, I don't believe that we're a damn bit happier. I think that we have to stop, turn around and take a long look at what we're doing and decide whether it is worthwhile. We need to freeze not only the arms race, but a helluva lot of other things too."

Reflecting on the ethic of acquisition that permeates America, Steve Hodges reveals how his religious beliefs lead him to be wary of the consequences of accumulation. He mentions that he agrees with biblical statements to the effect that "wealth imposes a great spiritual burden upon its possessors since you are continually tempted to protect and defend your property instead of attending to your other responsibilities." Most members of the peace community believe that this neglect has reached the status of a major cultural malaise. It prevents people from acknowledging their responsibility to the needy, not only in the United States but elsewhere. A number of the activists have lived in poorer nations, either as children of missionaries or as Christian service workers, and are today troubled by what Martha Osborne calls the "simple squandering of resources" and the lack of attention given to issues such as world hunger and the problems of refugees. Moreover, people in the peace community argue that the ethic of acquisition is actually an addiction that deflects attention not only from the needs of other persons but from our own needs as human beings. Having lost the capacity of personal diplomacy that establishes the personal contacts at work and in neighborhoods that make life meaningful, they believe that Americans pay an extortionist's fee for a self-defense budget in the form of fences, padlocks, alarms, guns, and continual distrust of others.

A similar emphasis on the themes of equity and responsibility can be found in the ideas which the members of the peace community express about the meaning of freedom in American society. The people to whom I spoke gave strong support to most of the causes that liberals have led during the past twenty-five years with respect to civil rights. Some of the veteran activists can remember marching in demonstrations and two Catholic priests to whom I spoke recall being influenced by the movement. Father Mike Schmeid, for example, tells of being influenced by a teacher at his seminary expressing irritation that all his students were going home at Thanksgiving to "eat turkey while some of us will be marching for open housing." Most people in the peace community were not active in politics during the integration struggles and, in fact, one person became involved while opposing them. As a young doctor in Florida during the early sixties, Jerry Gorman was a Republican county committeeman who worked to defeat John Kennedy because there were hints that he might be sympathetic to socialized medicine and because his campaign rhetoric indicated that he might adopt a forceful integration policy. Since those years, Jerry's outlook has been considerably modified, both by events and by exploring what the faith he professed actually required in terms of human relationships. He now holds the highest respect for the people who were involved in the struggle. In fact, one of his long-term fantasies is that the memorial statues of Confederate war heroes which grace Monument Avenue in Richmond will someday be removed to make room for sculptures of Martin Luther King, Jr., and other martyrs to the cause of peace and justice.

Members of the peace community also emphatically support women's rights with regard to sharing of home and family responsibilities, reducing coercion concerning sexual roles, and an increase in the capacity of women to enter the world on terms which they themselves define. Since many of the local activists are Catholic, the support of women's rights rarely involves a vocal defense of abortion, but it is equally unusual to hear vocal opposition to it. Donna Gorman, a Catholic who has become a feminist activist after bearing thirteen children, remarks, "I used to go to anti-abortion rallies, but I don't anymore. I just don't think that many of these people, especially the leaders, are really pro-life and concerned about women's problems."

Throughout the local peace community, women are not only present and active, but participate on an equal basis. Women in the peace movement frequently refer to the positive effects that have resulted from their understanding of women's liberation. Martha Osborne, for instance, attributes her previous inactivity with respect to social issues to the "socialization that I received about what a proper Southern woman should do." She has found the women's movement to be a source of strength that enables her to act more vigorously on behalf of others. Notes Donna Gorman, "I never got involved in politics [apart from the abortion issue] until recently because I always had a houseful of kids. But since I've understood the women's movement, I know that I have to find time to make my voice heard, even with a three-year-old at home. Patriarchy, war, poverty—you name it—it's all tied in. And it's important that I use my experience as a woman and a mother to provide another perspective on these issues."

Men in the peace community generally speak favorably about women's rights. Few seemed to be threatened by these issues and most take obvious pleasure in knowing that peacemaking is an activity they undertake with their wives and occasionally the entire family. Jerry Gorman observes that "women's rights is an important issue that needs to be addressed, not only by the society but also by the church. I think that I have become much more sensitive to the issues of patriarchy in our society and how women have been oppressed. I've also become more aware of the connections between patriarchal societies and the inclination of governments to make war." Not infrequently, men speak of the needs which have yet to be met in this regard. John Gallini remarks that "the church does not do a particularly good job with women. In time, I'd be in favor of married priests and women priests."

The activists' conception of feminism frequently includes the assertion that women bring special talents to the movement, not only in terms of task-oriented skills but also in outlook and approach. Due to their biological and historical association with activities such as bringing life into the world, nurturing the young, and reconciling domestic conflicts, women are often favorably compared to men, who have presumably been taught to revel in competition and pursue power ruthlessly while their skills at negotiation remain woefully underdeveloped. The household values that personalists want to make politically relevant, such as compassion and nonviolent resolution of conflict, are those that have been traditionally associated with the experiences of women.

To some degree, members of the peace community also hold ideas consistent with the traditional liberal encouragement of tolerance and diversity. Priests who were influenced by the liberalization of the Catholic church in the wake of Vatican II espouse conceptions of morality different from those prevalent when the hierarchical Church was taken for granted. Father Mike Schmeid thinks it regrettable that "so much of Catholic social doctrine was reduced to a series of no-nos about sexual morality." Since his ordination, he has made an effort to broaden the application of Catholic morality to social issues and to show his congregation that individual conscience is accorded a prominent place in Catholic moral philosophy when it is properly conceived. In a similar vein, Father Tom Magri deems it important that his parishioners develop their own conscience and even remarks, "One of my faults is that sometimes I don't understand people who refuse to think for themselves and I tend to get impatient with them quickly." And, as seen in chapter 2, John Gallini attributes much of his interest in peace issues to the outgrowth of a conversion experience he had in the early seventies under the guidance of a priest who had been influenced by Vatican II and who stressed the importance of individual growth and exploration.

Despite their support of the liberal agenda on most issues touching on equal rights and social tolerance, it would be inaccurate to characterize the members of the peace community as liberals. Examined in depth, their ideas are not really much akin to the nineteenth-century individualistic beliefs that actually underlie so much of contemporary liberalism. They do not believe that genuine freedom can be associated with the satisfaction of desire and they maintain a commitment to acting responsibly that is far more demanding than the liberal standard that anything goes if it does not infringe on another's freedom. When peace educators such as Makanah Morris and Martha Osborne remark in precisely the same words that they "cannot think about freedom without thinking about responsibility," they do not mean that people should give only passing attention to others, but that we are obligated to make positive commitments to them, even if this requires sacrifice of cherished desires so that strangers may also prosper.

As with their criticism of a materialistic economic order, members of the peace community maintain that the culture's prevalent ideas about freedom are ultimately harmful to the individuals who uphold these notions. They are disturbed by the breakdown of family life in the United States, the isolation that is often evident in residential neighborhoods, and the difficulty of forming relations that can sustain and nourish individual growth. As Wendy Northup puts it, "I see our inability to make strong commitments as a limiting factor on our freedom." A recurring theme in our talks was that individuals who are unable to develop relatively permanent attachments are likely to experience more personal difficulties and are prone to have the quality of their lives diminished. Given this perspective, it is not surprising that the peace activists in Richmond attribute so much importance to the development of community as a counterweight to the anomic drift of modern life.

An ambivalent attitude toward modernity lies at the core of the beliefs expressed by many of the people to whom I spoke. Peace activists do support many of the substantive goals that motivated much of contemporary liberal politics. They want greater economic equity, more respect for human rights and individual conscience, and the incorporation of women into the Church and the society at large as equal partners. Even Jerry Gorman, who thinks that we haven't "fully understood the costs associated with modernity," believes that it is important to be very supportive of women's rights. It would thus be inaccurate to portray the peace movement as simply a protest against modern life. None of the activists to whom I spoke would be comfortable with a politics of traditional values as this concept is presently understood and promoted by the New Right. At the same time, their personal background and intellectual dispositions make them reluctant to dispense with tradition and unreflectively embrace all of modernity. They worry about the decline in the level of personal responsibility. They understand the benefits of neighborly relations and believe that the shattering of community has damaged the fabric of American life. In short, they want central features of modern life to endure and even to be strengthened, while they also work to understand and ameliorate some of the problems that have accompanied it.

To argue that it is not completely accurate to characterize the Richmond activists as liberals is consistent with the ideas of scholars who have written about the development of "postmaterialism" in contemporary societies. Ronald Inglehart, for example, argues that a significant minority of citizens in Western nations today have focused their energies on values that are not strictly materialistic. According to Inglehart, postmaterialists are typically more concerned with quality-of-life issues than with obtaining economic benefits. A perceptive and thoughtful scholar, Inglehart also draws attention to the ambivalence people feel about modernity and to the increasingly middle-class nature and moralistic tone of contemporary reform movements. In all these ways, the postmaterialist label fits well with the sentiments expressed by the activists in Richmond.⁴

The problem with the postmaterialist label is that it does not really tell us enough about the specifics of the politics that these views may encourage. Inglehart, for instance, notes the possibility that postmaterialists may turn away from the world and toward mysticism. Yet he does not fully explore the tensions and ambivalences in their own positions about citizenship, politics, and community that could lead to either feverish engagement or mystical withdrawal. I am also wary of the postmaterialist category because in the hands of less sensitive observers than Inglehart it may be used to connote a superficial and somewhat privileged view of the world. It can be employed, as it is by some "new-class" theorists, to suggest that the problems which concern postmaterialists are not genuine because they are not primarily focused on economic conditions. This approach permits scholars to ignore the historical conditions that have given rise to these movements, the sacrifices often undertaken by those who participate, and the substantive content of the issues under consideration.

Attempts to categorize the activists in Richmond might also refer to the New Left of the 1960s because it too attempted to synthesize personal development and socially responsible action. As observers such as Wini Brienes and Marshall Berman have noted, the New Left sought to realize the romantic ideal of individual authenticity while working to restructure the political order. Certain slogans and concepts—the personal is political, community power, and participatory democracy—were shorthand expressions for the belief that individual fulfillment, the establishment of community, and the reorientation of American national politics were goals that could be, and indeed had to be, pursued simultaneously. Participants believed that it was essential to counter the dehumanizing tendencies of modern society as well as to attack the mistaken policies of the American government.⁵

The personalist orientation of the activists in Richmond has much in common with the approach of the New Left. Personalists also maintain that genuine reform must address cultural problems of dehumanization as well as concrete dilemmas of arms control and poverty. They believe that activists should work to build communities that can serve as a model of what the new society can be. The men and women in Richmond echo the community-power argument when they assert that attention has to be

focused on local politics and culture if the redirection of national legislation is to be rooted and enduring. In fact, the attempt to develop a politics
that is both cultural and pragmatic posed a similar set of problems for both
movements.

Yet it would be wrong to view the religiously inspired activism of the
1980s as simply or primarily an updating of the New Left. The differences
between the two orientations are also substantial. Perhaps the most important distinction is the role that "tradition" occupies in the personalist
approach. The New Left self-consciously professed its "newness." Members drew attention to their own youthfulness; they denigrated the Old
Left for its supposedly inflexible politics; and when they spoke about
building an alternative culture, they contrasted what they would create
with the narrow and repressed values of their parents. Personalists use a
different vocabulary. They emphasize how traditional values such as religion encourage them to work for political change. They frequently justify
their activism by referring proudly to their responsibilities as parents.
Their talk about developing an alternative culture places little or no emphasis on the desirability of liberating sexual impulses as a program of political
reform. One might argue that these differences flesh out into very different
notions about the nature of freedom.

From Theory to Practice

The ultimate goals of the peace community to demilitarize American society, reorient a materialistic economy, and develop a communal
environment that is tolerant of diversity would require a massive alteration
in institutional practices and personal values. Men and women who are
interested in accomplishing these aims are, in a sense, groping in the dark.
They do not have many successful models to follow and are often unsure of
how their activities will end. In fact, they are confronted on a daily basis with
a series of questions that could immobilize even the most well-intentioned
of activists. What are the first steps toward creating a less materialistic
society? How can the dominant consumerist ethos be reordered? Most
important, what could be done on a local level to further these aims when
the business and governmental practices of the nation are becoming increasingly concentrated and centralized?

Let me offer a small example of how this difficulty manifested itself in
Richmond. In the latter part of 1980, a group of approximately ten lay
people and clergy in the city's Catholic churches decided to form a local

chapter of Pax Christi. Pax Christi International had been in existence since the end of World War II when it was founded by a French bishop to promote reconciliation between the Germans and the French. Until recently, however, it operated primarily at the national and transnational levels. Catholic leaders in Pax Christi issued statements about international peace concerns, lobbied at the United Nations, and sponsored campaigns on behalf of various social justice concerns. Local "members" of Pax Christi gave moral and financial support to its efforts, but did not actively participate in the formation of a Pax Christi agenda. Nor did they attempt to adapt that agenda to the particular conditions of the locality in which they resided. When the group of Catholics in Richmond decided that Pax Christi should have a presence in the area, their first problem, as John Gallini remembers, was to answer the question, "What does a local Pax Christi chapter do?"

One of the principal virtues of the nationwide freeze campaign organized at the beginning of the decade by Randall Forsberg was that it provided a simple yet meaningful task around which activists and groups like Pax Christi could mobilize their energies. As it was developed in Richmond, the freeze campaign enabled activists to establish short-term goals for their efforts and to enlist the support of others by providing them with concrete tasks that they could perform. Pax Christi, for example, decided to make presentations to the parish councils in area churches asking for an endorsement of the freeze; it lobbied priests, encouraging them to include peace issues in their homilies; it requested permission to speak to parishioners inside and outside the church on Sundays; and it volunteered to provide speakers for parish forums. The Richmond Nuclear Freeze campaign set target numbers for signatures on petitions supporting the freeze, sponsored "freeze parties," and circulated petitions at the state fair, outdoor concerts in the summertime, and other public events.

The freeze campaign gave public visibility to the peace movement in 1981 and 1982 and also served to energize activists. In meetings of the peace groups which were active in the city, a strong emphasis was placed on bringing the message to the wider community. Letter-writing campaigns were organized, announcements were made about vigils, demonstrations and other actions were planned, and there was an informal exchange of information about strategies that had worked or had been notable failures. Newcomers to the movement who may have been reluctant to staff a table or leaflet a concert were invited to do so in a buddy system where they would work alongside a more experienced political hand. At one session of the

Richmond Nuclear Freeze campaign, Phyllis Conklin offered encouragement to the reticent by noting that "there's no reason for anyone not to be
out on the street today. They don't even say nasty things to us anymore."

The attention that the groups in the peace community paid to the freeze
campaign was complemented by the energy devoted to its broader purpose
of building an enduring peace culture in the area. The Richmond Peace
Education Center, Pax Christi, and the War Tax Alternatives Group stressed
a much broader array of social and political goals, and most of the people
involved in the freeze campaign also participated elsewhere. Indeed, in 1983
the freeze campaign officially endorsed the strategy of working with other
groups in the city to build a progressive alliance. The activists frequently
characterized the freeze as a "sensible first step," a way "for individuals to
register their dissent and unhappiness with existing trends," and a "good
way for individuals to become involved." Viewed from this perspective, the
freeze actually functioned in Richmond as an introduction to the peace
culture, to the activists' broader outlook on contemporary life.

The long-term task of building a peace culture was so important to
many of the activists that they occasionally expressed reservations about
the rapidity with which the idea of the freeze had been adopted by large
numbers of the public. While they certainly were not unhappy with the
movement's early successes and did not believe that it could ever be too
soon to begin reversing the arms race, they also recognized that their
ultimate aims were not to be accomplished overnight and that it would
have been self-defeating to become euphoric about the freeze campaign's
appeal in 1981 and 1982. Wendy Northup, for example, felt ambivalent
about the successes which the freeze had in the elections of 1982 precisely
because she thought that electoral politics needs to be supplemented by the
kind of work that can generate deep and permanent attachments to a
peaceful way of living. Jerry Gorman's delight was tempered by the worry
that the freeze was becoming another fad which he labeled "nuclear chic."
Buoyed by their success, activists still feared that the movement would
eventually be reduced to a nostalgia clipping in which people would remember 1982 as the year when they joined Jane Fonda workout clubs,
danced to the Go-Gos, and voted for the freeze.

The commitment to exploring what it meant to build an authentic peace
culture was evidenced in a variety of ways. Since joining the movement, a
number of activists have altered their consumption patterns and explored
in more depth their conception of what constitutes a worthwhile life.
Many now purchase their clothes from secondhand stores and trade with
other families for their children's apparel. Father Tom Magri remarks, "I

know that world hunger is a structural problem and that I'm not going to solve it, but I've reduced my consumption of red meat and want to experiment with vegetarianism as a way of reminding myself what needs to be addressed." Many activists devote a significant portion of their income to their churches, to social justice causes, and to world hunger. Steve and Diantha Hodges are attempting, in Steve's words, to be "downwardly mobile. We've reduced the number of hours we devote to paid employment so that we might have more time to raise our child, to be with each other and to spend on peacemaking. We're very happy this way and we no longer have the burden of deciding what to do with our money." Harold Houghton, a young Quaker schoolteacher who has struggled with his conscience during the last five years to determine whether he should resist "war taxes," expressed an attitude that was frequently exhibited by members of the peace community when he said, "I have a need to live my life as consistently as possible. I really believe in an old Quaker statement that we have a duty to let our lives speak."

Peace activists complement these practical efforts to reorient their individual lives with attempts to establish relations with others and build communities that support them in the practice of their beliefs. It might be said that they are trying to do what the Wobblies once identified as "building the new society in the shell of the old." Wendy Northup, for example, suggests that "at one time we had strongly identified local communities that are now lost. Community today has to be based on the recognition that we often don't have roots anymore, but that we still have mutual concerns which should lead us to work together. And the community we do create has to be tight, but not exclusive. . . . We talk a lot about building communities and devote a great deal of time to it."

One might add to her commentary by noting how difficult a task it is. Although the decline of community and the need to revive it are commonplaces in scholarly analyses of American life, there is hardly any understanding of how this might be accomplished, let alone much experience with its successful achievement. Peace activists struggle to discover small, realizable actions that may help to generate a deeper sense of community. Says Steve Northup, a leader in Pax Christi and board member of the Richmond Peace Education Center, "We are novices at this and still have a lot of learning to do." This learning process is not a glamorous crusade designed to attract significant media attention or to harvest a bushel of votes come election time. In practice, it boils down to a variety of mundane yet responsible and thoughtful activities that attempt to replace communities that have been shattered with ones built from an awareness of what has been lost. It might be plans for having common meals once a week during the Lenten season; or it might be writing in the peace education newsletter about the difficulties of raising children in a materialistic culture; or it might simply be committing oneself to be a better representative of the peace community's values at one's work place and among people with whom one does not necessarily agree.

At times, the results of these groping and uncertain efforts at building a community can be palpably seen and touched. One good example is the manner in which Pax Christi combined its function of educational and political outreach with building a community that offered sustenance to its members and explored the implication of their commitment to peacemaking for the actual ordering of their lives. Their monthly meetings always began with prayers and songs that related their religious faith to their commitment to peace and justice. The liturgy was composed with considerable care by the Spirituality and Justice Committee and considered an essential part of the meeting. After the opening prayers, an invited speaker presented a Catholic perspective on an issue such as tax resistance or simply offered information about conditions in Central America, Lebanon, or Poland. Questions were usually raised and occasionally the group broke into smaller circles to discuss the implications of the talk for their own activism. Some time was then allotted to announcements about the various peace-related events that were taking place in the area and comments were offered about strategies for becoming more effective and coalitions that could possibly be formed with other groups in the city. The meeting officially ended with a closing liturgy, again composed by the Spirituality and Justice Committee. A social hour followed and a genuine effort was made to welcome new members, while others further explored questions related to the group's shared concerns.

The communal affirmation of values that occurs at a Pax Christi meeting serves a number of purposes. On the most rudimentary level, it helps to alleviate some of the loneliness and feelings of futility frequently experienced by people involved in promoting social change. Activists are quick to mention that it is important to have other people share your beliefs and to know that they are working with you. People involved in Pax Christi are also given affirmation that their activities are deeply rooted in their faith: at each meeting, the liturgy provides an interpretation of Catholicism that supports their undertakings in the secular world. Moreover, this interpretation is often addressed to the emotional needs that activism generates. Themes such as how to handle disappointment, why it is important to persevere when the outcome looks disappointing, and how change occurs in startling and sometimes miraculous ways are regularly connected to the teachings of Jesus Christ, to the sufferings he experienced, and to the lives of his followers. Finally, there is also the implication that Pax Christi itself is an experiment in creating the new world that the activists hope to bring into existence. This is manifested in the internal workings of the organization, in which hierarchy is discouraged, women hold prominent positions, and community is consciously built. It is also present in some of the liturgies, which suggest that a significant purpose of the group is to be a living experiment for people interested in understanding what it may be like to follow the teachings of Jesus in modern America.

Another example of the peace activists' concern for building community is the emergence of a group called SPAN, the letters an acronym for Spirit, Politics, Alternatives, and Nonviolence. SPAN's origins were in a series of study groups on nonviolence held in the fall of 1982 and the winter of 1983. Steve Hodges, coordinator of the Richmond Peace Education Center, was interested in ensuring that the focus on the nuclear freeze did not deflect attention from the ethical and religious roots of the local movement. Personally committed to nonviolence, Steve wanted this to remain an integral part of his educational focus. He therefore began a study group in which the participants read and discussed work by Mohandas Gandhi, Martin Luther King, Jr., and Gene Sharp. Members of the original class then agreed to volunteer as instructors for the others which were formed.

The five or six study groups that started in 1983 and 1984 were not large, sometimes as small as four people and never more than twelve. The themes of the seven-week sessions normally included some background on the philosophy of nonviolence, the use of nonviolence in previous efforts at resistance and social change, its relevance to interpersonal life, and its potential for bringing peaceful change to the contemporary world. Besides reinforcing the spiritual and philosophical bases of some of the activists' commitment to peace, the study groups prompted most of the participants to wonder how the insights they gained could be applied to the antinuclear movement, both in Richmond and in the nation at large. Prompted by Steve Hodges, about ten people from the study groups came together to think in more detail about the possible use of nonviolent action in Richmond. The result of these meetings was the formation of SPAN, a group that would experiment with combining a spiritual commitment to nonviolence with regular political involvement and ultimately a professed willingness to consider alternative means of conducting one's life.

Ecumenical in orientation, the participants in SPAN agreed to the statement that God is on the side of justice and desires people to act accordingly. Again, the spiritual orientation was not incidental to the actual conduct of SPAN's meetings, as one quarter of the biweekly two hours was allotted to relating the goals and strategies of the group to spiritual development. One member would be responsible for leading an extended prayer or meditation relating the goals of peacemaking to its spiritual roots or would speak about the importance of building communities in the effort to bring peace to the world. The rest of the meeting gave evidence to what has previously been called the pragmatic utopianism of the activists. At the outset, the group's goals were defined and thereafter potential actions were designed which could give witness to this belief and, hopefully, show others the possible efficacy of nonviolent action. In the summer and fall of 1984, SPAN decided to become part of the nationwide watch about the nuclear White Train and organized a vigil composed of people willing to participate in a protest at the tracks if it passed nearby. In 1985, SPAN became involved in the local organizing for the Pledge of Resistance to escalation of the American presence in Central America and in the Free South Africa movement. Members also developed a plan to urge churches to resign from various plans to have them function as emergency shelters in case of nuclear attack.

With the exception of their position on how to reduce nuclear weapons, the women and men to whom I spoke were not very assured talking about the national policies that might be required to implement their beliefs about the necessity of changing American culture. Peace activists believe that something is wrong with American society, but they acknowledge their present uncertainty about more adequate solutions. They typically exhibited a general consensus on the direction in which the nation should move, but were uncertain of and sometimes divided about the practical steps that ought to be taken.

This was especially true of their thoughts about the redirection of American economic life. Possible solutions to the problems raised were qualified with "Perhaps," "I'm not really certain," and "Maybe we ought to give this a try." Phyllis Conklin thinks that a "socialist government might work," but Makanah Morris believes that "equality cannot be imposed by the government. People will have to be brought to it voluntarily because it will never work if they are coerced." John Gallini knows that "we haven't adequately applied the Christian ideal to economic reality," but admits, "I'm seriously struggling with what this means and I have to study it more."

This mix of assuredness about misplaced priorities and uncertainty about practical solutions was best expressed by Steve Hodges. Speaking about his economic beliefs, Steve mentioned that he was attracted to the ideas contained in a passage in the Bible drawn from Leviticus. The passage, he relates, tells of a "system in which every seven years the land lies fallow and the slaves go free. With every seven cycles of seven years, all people go back to their original allotment of land, no matter what was bought and sold in the previous forty-nine. I'm intrigued by this idea of a periodic redistribution of capital. It is a little simplistic, but it provides that the poor will be taken care of, not by welfare but by giving them the means to provide for themselves. It doesn't hold people to a rigid equality. It allows them to buy, sell and accumulate. But it still provides for a basic check on the problems that accompany accumulation." The one drawback to this idea, Steve confesses, is that he "wouldn't know how to go about implementing it," though he finds "the principles very appealing."

Various reasons help to explain the inability of the activists to furnish specific recommendations about national policy. First, they simply do not possess the political experience that would permit them to address these issues in a compelling manner to people who are practically minded. Second, they are only beginning, as John Gallini admits, to think about how to relate their ideas concerning peace and cultural change to economic reform. Third, the broader movement in which they participate has exhibited many of the same limitations. The pastoral letter of the Catholic bishops is a case in point. Although the bishops performed a valuable function in pointing to the persistence of poverty and hunger in the midst of an economic recovery, they were unable to detail innovative and politically feasible solutions to these problems. Taken together, these considerations indicate that strategic thinking tends to be one of the weakest aspects of a personalist approach to politics.

Community Building and Social Change

The attempts by the participants in the Richmond peace groups to alter their own lives and to build a local community grounded in their professed commitments are key features of the personalist approach to political issues. These efforts are based on the assumption that the steps taken will, in the long run, help to develop a sturdier foundation for the peace movement. But is this necessarily true? Does the personalist emphasis on reorganizing individual lives and constructing exemplary communities promote political change or deflect energy and attention from the reforms that the activists endorse?

I raise this question because a case can be made that a politics grounded in exemplary communities can become so inward-looking that it loses sight of its political goals. Groups which simultaneously seek to promote social change and to establish a nurturing community are continually tempted to retreat from the effort to change the wider culture. They may adopt a posture of detachment and even haughty arrogance toward the very people they are supposedly trying to reach. During the sixties, for instance, numerous authors spoke of an emerging counterculture among American youth as an element of the New Left. At its best, this countercul- ture represented a sincere and imaginative effort to protest against a mis- guided war policy conceived in secrecy, to proclaim to the nation that there was a standard of living more important than the level of affluence, and to testify that citizens had the capacity to shape the nation (and the world) in a more humane fashion. It inspired many young Americans to actively embrace an idealistic commitment to improving the quality of American life and it challenged the complacency of adults who had become resigned to its inequities.

Unfortunately, there was another side to the counterculture in which criticism of the established order was reduced to derisive mocking and strategies for political change were replaced by a cultural separatism which assumed that the majority of the population was incapable of enlighten- ment. The exclusionary side of the counterculture had its most egregious manifestation in the half-jesting, half-serious slogan not to trust anyone over thirty. But it was also evident in the flag patches worn on the seat of the pants, the symbolic burnings of American flags, and the taunting attitude often exhibited toward ordinary Americans. Ironically, the move- ment was only broadened when advertising executives divested it of its critical edge by coming to understand how its hedonistic celebration of youth meshed perfectly with the vision of America they were striving to promote.

The self-isolation of the counterculture in the sixties was a manifestation of a more familiar process. A group is started with the intention of bring- ing its point of view to the wider public. But as it does so, and especially if it achieves a measure of success, people opposed to its point of view defend their power and respond with charges of their own. Many of these accusa- tions are presented fairly and contribute to the deepening of democratic debate. But some are not so evenhanded. A few vicious newspaper editori- als are published. Supporters of the movement may occasionally find that their co-workers do not approve of their activism. Letters to the editor cast doubt on the participants' patriotism. Scarred by the assaults, members of the group seek solace in the warmth of community, hoping to become less vulnerable. Participants now begin to define themselves as victims of a repressive society rather than as people who come under intense scrutiny because of their desire to change that order. The group now serves primarily as a shield to protect its members from the harshness and bitterness of the outside world. As this happens, the original purpose of the organization is subtly transformed and it loses its identity as an agent of social and political transformation.

Perhaps the most critical intellectual argument about the consequences of this process has come from the sociologist Richard Sennett, who has claimed that the formation of community is inherently antagonistic to the pursuit of significant political goals. In his book, *The Fall of Public Man*, Sennett maintains that politics should be viewed as a process in which interests are pursued rather than as an activity that helps to satisfy emotional needs. In essence, Sennett takes the common dilemma just mentioned and elevates it to the status of an iron law. Sennett's immediate target in the book is the New Left and the communitarian rhetoric of the sixties, but his attack is more generally directed against all plans to infuse politics with the values of intimacy, nurturance, and friendship. Coming to the public arena for these purposes, Sennett argues, is only a prescription for failure. Because political action can rarely, on an enduring basis, meet the needs for warmth and intimacy, people inevitably become disillusioned with the process and retreat to the places where they feel wanted, though these locations rarely have anything to do with challenging the structure of the wider society.[6]

Sennett's argument is not entirely without merit. Groups frequently do retreat from their original commitment to more insulated communities. The reasons for this are not hard to understand. Political activity has always functioned, to some extent, as an emotional haven for people more interested in meeting psychological deficiencies than in furthering any actual cause. Less pathologically, people find themselves more comfortable around those who share their view of the world. The segregation of activist groups from the wider society is, in one sense, a retreat to normal, everyday existence in America where informal lines of class and racial separation hold sway. People simply find it easier to remain in the company of like-minded men and women than to commit themselves to the less comforting activity of political change. I think that this is the case, to some degree, with the activists in Richmond, inasmuch as they have not been especially innovative in thinking of how to approach working-class whites about the peace issue and seem to believe that very little can be done in that area.

Still, Sennett clearly overstates his case. He ignores the positive effects of communal relations on social involvement and thus transforms what is a genuine dilemma of political change into an inherently fatal weakness. Put simply, though the warmth of community can deflect attention from political endeavors, it can also be essential to their inception and endurance. From where, one might ask, does the motivation come that can generate the commitment to change society? Why do people persevere? How do they cope with the potential for despair? Perhaps there are steel-tempered individuals who can persevere simply by drawing on their own vast internal resources. But most people are not so autonomously motivated. They cherish the support of others and want to have their commitment affirmed by people for whom they care. Without a vibrant community to nurture their involvement, temper their disappointment, and crystallize their inchoate beliefs into a compelling vision of how the world should be organized, they are likely to lapse into resignation, becoming unable to pursue even their own interests with sufficient vigor.

This is particularly true in an area such as Richmond that has never had a well-defined peace movement and where the Democratic candidate for Congress in 1986 avowed that, if elected, he would be "one of the most conservative members" of the House of Representatives. If Sennett's advice were taken in this milieu, there would never be progressive activism because it would be impossible to pursue political "interests" with any success at all. Short of accommodating themselves to the very conditions that they desire to change, clear-thinking activists would retreat from political involvement and carve out a tolerable niche for their personal lives—precisely the development that Sennett wishes to condemn. Indeed, it is only the communities they form and the nurturance they receive that enable them to persist in their efforts to establish a presence which represents an ongoing challenge, however small it may be, to the outlook and institutions they want to reform.

Among the peace activists in Richmond, their budding communities clearly serve these functions. Chapter 6 shows how this is evident among people who are resisting what they consider to be war taxes. Yet the same purpose is realized among those who participate in entirely conventional activities. The community provides friends for people who may begin to think a little differently from their neighbors. It provides a constant challenge to think of ways in which the commitment may be manifested in everyday life. In fact, it seems to me that it is practically impossible for significant political change to occur today without the development of an intense group life among the people committed to it. The real question is not whether communal feelings should be nurtured or not, but how to go about doing this so that the broader purposes of the group are not undermined by the functioning of the community.

Besides the possibility that constructing exemplary communities may represent one of the only hopes in helping to build a progressive presence that will have long-term implications, there is another reason to take the personalist approach seriously. I alluded above to the frequency with which scholars have lamented the decline of community. During the last fifteen years, a number of our most perceptive writers have criticized American society from a communitarian perspective. One particularly interesting feature of these criticisms is that they have been put forward by people of widely differing ideological stances. There is a communitarianism of the Right that stresses values such as the defense of the traditional family, the desirability of maintaining neighborhood schools, and the government's obligation to legislate against pornography and abortion. We think in this regard of people like the Reverend Jerry Falwell and his Moral Majority, along with a commentator such as George Will, who believe that the pursuit of self-interest has become so prevalent as to leave us unwilling to judge anything right or wrong. Left communitarianism tends to emphasize how American capitalism has undermined traditional institutions such as the family, violated the integrity of neighborhoods and local economies, and robbed significant numbers of Americans of their craft skills. Evidenced in writers such as Harry Boyte, Jean Bethke Elshtain, and Michael Sandel, this perspective calls for a challenge to the organizing ethos of the American economy as a way of restoring the communal health of the nation. Between Right and Left communitarianism lies a body of writing that combines themes in such a way that it becomes very difficult to place these works within traditional categories. Authors such as Wendell Berry and Christopher Lasch seem to be alternately radical and conservative as they condemn both American capitalism and most of the movements that have been organized to oppose it.[7]

All these criticisms originate in a belief that there is something profoundly troubling about American life. At times, of course, these arguments may be nothing more than a romanticization of bygone times and a yearning for a past that never existed. Even worse, the arguments occasionally represent a new intolerance cloaked in the garb of traditional virtue.. But just as often, something important is being said about the paucity of thought given to the way society has been organized and the lack of care shown to one another in daily relations. Though we may argue bitterly about how these ideas should be manifested in public policy decisions, they are nonetheless heartfelt sentiments that give expression to powerful feelings about contemporary life.

It is not clear, however, that these sentiments can be easily translated into practices that can appeal to modern individuals. We often wax nostalgic about the decline of community and lament its passing, especially today when terms such as alienation, narcissism, one-dimensionality, and the me-decade have become common descriptions of everyday life. But these longings are often tempered by memories and experiences that point not to warmth and support, but to uniformity, repression, coercion, and intolerance as the characteristic elements of community. Jim Jones and the People's Temple, the smiling but empty faces of converts to the Unification Church, the emotional extortion of supposedly close friends, and the viciousness of small-town gossip—all these memories constitute the dark underside of community, one that ensures that nostalgic longings for it are rarely followed by any concrete activity designed to reconstruct this way of life.[8]

For this reason, it seems especially important that efforts to build community in contemporary America are not summarily dismissed as politically useless. If the writers who have pointed to the decline of community are in any way insightful, we will need to pay more attention to those who have maintained a sense of community and those who are trying hard to build it. We will want to have stories written that can describe these efforts, illuminate the achievements that have been made, and point out the inventiveness of ordinary people and the destructiveness and manipulativeness that can also be present.

The antinuclear activists in Richmond are trying to combine an effort to sensitize people to the possibility of global annihilation with an attempt to reconstruct a local community of conscience. In doing so, they are involved in a practical experiment that speaks not only to the survival of the world, but to the quality of everyday lives within it. They are sometimes not quite sure how these connections should be drawn, but they are convinced that it is a task not to be ignored. They believe that global transformation must be rooted in local action and must be grounded in the values of nurturance, cooperation, and mutual respect that characterize their own communities.

Considerable work remains, however, for the activists to perform in this regard. If they are convinced that American society ought to recognize more explicitly the communal needs of individuals, they must concern themselves with how communities can proliferate and how they can be presented to the rest of the public in a more appealing manner. If they believe that values such as nurturance, friendship, equality, and frugality have relevance to the workings of nations and their relationships with one another, they must become more attentive to the specific meanings of their assertions. They must be able to tell people what a different economy would look like, show them the benefits of more cooperative relations, and persuade more citizens that such changes are possible. Admittedly, these are formidable tasks that will not be resolved by any particular group of activists in one specific location. But these are also the kinds of questions that will have to be addressed if personalist notions are to be as socially effective as they are psychologically appealing.

5

Bringing the Message Home: The Family, Children, and Peace Education

THE NATURE of a perceived threat frequently influences both the form and the content of the opposition which takes shape against it. Given the potential of a nuclear conflict to eliminate all human life, it is not surprising that children occupy a special place in the resurgent movement against nuclear arms. It was almost impossible to attend a session about the threat of nuclear war without hearing at least one speaker or member of the audience relate to the gathering a chance remark of a child which indicated his or her awareness that the future itself may be extinct. Such remarks were normally followed by expressions of parental concern that the world may be extinguished before one's children can experience the joys, rewards, and pains of being fully human. This ominous possibility has given the recent peace movement its distinctive coloration as not only a protest of idealistic youth, but also one of young and not-so-young mothers and fathers disturbed by the arrogance of governments which contemplate genocidal actions in which the death of children is described, in the sanitized parlance of nuclear jargon, as collateral damage.

Antinuclear activists do more, however, than merely speak in the name of their children and carry cute signs at demonstrations testifying that you can't hug your kids with nuclear arms. Children are frequently the objects of their activity as well as the ultimate justification for it. Peacemaking is often connected to creating family environments and developing educational plans that will expose children to the values and ideas that peace activists believe can bring positive change to the world. A recurring theme is that the lives of children threatened by the existence of nuclear weapons are also diminished and damaged by a materialistic culture. The peace community's interest in children and the family is indicative of the movement's personalist orientation, which holds that changes in daily life should accompany and sometimes precede structural alterations in the wider society.

Recently, a good deal of controversy has surrounded the question of whether children are psychologically damaged by the threat of nuclear war. Robert J. Lifton, for instance, has written that the self-development of the young is hampered by their often unconscious recognition that they have no future.[1] Others have responded to this claim by maintaining that such worries affect only a small minority of children. They argue that most young people are primarily occupied with the traditional problems of growing up—learning to coordinate body and mind, getting along with peers, making it through school. Robert Coles suggests that fear of nuclear war is a class-based phenomenon present only among children of the affluent. "In the ghettos of Boston, I do not find children worrying about a nuclear bomb. I find children worrying about other things. Who has stolen what from whom? Who can possibly get a job?"[2]

There has also been much discussion about the curriculums used in the schools to introduce students to some of the issues involved in the arms race and the formation of nuclear strategies. Supporters of these curriculums often claim to be meeting a responsibility that the schools have been terribly delinquent in addressing. In Richard Barnet's words, the "teaching profession has failed to prepare young people to live in the nuclear age."[3] Robert J. Lifton has applied the indictment to higher education. "In our universities, we have done virtually nothing to address the situation, to explore it as compassionate thinkers and scholars. This is an intellectual and moral scandal and we should not forget that."[4] Conservatives have responded by charging that the messages given to children by the movement and the curriculums that have been developed are nothing more than propaganda on behalf of the freeze and a pacifist approach to foreign policy. They claim that such curriculums distort reality, generate unreasonable fear, and encourage utopian illusions.

These debates about what children really think and what they should be taught about nuclear war are important. At the crux of the controversies are critical questions about the health of American culture, the best strategies for ensuring continued survival, and the values that ought to be passed on to the young. At the same time, there is something problematic with the form that these quarrels have frequently assumed. The arguments that are so heatedly presented in the newspapers frequently have very little connection with what the activists in the movement are actually doing. First, most of the efforts undertaken with children envision the family and not the schools as the locus of change. Questions about parenting are just as important as the form and content of instruction in the schools. In a sense that has gone largely unnoticed, the antinuclear debate is part of the controversy about the role of the family in American society. Second, many of the educational materials subsumed under the category of nuclear education only indirectly address the question of nuclear war. They focus instead on self-esteem in children, on possible methods of resolving interpersonal conflicts peace- fully, and on the meaning of personal responsibility. In this respect, anti- nuclear activists are also struggling to discover a proper role for education about values in a modern, democratic society. Third, little attention has been paid to how the successes and failures of developing and implementing peace education programs in the family, the churches, and the schools reflect on the promise and the difficulties of the movement at large.

This chapter is based on an analysis of the materials used in programs for parents and children, interviews conducted with members of the peace community, and observations of religious education programs. I begin by placing the educational assumptions of many peace activists in the context of the current reassessment of the family undertaken by people of the liberal Left. I then move to investigate the principal ideas contained in the curriculums designed to acquaint children with the principles of nonvio- lent conflict resolution. I show how antinuclear educational programs draw upon personalist assumptions and reflect the ambivalent attitude toward modernity described earlier. The chapter concludes by assessing the short-term and potential long-term effects of these educational endeav- ors. I suggest that they have been successful in sharpening the activists' sense of self-definition and in giving shape to their community. To date, however, it is not certain how their practices will affect the development of their own children. This is surely understandable, given the incipient state of the movement. But mere passage of time alone cannot guarantee a more favorable response, because of the formidable obstacles involved.

A Changing Perspective

During the sixties, a number of writers and activists on the Left spoke critically about the role that the family played in American society. People hostile to American capitalism argued that families encouraged anti- social behavior by teaching children to be exclusively individualistic, possessive, and compulsive. Critics such as R. D. Laing and Jules Henry saw the family as depotism writ small. Arlene Skolnick compared the position of the "helpless" child to that of a prisoner: "All activities are under the total control of a single authority, empowered by the state to employ corporal punishment to enforce his rules, however arbitrary they may seem to the child."[5] From a militant feminist perspective, authors maintained that traditional family structures oppressed women by dividing labor unequally in the home and hindering the development of women's full potential. Believing that the family was tyrannical and pregnancy "barbaric," Shulamith Firestone went so far as to recommend that women be relieved of the burden of childbirth either through the development of artificial means of reproduction or by implanting manufactured wombs inside men.[6]

The various criticisms of the family accompanied a period of rethinking and experimentation in American society. On college campuses across the nation, students examined the Israeli kibbutz system and child rearing in socialist societies as possible alternatives to family life in the United States. Thousands of young Americans deliberately chose to live together in groups ranging from two couples sharing a household to full-blown communes with upwards of two hundred members. Some of these experiments were grounded in monogamous sexual relationships, while others preferred to chart a course beyond the presumed possessiveness of bourgeois sexual morality. These more radical experiments were complemented by a series of practical reforms in the mainstream of society. Liberals endorsed proposals for better day-care facilities, more sensitivity to the contradictory demands on women in the workplace, and a refashioning of educational curriculums to stress the advantages of sharing and cooperation.

The attacks made by people on the liberal Left against the traditional family and the vision of liberation contained in these indictments became part of the ammunition that the New Right fired back at them in the mid- and late seventies. In the oratory of Jerry Falwell, Tim LaHaye, and Ronald Reagan, liberals and other secular humanists were accused of conspiring to destroy the very foundation of American society. Reversing the charge that had been leveled by the Left, these men now argued that most of our serious problems—crime in the streets, the decline of the work ethic, and teenage promiscuity—were the result of the breakdown in the family that had been promoted by critics of American society in the previous decade. To the extent that liberals approved of women in the workforce, legitimized abortion, and increased government aid for the poor, they accused of having adopted the radicals' agenda.[7] For television evangelists, the moral bankruptcy of those who wished to experiment with relationships outside the family was amply confirmed by the widespread herpes epidemic and the discovery of acquired immune deficiency syndrome in the homosexual population.

By the end of the seventies, however, people on the Left had started to rethink their position about the function of the family, viewing its role in rearing the young and its potential for making a positive contribution to society in a more favorable light than previously. To be sure, these people did not simply embrace the position that had been advanced by the New Right. In particular, they argued that conservative endorsements of traditional family values ignored the legitimate aspirations of contemporary women and underestimated the stress placed on the family by institutions such as corporations, about which conservatives were largely silent. But they also acknowledged the theoretical shortcomings and practical difficulties of the outlook that had been prevalent in the previous decade. For some participants, experiments with communal living had been psychologically damaging. The research about children who had been raised in countercultural communes was, at best, less than reassuring. Many women who considered themselves feminists did not share Shulamith Firestone's aversion to childbearing and child rearing, but eagerly anticipated the opportunity to become mothers. And, herpes aside, serious doubts were also raised about some of the practices associated with the sexual revolution, especially the casual nature of relationships and the cool switching from partner to partner undertaken in the name of liberation. As Jean Bethke Elshtain put it, "The right's portrayal of feminist and radical antifamilialism is of course drastically overdrawn, but there is just enough truth to make the charge seem plausible. . . . The right has been able to portray itself as the defender of family life in part because of the early and dramatic hostility of many, though not all, feminists and radicals to traditional forms."[8]

This rethinking came full circle when some intellectuals began to argue that the family was not necessarily a repressive institution, but one that could be organized to provide a first experience with love, discipline, commitment, and community—experiences that were invaluable prerequisites to developing the vision and sustaining the effort that would be required to change the culture and the political order. Viewed in this light, the principal problem for the family was its permeation and subsequent erosion by American capitalism and the state bureaucracy. This created, in Christopher Lasch's phrase, a culture of narcissism that rendered people unable to form valuable and long-standing relationships with one another, let alone an enduring commitment to a political cause.[9] The task of people interested in changing American society was to protect the family from its attackers and to cultivate within it the values and discipline which run counter to the general trends of society at large, and, in Elshtain's words, "to refuse to build familial alternatives on the shaky sands of accommodation to the status quo."[10]

The Family and the Movement

I have quoted Professor Elshtain in the last two paragraphs because the views of the people to whom I spoke seem to correspond with the essential features of her argument.[11] The devotion that activists have to their families is reflective of their traditionalist sentiments and their own self-definition as "establishment-type people." They are interested in preserving the institution and are often fervent defenders of it. But they have also come to believe that their efforts to construct a rewarding family life are threatened by the workings of the American political and economic order. This trend is most noticeable, they think, in the military preparations currently being undertaken by the nation's political leaders, particularly the Reagan administration's nuclear buildup. But they suggest that it can also be discerned in the media's glorification of acquisition and in the lack of attention paid to notions of social responsibility.

There is much discussion within the peace community of how the values of nonviolent conflict resolution can be most effectively taught to children and of how they might be raised to resist the blandishments of a materialistic culture. Activist Wendy Northup writes a regular column on parenting that addresses these issues in the peace center's monthly newsletter. This concern is also reflected in the outreach efforts of the peace groups. Wendy and her husband Steve coordinate presentations at local churches and community forums for the Parenting for Peace and Justice program; religious educators adapt and develop curriculums for teaching peace issues to church education classes; and the peace education center collects materials and maintains a bibliography for parents and educators interested in acquainting their children with the principal themes of the movement.[12] The importance given to these concerns by the other members of the peace community is readily apparent in their favorable references to the activities of the people who are working with children.

The column that Wendy Northup writes about children and the family is a good illustration of how people are encouraged to incorporate the principles of the movement into their daily routines. In a typical contribution, Wendy begins with reflections on a general theme that she then relates to everyday realities, often by speaking about how she and her husband Steve translate their religiosity into the warp and woof of family life. The following column, which addresses the question of whether and how parents should expose children to their social beliefs, provides an example of how general reflections and practical advice are combined:

> Is it fair to our children to expose them to social problems? What about their childhood—don't we deprive them of that innocent carefree stage? These are legitimate questions with which parents need be concerned. But honest investigation of these questions still leads us to believe that our children need to be concerned about the world they live in.
>
> First of all, the discovery of evil in the world can be a paralyzing discovery for our children if they have been raised in a fairy tale where all ugly toads are princes in disguise. This doesn't mean that we should expose our children to unlimited ugliness or heap on too many of the world's problems. But it does mean that we can show them the pain and suffering in the world so that they, too, may feel sorrow and the desire to change things.
>
> And this leads to the second reason that we believe in exposing our children to social justice issues. We want them to be caring people whose meaning and mission in life involves service to others. We believe that the best way to do this is to provide them with opportunities to think creatively and compassionately about the problems they encounter.
>
> We want our children to be caring and hopeful, believing in the possibility of the Kingdom of God even in a world that cynically denies that possibility. We want them to believe that social change is possible, even if it is never easy and always very slow. They can only have this hope if they participate with us in the slow, ongoing efforts that characterize work for the Kingdom.
>
> But we involve our children with us in social action as one of the many parts of our family life. We also share their ball games, school plays, ballet recitals. And when we choose experiences to expose them to, we take the time to explain them on their own level so that it's not just a confusing adult activity. We encourage them to bring a friend along—even we would rather do something with a friend than do it alone. And we make sure that they have something concrete to do—sing a song, pass out leaflets, help serve a meal—at one demonstration at the Pentagon the children put on a play.
>
> They gain confidence when we and other adults treat them as important and let them participate in grown-up activities. And they will need this confidence as well as compassion and concern if they are to grow up to be caring, serving people in a world that often rewards those qualities as weakness.[13]

Because of her interest in relating general notions to the ordinary concerns of daily life, Wendy Northup's column contains much of the same kind of information found in a newspaper's "Helpful Hints" section. The principal difference is that hers is primarily directed toward the peace community and other parents who are socially concerned. In 1982, when the local paper published an article noting that a "new national mood" was creating a more profitable climate for war toys, Wendy asked other parents "to look seriously at this new national mood and how it might affect our children. We need to alert them to the possibility that they may see these ads—let them play detective and keep a sharp eye out for this new affront. Then we need to watch these ads with them, pointing out the glorification of killing and openly expressing our outrage. Our children need to see that we are really moved by these issues."

On one occasion, the column explained how the Northups dealt with a question raised by their five-year-old daughter, who wanted to know whether she would have a spear thrown at her if she ever met an Indian. It began by remarking how Wendy and Steve were taken aback by the comment, having simply assumed that their children would not be influenced by cultural stereotypes. Acknowledging that this was not the case, the family held a meeting to discuss the possible ways of gaining a better awareness of native American culture. The Northups ultimately decided to visit a nearby museum, see a documentary which provided a more accurate portrait of native American life, and visit a reservation in Virginia where a tribe is now located.

The Parenting for Peace and Justice program is the instrument with which Wendy, Steve, and others in the peace community attempt to reach a wider audience with their ideas about American society and the problems and possibilities of enriching family life within it. The program is based on two books written by James and Kathleen McGinnis, a couple in St. Louis who have devoted considerable energy to relating their ideas about Christianity and social justice to the daily routine of family life.[14] The program centers on various ways that *shalom*, the Hebrew word for peace, can be introduced into daily living. Shalom is interpreted broadly so that its meaning includes the connotations of harmony and wholeness as well as the simple absence of overt conflict and violence. Wendy and Steve conduct the Parenting for Peace and Justice session in a few different formats. There is a "Parents Only" session which describes the program's intellectual rationale and fosters discussion about the problems which parents experience in raising their children in a materialistic and militaristic society. The other formats, which the Northups find more valuable, bring parents and children together to explore their respective visions of peace and to think about how these might inform family activities. Wendy and Steve also tailor the content to the needs and wishes of their particular audience. When the session was held at the local Mennonite Church, for example, the congregation's long tradition of singing together and at home was drawn upon by including such hymns as "Peace Like A River."

The program begins with an emphasis on the significance of families to God's plan for people on earth. The importance that peace activists attribute to the family is, in some ways, similar to the arguments advanced by conservative evangelists. Both groups see it as an institution blessed by God in which children learn (or at least should learn) lessons that will shape their character and serve them well later in life. Both movements also object to the forces that they believe are weakening family life and undermining their capacity to raise their children properly. Yet the family in the Parenting for Peace and Justice program is not the same family extolled by Jerry Falwell and Jimmy Swaggart. This is most evident, I think, with respect to the position of women. Parenting for Peace and Justice explicitly endorses a more contemporary, egalitarian stance that almost goes so far as to imply that the Bible advocates affirmative action. Instead of quoting biblical passages that might lead to the conventional and conservative position that men and women occupy segregated yet complementary roles, Jesus' treatment of Mary Magdalene and the Samaritan women at the well are referred to as examples of his providing special treatment to bring out the potential of women who were crushed or living under a form of oppression.[15]

The basic premise of the program is a principal personalist tenet, namely, that the conditions for harmony in the world ought to be rooted in the everyday life of individuals. Families offer a training ground for dealing constructively with conflict, for learning that peace is a goal toward which we must continually strive, and for experiencing the deep satisfaction that comes with making progress toward that goal. During the session, Wendy and Steve frequently speak about the experiments they have initiated in their own family. They might talk about building a "shalom box," in which suggestions are placed by all members about how to make family life more peaceful, or the steps they have taken to ensure that meals would be rewarding even when everybody seemed more irritable than normal. Lest anyone think that the Northups have resolved all the dilemmas that bring conflict to the home, they also mention those efforts that have been absolute failures. They invite people in the audience to share their experiences with everyone and they may also ask people to form small groups to discuss how they might introduce the ideals of shalom more fruitfully into their household.

The discussion of shalom is not, however, confined to the family, for it is a premise of the program that while peaceful action has its roots in the family, it must also spread out into the world. The values that make for a good family life are also said to be politically relevant in contemporary times. The discussion of shalom is thus expanded to include the neighborhood, the nation, and ultimately the global village. Here, the principal emphases are on the biblical call to stewardship of the earth's resources, the necessity of respecting human diversity, and the solidarity of all peoples in God's kingdom. There are appropriate citations from the Bible about the proper use of resources and the problematic character of wealth. There are also references to other religious sources such as Chief Seattle's statement: "One thing we know which the white man may one day discover. Our God is the same God. You may think you own him as you wish to own the land; but you cannot. He is the God of all people, and his compassion is equal for all. The Earth is precious to God, and to harm the Earth is to heap contempt upon its Creator." Once again, a rich variety of activities that can be incorporated into daily living patterns are presented to the audience as possible ways of making a commitment to the values of shalom. These ideas range from examining textbooks and media for stereotypical portraits of minority cultures to thinking about the food we eat, the clothes we wear, and our leisure activities in terms of efficiency of resource use.

The program also encourages mothers and fathers to involve their children directly in social action. This includes traditional works of mercy that have been practiced for years by members of religious communities, such as staffing a soup kitchen, visiting the elderly, or opening one's home as a shelter for victims of injustice. The rationale is that works of mercy are both time-honored elements of the religious tradition and one of the most appropriate means of motivating children to take a personal interest in opposing injustice. At the same time, the program urges parents to broaden their involvements beyond merciful actions. It encourages them to be attentive to the structural problems that can be at the root of injustice and to the courage needed to remedy these. Parents are advised to acquaint their children with the nobility of a hero like Martin Luther King, Jr., who gave vivid witness to the depth of his commitment through political action. And the program offers a justification for civil disobedience through its favorable portrayal of activists such as Dorothy Day and Daniel Berrigan.

In sum, four themes appear relatively consistently in the peace community's discussion of family life and its outreach programs on parenting.

1. Children are taught in American society to be excessively militaristic and materialistic. They are exposed to more glorification of warfare than is proper; they learn about other cultures through dehumanizing stereotypes; and the media make a strenuous effort to socialize them into the consumer mentality. It would be preferable if children were instructed in the horrors of warfare and the sacredness of life. They should appreciate

Gandhi's notion that "there is enough in the world for everyone's need, but not for everyone's greed." Children should be encouraged to understand that they are stewards of the world's resources and that war and waste are antithetical to this identity.

2. A deformation of character is taking place in subtle and insidious ways in contemporary America. Our society tends to be competitive in the wrong ways and to foster narrow-mindedness in its children. Certain critically important character traits such as a disposition to care for others, to sacrifice immediate self-interest to higher principles, and to be socially responsible are neither encouraged nor rewarded in American society. Children should be taught to relate to each other more cooperatively and to emulate people like Dorothy Day and Martin Luther King, Jr., who embodied Christian values in a worthwhile and ennobling life.

3. Families that oppose the general drift of American society are, in many ways, under attack by the major economic, political, and cultural institutions. To the extent that families are the repository of Christian values such as compassion, equitable sharing, and community, they are in opposition to the prevailing trends in the culture. This can be observed in the daily struggle of parents to minimize the influence of television advertising on children. It is also evident in the battle over militarism that begins at a very young age with the controversy over whether war toys are acceptable gifts for children.

4. Responsible parents ought to counter the attempts to shape their children in accordance with the twin dictates of militarism and materialism. Parental obligations assume two general forms. First, parents should become politically active in order to inhibit the existing powers from carrying out policies that are harmful to their children and the rest of the world. Second, responsible parents are called to move beyond negative actions. It is their obligation to create a family life that will compensate for the sacrifices their children will make by not adopting the values of the dominant culture. The family should become an institution of alternative education, a place where children can learn to be independent, creative, and socially responsible, where they can develop the treasured memories that will serve them and other human beings well as they enter the adult world.

Self-Development and Social Responsibility

Peace activists in Richmond have attempted to translate their concern about how children are raised in American society into specific educational programs. Speakers from the Richmond Peace Education Center have been invited to a number of local high schools. The center also provides an overview of the arms race and a discussion of the principal positions taken about it for the in-service training of social studies teachers in one of the county school systems. A number of churches explicitly address the connection between faith and nuclear arms in their religious education programs. At times, this has simply meant the appearance of a spokesperson from the peace community at religious education classes. But a heavier emphasis has been placed on the development of six-week or summer-length programs that systematically present a nonmilitaristic perspective on peace issues. The form and content of these programs are modified according to the age of the group involved. Because the Catholic hierarchy is concerned about implementing the educational proposals of the bishops' pastoral, peace-related themes have also been introduced into the curriculum at the diocesan high schools.

While the necessity of arms control and superpower cooperation are central features of the message that the religious educators impart, the materials also stress the importance of developing a more peaceful psychological orientation, the benefits accruing from cooperative interpersonal and group relationships, and the relevance of adopting a global perspective on world issues. Interdisciplinary in approach, the programs reinforce the personalist nature of the movement by assuming that teaching children to deal peacefully and constructively with their emotional turmoils will predispose them to seek constructive solutions to social and political conflicts in later years. This approach is also manifested in the message that children should begin at a relatively early age to take small personal steps that show their interest in becoming responsible for events in the wider society.

My initial understanding of the activists' educational intent was corroborated by my conversations with some of the people involved in the actual design and teaching of the local programs. Martha Osborne is a religious educator who is currently dean of students at the Presbyterian School for Christian Education in Richmond. When she was employed in downtown Richmond by the Second Presbyterian Church, she organized Living in Harmony, a summer program that took children from different racial groups and social classes and exposed them to the diversity of urban life, including some of its most serious problems. Today, Martha remains active in adapting peace curriculums for local use and in speaking to people about how these might be utilized in religious education classes. She notes that she has a "holistic understanding of what it means to be a Christian" and believes that a genuine Christian education incorporates lessons about human character development through biblical and theological study. Martha describes the Living in Harmony program by saying that a "lot of our education was centered around affective and cognitive learning," especially since the "group itself was a microcosm of the world at large. Children had to learn to get along with others from different backgrounds. We spoke to children about their feelings for each other and their reactions to the people and places they saw. It was a good experience, if only because children are often very honest in expressing their feelings."

Makanah Morris is a Unitarian minister who directs her church's religious education classes and has undertaken some initial efforts "working from the ground up" to encourage social studies teachers in the area to incorporate peace-related themes into their courses. While she has a "grand vision that every school in Richmond would offer courses about peace," she does not think that it will become a reality in the foreseeable future. Most of her energies have been devoted to designing and organizing a six-week Sunday-school program that the Unitarians offer every other spring, alternating it with a program on ecological responsibility. Her methods in the course are similar to those of Martha Osborne inasmuch as Makanah consciously follows a holistic approach, maintaining that "we have to use our intellects, our bodies, our feelings, our games, and our art" to examine peace issues. With younger children, "we start with ideas about self-worth and family relationships and from there move on to discussions of peace in the world and what can be done to further it. We spend a lot of time asking children about their experiences with violence and conflict, exploring their vision of peace and why they believe it is important to have peaceful relations."

The curriculums designed or adapted by members of the peace community contain materials that attempt to reconcile a psychological orientation that stresses the importance of individual choice with a social outlook that encourages individuals to be responsible to their community and to develop a cosmopolitan or global outlook on world affairs. The psychological assumptions found in the books, games, and songs that peace educators use are derived from notions popular in progressive education circles during the past two decades. The self is conceived not as a demon to be exorcised but as a seed that should be allowed to grow into maturity. Children are encouraged to "accept their feelings" and to express them openly, though each and every feeling is not validated as an adequate guide to action. A definite effort is made to acknowledge that though a violent reaction to certain provocations is normal and understandable, acting upon this impulse may be detrimental to all involved. Still, the teachers accept the naturalness of the response and maintain that it is most effectively channeled into constructive paths by confronting it directly through its open expression. Younger children are especially encouraged to speak about occasions in which they have been prompted to deal with anger through violence. Afterward, alternative forms of action and their possible consequences are discussed. People such as Martha Osborne and Makarah Morris envision the teacher's responsibility as being primarily concerned with drawing out the problems which violence brings to personal relations and enabling children to develop the skills needed to deal creatively and nonviolently with conflict situations.

The social ethic that peace educators promote stresses the benefits of diversity, the necessity of limiting self-interest for the common good, and the advantages that accrue to groups, communities, and nations that develop the talent for nonviolent action. On an interpersonal level, their intent is to combat parochialism and nurture curiosity about the people and customs of different cultures. These lessons are grounded in the notion that there ought to be solidarity among all people in God's kingdom. At Martha Osborne's Living in Harmony program at the Second Presbyterian Church, the refrain of the theme song was "Different is beautiful / God bless variety / Just look around and see / Different is beautiful." The outlook expressed here is obviously equivalent to the idea present in the Parenting for Peace and Justice program that people ought to develop an awareness and appreciation of other cultures. In the session for preschoolers, a number of lessons began by focusing on how relationships in the family could be enhanced by peaceful values. Having done so, subsequent sessions examined "families throughout the world," explaining the similarities and differences among these primary structures. Children were then urged to learn about the cultures of various nations, especially as these were manifested in the conduct of daily life.

Peace educators occasionally use their emphasis on diversity to speak of the importance of not equating self-development with selfishness. At the Living in Harmony program, breakfast one morning came from a Kellogg's Variety Pack that was placed at each table where the children sat. At most of the tables, the children grabbed for their favorite cereal without hesitation and without regard to the likes and dislikes of the friends with whom they were eating. Arguments ensued and more than a few children were dissatisfied with the results of a distribution by first grab. Much of the morning program then focused on a discussion of the turmoil at breakfast. The battles over Rice Krispies, Corn Flakes, and Raisin Bran were thus translated into a consideration of whether might makes right and whether cooperation provides advantages that might not be obtained through conflict. Ultimately, many of the children themselves maintained that people have to acknowledge the limited quantity of life's goods and apportion them more equitably.

The activists' actual efforts to develop this socially responsible outlook appeal to what the guidebooks label "the child's innate sense of fair play and justice." But it is also repeatedly mentioned that social responsibility does not require individuals to sacrifice their own fulfillment. Curriculum materials assume that most deep individual needs—friendship, love, and esteem—are best met by sharing thoughts and kindnesses with others, giving love wherever possible. An enlightened pursuit of self-interest will lead to the recognition that true happiness emerges only when people agree to modify their crassest desires and impulsive reactions. Children are again informed that it would be best if they emulated important social and religious figures who realized their own identity more fully through service to others. One of the exercises used by peace educators in Richmond, titled "Because God Loves Us," uses the Lord's attitude toward the human race as a model for children to imitate in their relations with each other. The exercise informs the children that if they are to experience the friendship and happiness that mean so much to them, "love cannot stay at home. It must be spent and given away."

In most of the curriculum materials I examined, students were urged to adopt a global perspective on world problems. They are taught to perceive the interrelatedness of problems such as pollution, world hunger, and war, and are urged to see themselves as having some personal obligation to ameliorate these conditions. Children are also exposed to ideas which suggest that nationalism can be a malignant force in the world arena. One teacher's manual suggests, for instance, that students be asked to respond to the statement of H. G. Wells that "our true nationality is mankind," to another remark which suggests that "nationalism is an infantile disease . . . [and] it is the measles of mankind," and to Martin Luther King's assertion that "we cannot long survive spiritually separate in a world that is geographically together." Children are encouraged to read books like *Penguins of All People, On the Other Side of the River,* and *Walter the Wolf,* which focus on the connectedness of citizens of all nationalities and the inappropriateness of conflict as a means of settling political disputes.

Given the encouragement of internationalism present in these curriculums, it is not surprising that institutions such as the United Nations and the World Court are favorably portrayed in the materials used by children. As early as the second grade, children are informed of the various functions of the United Nations, and as they advance up the educational ladder, they are encouraged to report on its purposes, simulate Security Council debates, and learn of its efforts to arbitrate disputes. Occasionally, the curriculums do treat some of the recurring dilemmas which the United Nations and other regional organizations have experienced in meeting their established goals. These are typically described as problems to be overcome and not as sufficient reason to scrap the idea of supranational organizations and the cooperative approach to world problems.

The implications of the materials used with children about patriotism, nationalism, and internationalism may not, however, be fully consistent with the ideas that the activists express about citizenship and American political ideals. As I mentioned above, participants in the movement maintain that they have "old-fashioned ideas" about citizen responsibility. Many of them profess to embrace American political values, but contend that the nation's political leadership no longer faithfully adheres to these. I suggested that this pattern of belief constituted an important source of the movement's appeal. Participants could point to a set of beliefs that other citizens share and then show how existing policies contradict these commonly held notions. To put this in terms sometimes used by scholars, activists used the American civil religion as a critical tool to judge current policies and to sketch a direction for reform.

This style of argument is not prominent in the materials designed for children. The intention of promoting a commitment to human solidarity, the desire to counter the assertion that "one's country right or wrong" is an adequate ethical position, and the presumed need to break down stereotypes about people in other nations appear to be the guiding principles of the literature used with children. These may be valuable and laudable objectives. The problem is that they are often presented in such a way—nationalism is "the measles of mankind"—that loving one's country and maintaining a global vision become incompatible. The materials that I examined rarely spoke of the idea that American values might lead citizens to oppose official policy. In other words, the distinction between a civil religion critical of the state and the official definition of patriotism frequently dissolves into a univocal condemnation of national pride.

Peace Education and Its Limits

It is too early to judge adequately the outcome of the peace activists' efforts to strengthen their families, persuade children that there are viable alternatives to violent resolutions of social and political conflict, and convince other parents to follow their lead. Most of the activists profess to be glad that they have discovered steps that they can take with their loved ones to affirm their commitment. They testify that their lives are marked by a harmony, a sense of wholeness, and a consistency that would not be present if they had not made this effort. They feel better thinking that their families have a purpose other than accumulating goods and furthering personal ambition. Indeed, their commitment is reinforced by the positive changes that they see occurring in their own lives.

Many of the men and women in the peace community think that their involvement in antinuclear activism has also served their children well. They believe that children benefit from examples of care and commitment in a world that the activists feel is often cynical and self-serving, and they are eager to point to instances where their sons and daughters seem to have grown in their understanding of social problems and the meaning of personal responsibility. Although parents are glad that they are making this effort, they are also quick to point out that they have achieved only mixed success. This is partly because of the broader dilemmas of the movement. I have mentioned in other chapters that while the personalist orientation of the activists is appealing, it can also appear overly demanding. People may think that the movement is doing something important, but consider themselves too busy to make an active contribution. They may, for instance, support the freeze, but not assume that this entails changing their manner of living.

The Parenting for Peace and Justice program is a good example of how this tendency is manifested in response to the efforts of the activists. Wendy Northup believes that people who attend the session typically react favorably to its content. Much of this can be explained by the fact that the audience is usually self-selected and may already share the basic outlook of the peace activists. But even when Wendy has conducted the program in churches or civic organizations whose members are not especially sympathetic to the peace movement, the response has been generally positive. This can be attributed, I think, to the use of traditional Christian themes such as antimaterialism, personal responsibility, and the imperative of helping the disadvantaged within the framework of strengthening the family. At the same time, most people who attend the program do not ultimately make the kind of commitments that it promotes. They are apt to praise Wendy highly while implying that they could not really follow her example. "One of the most disappointing responses I get is when someone comes up afterwards and tells me, 'you're really wonderful, I admire you so much,' but makes it seem that I'm so unusual that nothing which I've said has any meaning to them."

However disturbing this response may be to activists, its prevalence is understandable. The Parenting for Peace and Justice program asks people to make considerable adjustments in their manner of living. If they were to implement some of its advice, parents would more consciously find ways of challenging their children to think differently. They might be compelled to alter their long-standing habits of television viewing and would replace some of their leisure time with political action. Living consistently could require mothers and fathers to examine how they might be in complicity with disturbing trends in the larger culture, to ask themselves about what kind of role models they are, and to consider how the ambitions expressed in their own lives reflect on the ideals they profess to be transmitting to their children.

If people were to act on the message of the Parenting for Peace and Justice program, they would have to be willing to raise children who are, in a sense, different from most of the kids growing up in the United States today. Most parents, I think, have ambivalent reactions to the prospect of placing their families in an adversary relationship with the culture. They do want their children to stand out from the rest by excelling in athletics, scholarship, or even general moral demeanor, and they do not want their sons and daughters to jettison all the values they have been taught in favor of the prevailing fad. But, at the same time, parents are reluctant to encourage their children to be too different. They are aware of the pressures on young people to conform to the expectations of their friends and they know how lonely children can be when rejected by their peers, particularly with the special viciousness that youth can exhibit. These considerations are likely to bear most heavily on the very people whom the activists are most interested in attracting—men and women who have an intuitive sympathy for the movement, but whose daily routines lie entirely outside the culture of the peace community.

Directly approaching children through the Catholic schools and religious education classes may seem, at first glance, to be more promising for the activists' position. During the last few years, an informal alliance has developed in the Catholic church and in a number of Protestant denominations between grassroots reformers and the clerical hierarchy. One consequence of this in Richmond has been the attempt by the diocesan Office of Justice and Peace to promote discussion of the bishops' pastoral and to present a peace and justice orientation as a legitimate outgrowth of Catholic religious beliefs. The people involved in this process and others who know about it believe that this is a significant development. They think that children have been helped to deal with conflict more responsibly, that

they manage anger better, and that they see the possibility for reconciliation where previously they did not.

Nevertheless, the translation from diocesan encouragement to classroom
presentation is not automatic. Many principals and teachers simply may
not agree with the bishops' position, the statements of Walter Sullivan, or
the activities of Pax Christi. Moreover, even some of the people who are
sympathetic may be influenced by other considerations. Teachers and principals are more likely to feel constrained by parental misgivings than are
those people making diocesan policy. And parents who have enrolled their
children because they believe in the discipline that is characteristic of paro-
chial schools may not be happy with an orientation that legitimizes social
activism in a framework of traditional values. In fact, the back-to-basics
movement that has become so prominent in recent years argues that it is
programs such as peace studies and conflict resolution that destroyed education in the first place.

Besides potential conflicts with parents, the long-term influence that
religious education classes and peace-related themes in school curriculums
will have on children is uncertain. To be sure, there are children who are
powerfully moved by their teachers and can remember a very special one
who prompted them to reconsider their fundamental beliefs and reexamine
the direction of their lives. But there are probably many more people who
carry no such recollection of their school years, but instead recall them as
boring and unhappy moments which they were compelled to endure. In
particular, religious education classes may be thoroughly ineffective in
motivating children to examine critically the culture in which they reside.
For every parent who is sincerely interested in ensuring that his or her
children are adequately instructed in the foundations and implications of
the inherited faith, there is probably another who sends the children to the
classes in order to assuage guilt feelings about the lack of religiosity at
home or to have the instructors function as baby-sitters. In any event, it is
highly unlikely that most of the faithful perceive religious education classes
as a place where their children ought to make a deep examination of the
conduct of their lives.

The attempt by parents and educators to transmit their values to children is subject to continual frustration, both by the mystery that is each
child's own self-identification and by the forces in the larger culture—peer
groups, other relatives, teachers, and corporate advertisers—who may be
sending antithetical messages. Some children may wholeheartedly embrace
the values that their parents deem important. But others may already see
their mothers' and fathers' reservations about video games, war toys, and

the glorification of conflict as quaint habits that need to be humored or, even worse, as a personal embarrassment whose existence they would like to keep secret from their friends. It is not entirely out of the question that more than a few parents in the peace community will one day find themselves in the incongruous position of having contributed to the upbringing of ardent militarists and fervent consumers.

The problem that parents face here is similar to that confronted by anyone who wishes to promote certain value orientations in his or her children. How do you begin to promote your values when the culture is geared to alternative points of view? The problem is exacerbated by the growing recognition that television and peer groups are exercising increased influence on young children. Parents often feel a sense of powerlessness and resentment toward outside forces over which they have little control, and teachers defend themselves against attack by pointing to television, peer groups, and the lack of parental guidance in the home as the principal reasons for substandard achievement. In fact, this dilemma has been publicized most visibly by conservative men and women who maintain that their rights as parents are continually undermined by the liberal media and by liberal educators who teach that toleration of certain sexual practices is desirable.

This problem is doubly perplexing for people in the peace community because they adhere to ideas about self-development that cannot justify imposing values on their sons and daughters in a heavy-handed manner. When I spoke to parents about raising children and peace education, they frequently told stories and anecdotes about their lack of success in transmitting their values in a direct fashion to all of their children. Wendy Northup, for instance, noted that her son maintained that "peace was boring and he asked us to buy him fatigues so he could join the neighborhood 'guerrillas' and run around playing war." And after hearing about the importance of reaching her full potential, Wendy's daughter Kathleen insisted on dressing up on Halloween as a belly dancer. Similarly, Donna Gorman's effort to sensitize her children to how militarism has permeated the United States is resisted at home. "I want them to be able to understand how pervasive this is in our society." But she also remarks that one of her sons keeps a gun at home for hunting purposes. "I can see his point, even if I don't really like it."

Perhaps not much should be made from these anecdotes. But I think they are important because they reveal some of the dilemmas and contrary pulls posed by the commitment of people in the peace community. In particular, they illuminate once again the ambivalence about modernity that personalists exhibit. Quite attached to some features of contemporary culture, they remain bitterly opposed to its advance in other areas of life. The activists clearly believe that American society is overly militaristic and materialistic. They want their children to know about this concern and to be capable of resisting the enticements that a consumer society offers in favor of a more socially responsible stance toward life. They would be pleased if their children grew up to become active participants in the movements to which they devote their energies and monies. But they also adhere to many "modern" ideas about child rearing and the position of youth in society. They do not believe that parents should simply impose their values on their children. They want their children to develop their own consciences and to make free choices about their careers and beliefs. Indeed, one can almost detect a hint of pride in the stories and anecdotes they relate about their children's independence and their unwillingness to simply affirm all that their parents have deemed important.

Unlike some conservative educators concerned about revamping American society, activists in the peace community do not believe that going back to the basics should entail repudiating the politics of the past thirty years. They think it is important that young men and women should feel comfortable expressing their own ideas about significant personal and social issues; they want their sons and daughters to develop their talents to the fullest extent; and they believe that it is worthwhile to learn about history and politics from the perspective of people who are not necessarily part of the dominant class. But they also want to raise children who will not see individualism as a justification for riding on the backs of other people. The educational activities of the peace community attempt to show that a society that glorifies self-development must also develop a sense of responsibility and obligation in its populace if it is to avoid the worst excesses of individual self-expression.

Martha Osborne's reflections on her own activities capture the ambivalence ultimately contained in the activists' ideas about peace education. "Some people might think that what I do is indoctrination. And, in some small sense, they may be right. I rely on the power of notions such as hope, trust, and love and these basic Christian values might not always be rational in the normal sense of the term. To love people, to trust them, and to be hopeful about change does require a measure of faith. But I can't see how you can teach about life without expressing values and without showing what you think is important. Besides, I really don't try to indoctrinate, but see what I do as offering a basic Christian perspective that might help people make choices about living in the world as they become adults."

This work which peace activists are performing with children might be described as an effort to reconcile the needs of what Edmund Burke called the little platoon—family, neighborhood, church—with the needs of people outside this circle, whether they be located in a different economic class or in another part of the globe. In the past fifteen years, many people have gained a renewed appreciation of the importance of community, the potential value of family life, and the strength conferred by positive ethnic identities. Yet there is much work to be done in showing how these commitments can be disengaged from a parochialism and an exclusiveness that are the psychic underpinnings of a pernicious social Darwinism and militaristic adventuring. The men and women in the peace community are trying to make this effort. It is an endeavor that holds much promise, but it also reflects the practical difficulties that the movement faces and the intellectual challenges that it must confront.

6

When the Spirit Says Protest: Unconventional Politics and the Limits to Personalism

DURING THE fifties and sixties, many activists in the civil rights movement were devoutly religious. They did not speak in complicated philosophical terms to justify their beliefs, but referred to notions found in the Bible, such as simple justice, human decency, and respect for others. The adaptations they made of traditional gospel hymns provided ringing evidence of how their religious fervor could be used in the service of progressive politics. One of these songs, "Do What the Spirit Says Do," gave explicit testimony to the guiding power of religious conviction in the participants' lives. Led by Len Chandler and sung by over thirty thousand people at the Capitol steps in Montgomery, Alabama, following the march from Selma in 1965, it opened with a refrain that set both the form and the cadence for the succeeding verses.

> You've got to do what the spirit says do
> You've got to do what the spirit says do
> And when the spirit says move
> Lord you've got to move
> You've got to do what the spirit says do.

Acknowledging that you've "got to pray when the spirit says pray" and "love when the spirit says love," most of the verses were more highly politicized. The lyrics affirmed the righteousness of the marchers and sanctified the tactics of the movement. As the voices in the crowd crested, the protesters proclaimed that "you've got to vote when the spirit says vote," "march when the spirit says march," and, finally, "picket when the spirit says picket."

It is obvious that many participants in the recent peace movement in the United States have listened to the same voices that animated the civil rights marchers in the sixties. Once again, we have witnessed the birth and growth of a political movement that is grounded, to a significant degree, in the translation of religious conviction to the political realm. Furthermore, a number of people have been prompted to consider nonelectoral, nonconventional modes of political participation. There has been a modest resurgence of civil disobedience, designed to draw attention to companies that manufacture nuclear weapons and to governments that have contingency plans for their use. Efforts have been initiated to form a nationwide network of tax resisters willing to withhold a portion of their tax bill in protest against military spending and to notify the government of their rationale. Besides these protest activities, some participants in the nation's peace movements have founded small, ecumenical communities that function both as sources of emotional and religious sustenance and as collectivities committed to merciful action and social change in the wider society.

Civil disobedience has not been the most prominent feature of the activism in Richmond during the past few years. But neither has it been ignored in the peace community. A few individuals have broken the law as acts of personal witness to the sinfulness of the arms race, joining national protests such as the Pershing resistance or the American Peace Test in Nevada. The development of the War Tax Alternatives Group shows how some participants are connecting their thoughts about individual responsibility to the funding of nuclear weapons. Groups associated with the peace community have been arrested at sit-ins at the Richmond office of Senator Paul Trible protesting contra aid. In fact, by 1986 the option of employing civil disobedience was being considered seriously by more people in the area than at any time since the beginning of the movement.

This chapter examines and evaluates the practice of unconventional politics as it has taken form in Richmond. It begins with a sketch of Tim Lietzke, a Christian radical who participated in a Plowshares action in Orlando, Florida. Next, it describes the motivation undergirding tax resistance and the effort to transform it into a method of political action and public education. I then analyze an attempt by some activists to complement a politics of protest by living in an ecumenical setting—the Community of the Servant—that reflected their understanding of what a truly Christian life entails.

The chapter argues that the unconventional political activity of the Richmond peace community illustrates in a very pronounced fashion some of the key elements and central difficulties of the personalist approach. It highlights the deep religious motivation of the activists, their intention of having their own community function as an exemplary counterculture, and their willingness to experiment with a variety of participatory forms. At the same time, we see how demanding personalist ideals can be for even committed individuals and the difficulty that the activists have experienced in persuading others to embrace their beliefs.

Personal Conscience and Collective Action

To date, the most dramatic act of civil disobedience performed by any individual from Richmond was committed by Tim Lietzke. Along with seven other religious activists who call themselves the Pershing Plowshares, Tim entered the Martin Marietta plant in Orlando, Florida, at 4:30 in the morning on Easter Day in April 1984. Four of the participants symbolically disarmed a missile launcher by hammering on it, cutting wires and hoses, and pouring their own blood over it. Four others entered a Pershing Kit Building and hammered on components of actual Pershing missiles. Afterward, the eight reassembled and celebrated Easter and Passover with song, scripture, reading, and prayer. Security guards noticed the group when one participant blew a ram's horn, an instrument used during Jewish holy days to call believers to atonement. The eight were arrested and subsequently charged with conspiracy and depredation of government property. The Pershing Plowshares had intended to offer a justification defense at their trial. They wanted to claim that their actions were compatible with the norms of international law and that the American state was making it increasingly difficult for them to exercise their freedom of religion. The judge refused to permit this line of defense. The activists were convicted as charged and served sentences from one to three years in prison around the nation.[1]

Tim Lietzke's justification for his participation in the Martin Marietta action is twofold. He first argues that American foreign policy is guided by principles antithetical to basic Christian values. Echoing the indictments found in *Sojourners* and other radical Christian analyses of American life, he writes that we practice a form of "idolatry" that has "spawned a national security state which . . . to an unprecedented degree has usurped the place of God in our lives." He contends that the nation's participation in the arms race "represents an utter contempt for the American public, the peoples of other nations and most notably the poor and oppressed of the earth. . . . Simply put, the Bomb and the National Security State represent a massive theft from the 50,000 people who starve to death every day." In addition, he believes that in order to continue the race, the government has developed "taxation laws and laws against sabotage, depredation of national defense materials . . . and trespass . . . to establish and maintain the national religion of nuclearism and to prohibit the free exercise of the Judaeo-Christian faith based on the sanctity of life."[2]

The second part of his justification for committing civil disobedience refers to the responsibilities that he believes Christians ought to shoulder in idolatrous times. Tim contends that Christians determined to practice their faith will be compelled to resist the dominant mores of society. This resistance may entail becoming less dependent on material goods for personal security. It may be embodied in the creation of a faithful community that operates on norms different from those of conventional society. It may require the violation of existing laws in favor of presumably higher moral laws. In sum, Christians are required to ground their lives in gospel values that testify to the worth of all humans and not in secular norms. In the writings he penned in prison, Tim argued that simply doing this will result in the state defining a person as "an outlaw," just as Jesus was characterized by the political authorities of his era.

Of all the activists I interviewed and observed, Tim Lietzke was the person most committed to the perspective on "effectiveness" that Daniel Berrigan had articulated. Speaking about the actions he considered appropriate forms of witnessing, Tim never referred to potential influence as part of the criteria for choosing one possibility over another. He believes that making a moral statement that he finds personally fulfilling is much more important. Yet Tim does believe that ordinary citizens will respond to faithful action. In fact, he offers an extremely optimistic assessment of the mobilization that occurred as a consequence of his actions at Martin Marietta. "I see hope all over the place. There has been a positive feeling developing toward people working for the freeze. . . . After our own action, churches all over Sweden sat down and discussed the issue. We received a note of sympathy and gratitude signed by more than five hundred prosecutors and judges in Germany. And, in Orlando, a number of new peace groups were started in the wake of our arrest and trial. Even in prison, observing people's views change and their understanding deepen cannot help but to give me hope."

In general terms, most members of the peace community support civil disobedience as an appropriate response to the problem of reducing nuclear weapons. They hold that politicians must feel pressure bubbling up from below before they are willing to take stands of conscience on controversial matters, and the men and women whom the activists consider exemplary give further evidence of this. The movement's pantheon is populated not by elected officials who have cleverly shepherded legislation through Congress but by political prophets such as Mohandas Gandhi, Martin Luther King, Jr., and Dorothy Day, who captured the hearts and spiritual energies of their followers. Most of the activists to whom I spoke see civil disobedience as a necessary complement to other forms of politics. Some would go so far as to see it as a higher form, one which reflects a moral commitment that is not tainted and compromised by the daily responsibilities of getting along in the world.

The support for civil disobedience expressed by people in the movement is qualified by two considerations. First, the activists acknowledge that most people, including themselves, are unwilling to follow Tim Lietzke's example and go to jail for an extended period of time. In our interviews, this was occasionally described as a personal deficiency, as when one participant noted that he didn't "have the kind of courage that Tim does." More frequently, the activists pointed to other obligations that they had assumed as their reason for not wanting to go, as they phrased it, "all the way" with civil disobedience. The responsibilities of marriage and family were most often mentioned in this regard. We might recall, for example, John Gallini's comment that he would pay for his children's college education before he would contemplate actions that could land him in jail.

A second consideration raised by the activists had to do with the political effectiveness of civil disobedience. Steve Hodges, for instance, is as committed to civil disobedience as anyone in the local community. He admires Christians who have taken actions consistent with their professed beliefs and strives to live this way himself. He has been arrested at the American Peace Test at the Nevada weapons testing site, at actions in Washington, D.C., and in a local sit-in protesting a contra aid vote. But Steve has also been critical of the manner in which direct action has frequently been conducted. In particular, he thinks that pacifists should be more concerned with developing mass support for their ideas. Influenced by Gandhi and King, Steve is not convinced that the acts performed by Dan Berrigan and others in the Catholic pacifist tradition make the best possible use of their witness. He maintains that activists who engage in civil disobedience should give more thought to developing broad-based campaigns that involve people in mutually supportive acts of resistance that are both legal and illegal.

The development of tax resistance indicates how the Richmond activists have tried to apply these ideas about civil disobedience. Given their commitment to assuming personal responsibility, about two dozen people in the peace community have seriously considered withholding or have actually withheld a percentage of their federal income tax and placed it in a peace escrow fund as a protest against the use of tax monies to pay for nuclear weapons. Originally, a number of those involved resisted taxes as a matter of conscience and did not intend to persuade others to join them. Harold Houghton, a Quaker who teaches mathematics at a local high school, one year withheld 36 percent of his tax. He justified his decision by saying, "I feel that I must live morally, I cannot kill and neither can I pretend that my money does not pay for killing." Despite this commitment, Harold refrained from informing many of his acquaintances of his decision. "I don't tell people at work, 'Listen, this is what I'm doing, how do you respond?' Perhaps this is related to my concern about job security, but I think that I would just be terribly uncomfortable saying, 'Oh, by the way, I'm not paying my taxes and this is why.' I just don't want to confront people in that manner and I don't want to invade their privacy."[3]

Harold Houghton did participate in the War Tax Alternatives Group. For the first few years of its existence, WARTAG was basically a mutual support organization. It brought together tax resisters and those contemplating it to share thoughts and experiences with like-minded people. The group also organized seminars at local churches that explained to potential tax resisters the rationale for the act, the various legal and illegal mechanisms that could be used to register a protest about government spending priorities, and the penalties that were possible for war tax resistance. By the middle of the 1980s, WARTAG—under the impetus of Steve Hodges— began to move in other directions as well. Its activities were more highly publicized within the peace community and became a form of internal education. The group worked to increase the visibility of the issue by recruiting others to write letters of protest even if they were not actively resisting taxes themselves. Members began to pass out their literature at the post office on April 15 when citizens were filing last-minute returns. WARTAG also sought to recruit more tax resisters by drafting a resolution and circulating a petition in which those who signed agreed to resist a level of taxes if one hundred others in the area did the same.

These efforts to widen the scope of WARTAG achieved, at most, minimal success. Within the peace community itself, activists discussed both tax resistance and the general issue of civil disobedience. Steve Hodges' tax protest compelled the board of directors of the Richmond Peace Education Center to decide whether it would put a lien on his salary if the Internal Revenue Service issued this demand. The board ultimately stated that it supported individual acts of conscience such as Steve's, though it could not, as a tax-exempt organization, actually endorse civil disobedience. In other forums, activists debated whether tax resistance was the best possible way of bringing the movement to public attention.

Besides the internal discussion that tax resistance generated, protesters received a measure of public attention. Newspaper articles and television interviews permitted them to explain their rationale for their actions and to indicate their personal beliefs to a wider audience, and a few churches invited some of the resisters to discuss their perspective in Sunday-school classes or other special programs. But despite these accomplishments, tax resistance never extended much beyond its core group or caught on as a pressing issue of discussion in the wider community. In fact, it could be said that the effort to politicize it did not reach much further or deeper than the act which Tim Lietzke and the Pershing Plowshares committed in Orlando, Florida.

Besides tax resistance, members of the peace community have also been involved in other instances of civil disobedience. The SPAN group described in chapter 4 worked with local organizations that opposed the Reagan administration's policy in Central America and protested Senator Paul Trible's votes in support of contra aid. Rebuffed in their efforts to meet personally with the senator and explain their views, local opponents of contra support became more visible in their opposition. In the summer of 1985, eleven protesters were arrested for a sit-in at the senator's office and for refusing to leave at the end of normal business hours. They were removed from the office by the police while about one hundred sympathizers cheered their action outside.

Later that summer, those arrested used their trial to air their convictions and publicize their criticisms of both the Reagan administration and Senator Trible. The defendants took the stand on their own behalf and told how their moral commitments about the sanctity of life prompted them to disobey the law in order to oppose United States policy. To corroborate their arguments, an administrator for a prestigious local hospital testified to the destruction of health-care clinics by the contras that he had personally observed in Nicaragua and a former CIA official testified that the administration's support for the contras was based on a false premise, namely, that the Sandinistas were supplying large amounts of arms to the rebels in El Salvador. The judge's obvious antipathy to the political claims of the defendants and his relish in confronting and debating them clearly aided their efforts to publicize their beliefs.

The protest and subsequent trial did allow the activists to demonstrate how the movement could be broadened to include foreign policy issues other than the arms race. Moreover, it showed how a local political institution—the Richmond Circuit Court—could be transformed into an arena for public debate about the United States' role in international affairs. Yet its limitations shortly became equally evident. Not only did Senator Trible continue to vote in support of contra aid, but Chuck Robb, the state's most prominent Democratic politician, endorsed President Reagan's policy and chastised the Democrats nationwide for paying too much attention to the freeze movement and organized opposition to the contras. In addition to its lack of influence on mainstream politicians, the effort to broaden the movement was plagued by factional disputes that the freeze activists had successfully avoided but which have traditionally divided progressive efforts. Pacifists argued with supporters of revolutionary violence; nonreligious activists charged that the movement was too colored by religion; and the resulting divisions made it impossible for groups concerned about U.S. policy in Central America to formulate a coherent plan of local action in the months following the trial.

A Complete Action

Wendell Berry, in an essay titled "The Reactor and the Garden," has offered an interesting analysis of protest politics. The occasion of the piece was Berry's participation in an antinuclear protest against the construction of a reactor near his home in Kentucky. Berry's purpose in the essay is to explain his acceptance of the necessity of protest and his reservations about its use. He notes first how strongly he supported the ideas that motivated the demonstrators. People need, he thinks, to become capable of declining the "progress" that accompanies many technological innovations and to rely on sources of power less potentially lethal than nuclear energy. He felt that the protest was worthwhile and that during it he had experienced the camaraderie and solidarity that emerge from a commitment to a shared purpose. Yet Berry also maintains that there is something radically incomplete about protest politics, a feeling he expresses by noting that people very rarely protest "for" something. He contends that a demonstration can actually be an easy way of making a political statement, especially if it does not influence the manner in which people actually conduct

When the Spirit Says Protest

their lives. In the case of nuclear power, he avers that even the most vehement protester may also have a lifestyle that makes energy production of this sort appear to be an unfortunate yet necessary alternative. To supplement and complement the politics of protest, Berry calls for "complete actions," steps by which individuals incorporate their beliefs into their daily lives.[4]

I have tried to show that one of the most notable features of peace activism in Richmond is the attention paid to what Berry calls complete action. The personalist approach emphasizes the need for positive local activity that serves as a constructive complement to a politics of protest and resistance. This tendency, seen throughout the peace community, was even more pronounced among a group of young activists who formed an ecumenical community that combined their interest in living modestly with advocacy work on behalf of peace and social justice issues. The group, which called itself the Community of the Servant, was begun by Diantha and Steve Hodges, Tim Lietzke, and some of their friends in town and at the Union Theological Seminary in Richmond who wanted their ideas about Christianity and peacemaking to be manifested in their daily lives. The name of the community was chosen to be a sign of their dissatisfaction with what they considered to be the institutional churches' "neotriumphal identity." It was also to be a reminder to the members that Christian outreach was a primary reason for its formation.

The people who made up the community in 1982 were almost all between the ages of twenty and thirty-four. There were six males and five females in the group. There were two married couples and one couple who were planning to wed in the near future. Diantha and Steve Hodges' two girls were the only children in the community. Some members were in graduate school or the seminary. Those who held full-time positions were in service-related areas such as campus ministry, occupational therapy, or working with the mentally disadvantaged. There were, however, a couple of members who worked only part time and used the hours they saved to devote to various social actions. Most of the people in the community had strongly religious backgrounds. A disproportionate number were sons and daughters of ministers and almost everyone could recall their religious upbringing—even if it was conservative—being a decisive factor in shaping their beliefs. They wanted to retain these beliefs as a motivating force in their lives, yet desired to activate their religiosity differently than was common within the institutional church.

In 1983, the community occupied two homes in the Oregon Hill area of Richmond, a poor working-class white neighborhood notorious for its barroom violence and virulent racism. The decision to locate in Oregon Hill was the culmination of a lengthy process of deliberation among the members. It was a choice that revealed the twofold notion of community held by many people in the peace movement. On the one hand, prospective members of the Community of the Servant were searching for an area where they could find homes in relative proximity that would also be inexpensive. Given the rents in Oregon Hill, members of the community would have the opportunity to concentrate on personal and communal growth and use what monies they had to promote their goals. On the other hand, the people who formed the Community of the Servant also wanted to live in a neighborhood where they could do outreach work with local citizens. While there are a number of poor sections in the city, they finally settled on Oregon Hill because they believed it was important to learn about the race issue as it presented itself to people there if they were to make a contribution to defusing racial tensions.

The Community of the Servant met on Sunday afternoons for worship and fellowship services. It began with a moment of silence and meditation which was followed by a time of sharing in which members spoke to one another about their personal concerns. Someone might talk about a difficulty at work or a relational problem with another person in the community. There was also a conscious effort to share the positive features of the members' lives. Accomplishments at work, uplifting moments in a relationship, and the simple pleasures experienced in the day-to-day life of the community were mentioned as well. A discussion of business matters followed this. Here, residents spoke of the best way to use the money that had been pooled, possible efforts to serve the neighborhood, and plans for civil disobedience campaigns and peace-related events. This part of the meeting then concluded with a period called "outward journey" that typically consisted of a report which one member presented on an issue which he or she had been studying. These reports were wide-ranging and included themes such as the history and practice of tax resistance, Christianity and economics, and thoughts on the religiosity of the community and its relation to the institutional churches.

The second part of the meeting, open to people who were thinking of joining the community and to others who simply wanted to attend the worship, was the prayer and liturgy service. The coordination, planning, and direction of the service rotated on a weekly basis from one member to another. The purpose of the rotation was not simply to guard against the development of a priestly hierarchy, but to acquaint the members of the community with the practices of a variety of faiths. Depending on who planned the service, there would be a varying mix of song, meditation, prayer, and sermon. After this was completed, the meeting officially concluded with a common dinner, eaten in an atmosphere of song and prayer.

During the week, members of the community participated in a number of routine activities together. They baby-sat for the children of Steve and Diantha Hodges when they attended meetings. They cooked and ate dinners together. They watched television and worked on the home collectively. This last task was especially important because their inexpensive rents were dependent, in part, on their willingness to perform repair chores themselves. Much emphasis was also placed on bringing the "servant" ethos of the group to bear on local needs. A few people were involved with Richmond United Neighborhoods, a community action organization that helps to organize poor people for the purposes of political change. Tim Lietzke established a big-brother and big-sister program in Oregon Hill for children of broken and violent homes. Members of the community were instrumental in beginning Freedom House, a soup kitchen and laundry facility for the homeless and the hungry in the city.

When persons covenanted to join the Community of the Servant, they agreed to subsist on a poverty-level income or below in order to avoid the pernicious effects of wealth on religious faith and to demonstrate kinship with the poorest of God's kingdom. Any additional income that a person received was turned over to what was labeled the Servant fund. At its business meeting, the group talked about the most appropriate manner of using the accumulated money. Some of it was given to individual members to subsidize projects such as their participation in the Witness for Peace, but most of it was reserved for people and causes outside the Community of the Servant. The group committed at least 50 percent of its donations to organizations that were not simply charitable in intent but were also working for structural change in the larger society. By developing the fund and structuring its use, members of the Community of the Servant discovered that they collectively gave much more than they would probably have donated if they had merely added up their normal individual contributions. In 1983, for example, the Servant fund contributed $550 for buses to the Martin Luther King, Jr., mobilization in Washington, D.C., for people who were unable to pay. It also contributed substantial sums of money to Freedom House, Oxfam, Amnesty International, and Richmond United Neighborhoods.

The Community of the Servant made an effort to reconcile its members' individual needs with the necessity of sharing goals and performing common work. It did this by encouraging people to develop their talents and follow their calling. Given the vows of poverty, it was possible for some members to pursue highly unconventional vocations. Moreover, the pooled resources made it possible for those who wished to participate in civil disobedience or devote much of their time to volunteer work to do so without having to worry about their material sustenance. The group also tried to recognize that the communal experience is of such intensity that not everyone would be permanently comfortable within it. Though strenuous efforts were undertaken to preserve the community, it was understood that the goals of the members would change over time. For this reason, participants celebrated departures as well as entrances to the community, holding parties to affirm the contribution that the departing member had made to the life of the community and to offer good wishes for the success of future endeavors.

The task of reconciling individual needs with the shared purpose of the group was sometimes very difficult simply because of the commitments that the community had adopted. One good example was the belief of the members that it was their obligation as Christians to provide shelter for the homeless. Characteristically, a few members of the group viewed this responsibility in intensely personal terms. They felt that it was not adequate merely to contribute money to charitable organizations. Nor did they think that their obligation was fulfilled by the lobbying they undertook on behalf of the homeless or through the opening of Freedom House. Instead, they started their own hospitality ministry where they made their home and energies available to those who needed help. It was not uncommon for local agencies to call one of the households and ask it to provide emergency aid for a period of up to two weeks. The residents in the community had mixed reactions to this. They quickly learned that it was an imposition on their privacy that could easily aggravate personal relations. Yet it was a burden that did have its rewarding moments. Tom Campbell, a twenty-seven-year-old member of the group, acknowledged his ambivalent feelings about these commitments. "We've had personality conflicts with each other and sometimes the kind of people we bring in have serious problems and can be very frustrating to deal with. But there are positive aspects to our hospitality ministry and to all the sharing we do as a group. We enjoy being in the company of each other and we enjoy trying to live according to how Christ commands us to be."

Perhaps the most difficult task which the Community of the Servant set for itself was to lessen the virulence of racism in Oregon Hill. Although this was a principal factor in the decision to locate there, it was not an issue that was ever directly addressed. The need for indirection existed, I think, for two reasons. On a pragmatic level, there would have been absolutely no chance for success if the members of the Community of the Servant had taken to the streets with placards denouncing the racial backwardness of their neighbors. They might have received substantial media attention, but they certainly would not have achieved their purposes. A deeper reason for the indirection had to do with the conflicting feelings that members of the Community of the Servant had about the culture in Oregon Hill. They recognized the deep communal strength that had been built up over the years by living together, mutual aid, mutual bickering, and the perception of a common enemy. They felt that there was something valuable in this and wanted to be part of the neighborhood. But they were also detached and analytic about the culture. They had hoped to discover an effective way of suggesting that there is something wrong with a casual resort to violence as a means of settling disputes and something misguided about the scapegoating of blacks that is a prominent feature of the ethos.

The struggle by the men and women in the Community of the Servant to affirm the strengths of the culture in Oregon Hill while trying to dissipate some of its more unappealing elements is a microcosm of a dilemma common to American reformers. Moreover, it remains a baffling problem for anyone who believes that the development of a serious reform movement in the United States is dependent on forming a coalition of minorities and working-class whites. How do you convince people that their lives would be more rewarding if they became more critical of the economic system that has shaped their dreams of success? How do you convince white Americans that minorities and immigrants are not the principal cause of joblessness, but, rather, that it is an abstract economic system that disemploys people as the initial step in a "recovery"? And how do you convince generations weaned on the necessity of military prominence that their economic well-being may be enhanced by a reduction in military expenditures?

Ultimately, the Community of the Servant failed to answer these questions effectively. It was never able to become fully integrated into Oregon Hill and fulfill the dream it had originally possessed. Recalled Steve Hodges, "It was a worthy goal, but I am not sure that any of us realized how difficult it would be. Even the community action organizations which are doing good things are sometimes incredibly racist." Instead of understanding and working to change attitudes about race in Oregon Hill, members of the Community of the Servant eventually found themselves burdened by them. Black acquaintances were sometimes reluctant to visit them and the Hodgeses began to worry that their children would not only grow up without friends of different races, but could themselves be influenced by the ideas that permeated the neighborhood.⁵

The political difficulties of the Community of the Servant were matched by its internal problems. Between 1982 and 1984, it lost about half of its membership. Most frequently, people departed for reasons that had nothing to do with dissatisfaction with the community. For example, one person left to attend graduate school in Maryland and another to marry a woman who was attending a seminary in Boston. These people tended to believe that their lives had been enriched by their experience in a communal setting. As Phil Bauman put it, "One learns an awful lot about peace making and commitment when you try to really live a Christian life on a daily basis." But there were others who left the community because they were never entirely comfortable with all its aims. Some found it difficult to make the commitment of time to the Community of the Servant's social agenda and others became disenchanted with its economic philosophy that required them to forgo considerable income. Perhaps not too much should be made of these comings and goings because they are likely to characterize any new experiment with communal life. What may be significant, however, is that the Community of the Servant was unable to replenish itself at a time when the peace movement in Richmond was gaining popularity. By 1985, the departure of members and its lack of success in Oregon Hill resulted in a loss of purpose. The community officially dissolved, though a number of its members planned to move to a predominantly black neighborhood and see if it was possible for them to participate in a truly interracial fellowship.

Personal Conscience and Public Influence

The activities that have been described so far in this chapter indicate how seriously some people in the peace movement take the idea that their lives should reflect their professed beliefs. Tim Lietzke's hammering on the Pershing missiles at the Martin Marietta plant, WARTAG's quest to discover forms of collective action that can develop popular backing, and the Community of the Servant's experiment with basic Christian living all represent manifestations of this impulse that is so important to the movement. Yet these activities also direct our attention to the places where the movement has not achieved its goals and where it must strive for both a sharper self-definition and a deeper public influence.

The history of the efforts to develop alternative forms of civil disobedience and construct an alternative community point to three important difficulties in applying the personalist approach. The first is that personalist ideals can be extremely demanding, straining both the intrapsychic and the interpersonal lives of participants in the movement. Much of the commentary about people committed to social reform speaks about the psychological rewards that they receive. This is undoubtedly the case with the activists in the antinuclear weapons movement and evidence of this is shown in the next chapter. But it is also true that commitment carries its own set of demands and tensions. The decision by one partner in a marriage to practice civil disobedience can place formidable strains on the relationship of a couple who, in general terms, share the same outlook. A number of the activists in Richmond were compelled to deal with these pressures.

Elaine Shurie, for example, is a tax resister who has been penalized five hundred dollars on two occasions for taking what the Internal Revenue Service calls a frivolous deduction. It is hard to imagine anyone who could be more understanding of the reasons that impelled Elaine's husband, Tim Lietzke, to take the steps he did at Martin Marietta. Indeed, part of what attracted her to Tim was his unconventionality and willingness to stand up for what he believed in. Nonetheless, the prospect that Tim might commit another act of direct disarmament and risk an even lengthier jail term placed increasing strain on their relationship. Almost all of the first three years of their marriage had been spent apart because of Tim's prison sentence. The prospect that this could become a defining feature of their relationship simply aggravated the difficulties caused by the original separation. Elaine and Tim's divorce was amicable, but its very occurrence demonstrated how moral commitment can be detrimental to the maintenance of interpersonal relationships.

Harold Houghton also experienced the distress that can arise from trying to express one's opposition to nuclear weapons policy and to construct a successful marriage at the same time. While Debra Houghton supported Harold's decision to resist taxes—a step actually taken in the year before their wedding—the couple found the combination of fear and anxiety that permeated their young marriage almost impossible to handle. Unlike some forms of protest, a person resisting war taxes has no control over the timing of the consequences or the exact nature of the penalties. The Internal Revenue Service might choose to ignore it for years or take immediate action to garnish the salary of the resister and impose other fines. Interested in starting a family, the Houghtons would have been more comfortable facing a definite penalty at a specified time in the future. Instead, the computer-generated letters sent by the IRS at irregular intervals evoked fears of a catastrophic outcome to the protest. Harold mentioned that "when one of those bills arrives in the mail, your whole life gets blown into a nightmarish thing." Debra experienced similar fears, recalling dreams "in which people came at night and moved us out of our house." Eventually, Debra and Harold Houghton decided not to pursue this witness to its full limits. They paid the taxes that had been withheld, plus the interest and penalties that had accrued. Doing so, in Harold's words, "left a very bitter taste in my mouth. Writing the check and then mailing it seemed like an act of capitulation." At a minimum, it demonstrated how difficult it can sometimes be to harmonize the full complement of one's professed moral commitments.

In his generally sympathetic account of Mohandas Gandhi, Erik Erikson criticizes the pacifist leader for a tendency to become excessively rigid and even ruthless. Erikson argues that Gandhi's asceticism and denial of sexual pleasure not only limited his own self-development, but tarnished his relationship with his followers as well. Unable to understand that the pleasures and satisfactions of everyday life were not easily discarded in favor of a higher cause, Gandhi could be cruel and overly demanding. Erikson suggests that because of this "demandingness," elements of cruelty and even psychic violence could be discerned in Gandhi's activities. He implies that Gandhi's skills as a leader, impressive as they were, would have been enhanced had he experienced an ongoing and rewarding sexual relationship.[6]

I do not wish to assess the accuracy of Erikson's portrait of Gandhi here. It does seem to me, however, that he points to an issue that is important in any discussion of personalist politics. In particular, Erikson identifies a tension that can arise between some of the fundamental personalist precepts. The desire to make a morally appropriate statement that most purely represents one's perspective on nuclear weapons may conflict with the allegiance to family and household values that is so prominent in personalist politics. Commitment to one's family may be not only a justification for political action, but also an inhibiting factor. Individuals who decide to follow their conscience and commit civil disobedience need to recognize the strain that family relationships will undergo. And, as I think Erikson understands, the decision to go "all the way" with civil disobedience can sometimes represent a denial of the personalist outlook that resists isolating ethical considerations from the web of moral relationships that individuals have established throughout their lives.

The pressures that a commitment to social reform can impose on relationships is, of course, a recurring theme in autobiographies, novels, and films about political commitment. Authors sometimes wish to use this theme as a way of drawing attention to the hypocrisy that politics can engender. On other occasions, they merely intend to illustrate the blindness that can accompany lofty intentions or even the inevitable tragedies of social commitment. It should not be surprising that personalists experience their own version of what is probably a timeless dilemma. But however common this theme may be, its existence has to be especially troubling for the adherents of an approach that consciously attempts to infuse the political world with values drawn from the family.[7]

The second problem with the personalist approach is that personalist efforts to create exemplary communities are often perceived in ways that are quite different from the participants' intentions. The reaction of some of the neighbors in Oregon Hill to the Community of the Servant is evidence of this difficulty. In 1981 and 1982, members of the community made a genuine effort to avoid isolation in the neighborhood and to reach out to its residents. They realized that this would take perseverance because their neighbors were often suspicious of people whom they believed were students at the local university. Members of the community believed that they were making some small gains: a couple of people in need of food stamps asked their help in negotiating the bureaucratic labyrinth; they had a few interesting conversations about the need for poor blacks and poor whites to overcome racial divisions and join together politically; and some of the children in the neighborhood came to appreciate the concern that the Community of the Servant exhibited for them. But still, as Tom Campbell says, "many people just don't know who the hell we are. We once had a birthday party and, after it, some of the community members who have talent as clowns went on the streets entertaining the children. Word got back to us that a couple of the neighbors thought that we were on LSD. That was very disheartening, because we thought that we had demonstrated that we don't take drugs and that we're not interested in that kind of thing."

This response to the Community of the Servant is, in one sense, entirely predictable. The communal experiments undertaken in the United States are rarely given widespread publicity. When old or new communities do come to our attention, it is only when they exhibit antisocial or otherwise exotic behavior. We read about neighborhoods such as Oregon Hill, South Boston, or the Island in Chicago only when the racism becomes so virulent that innocent people are psychologically intimidated or physically harmed. In the last ten years, religious communities have been widely publicized, but the stories we hear are almost inevitably about cults that brainwash their membership while emptying their bank accounts so that self-proclaimed prophets can reign in splendor. It is therefore not difficult to understand the attitude of the Oregon Hill residents toward the Community of the Servant. Having heard and read very little about religiously based communities, they naturally filter them through the standard lenses that the culture has provided for seeing a sexually mixed group of young men and women who have chosen to live in a poor neighborhood.

The third major drawback of personalist politics is that acts of civil disobedience about the nuclear arms race have not been successful in engaging the hearts and minds of the populace. One way of approaching this is to compare the practice of civil disobedience in the new peace movement with its manifestations during the civil rights era. This is a particularly appropriate comparison because of the influence which the civil rights movement has exercised on so many of the activists. In the interviews that I conducted, for example, numerous members of the peace community mentioned Martin Luther King, Jr., as a person they would like to emulate. Furthermore, peace activists continually refer to King's example and often his very words when they speak about the necessity of civil disobedience, the importance of relating peace issues to social justice concerns, and the necessity of creating a black-white coalition around a progressive agenda.

When the civil rights movement began its civil disobedience campaigns, it generated a fevered response. Many southern officials responded with violence, as did any number of whites who felt threatened by the changes that the activists were intent on fostering. Buses were overturned; churches were firebombed; and civil rights workers and demonstrators were assassinated. Martin Luther King, Jr., was urged by many people, including the nation's highest elected officials, to call off the campaigns because of the dangers to which the activists, including child marchers, were exposed. The political and intellectual class of the nation took up the debate that the movement had initiated in the streets. A few commentators professed to support King's agenda, but maintained that his goals could be accomplished by other means. Others suggested that civil disobedience could not be condoned in a society that permitted peaceful change through the ballot box. But many commentators gave support to the movement. They noted that acts of courageous defiance were occasionally necessary to dramatize a grievance and they agreed with King's assertion that civil disobedience was the best option available to people whose democratic rights had been abrogated by the southern state governments.

Despite the intensity of the opposition that mobilized against the civil rights movement, King was able to speak persuasively to a significant number of Americans because the movement spoke a vocabulary and utilized a conceptual framework that the majority of Americans understood.

To many people, the civil rights movement stood for equality of opportunity and the removal of legal barriers to this on the basis of race. The movement, to citizens outside the South, did not seem to call for a revolutionary overthrow of the American way of life, only a less hypocritical application of the ideals in which we professed to believe. Why should blacks not be allowed to sit at the same lunch counters and use the same tables as whites? Why did states prohibit blacks from receiving the same educational opportunities that white children were granted? To be sure, this is a truncated and slightly inaccurate view of the movement's goals. King did speak eloquently of developing a communal alternative to American individualism, of the need to steer an economic course between the barbarousness of communism and the inequality of capitalism, and of the imperative of connecting peace and social justice concerns. But these were not the most important features of the movement to those who interpreted it to the rest of the country. Indeed, to this day, very little headway has been made with respect to this side of the civil rights struggle.

It is not self-evident that the antinuclear movement will (in the long run) be able to appeal to the conscience of mainstream America in the same manner as the civil rights movement did. Simply on the level of tactics, activists have yet to discover forms of unconventional politics that have the dramatic impact of the demonstrations in the American South during the sixties. Those people who are interested in mass campaigns have not found the way to involve large numbers of citizens in faithful acts of protest. As Phyllis Conklin puts it, "I think that civil disobedience is the way to go, but I don't think that the peace movement has found the way to do it yet. It's very difficult to do civil disobedience around the arms race, because it is so hard to develop a focused approach. The arms race permeates the entire society and it is hard to make people see that putting your little rowboat in the way of it is done out of love and that you're not a kook. On balance, most people don't see what has been done as a meaningful protest."

Tax resistance provides a good illustration of the problem that Phyllis identifies. Undoubtedly, tax resisters in Richmond have made progress in transforming lonely statements of personal conscience into a broader public action. They have also been attentive to developing strategies that will allow supporters of the movement to participate at a variety of levels, ranging from legal protest to civil disobedience. Yet there are some inherent limitations to tax resistance that may never be surmounted. One of the most critical is that the government can dampen enthusiasm for the strategy without engaging in heavy-handed public reprisals. If tax resistance ever threatened to become more widespread, there would be no need to arrest people in the streets or drag them from their homes while the neighbors watched. Sending a computer-generated letter from the Internal Revenue Service assessing a penalty of five hundred dollars for a frivolous deduction would adequately serve the government's purpose. It might not dissuade those people who were already resisting, but it would certainly discourage other people from taking a war tax deduction and, most important, it would do so without casting the U.S. government in a particularly malevolent light before the rest of the American population.[8]

Antinuclear weapons activists have developed imaginative ways of politicizing their concerns in local settings. Debates in parish councils, efforts to create nuclear-free zones, and local referenda have compelled millions of Americans to think about issues related to nuclear weapons policy. But passionate though these debates have sometimes been, there is a significant distinction between influencing a vote and recruiting supporters for civil disobedience campaigns. For civil disobedience to be successful, citizens have to come to see the issue with more urgency. This has been difficult because antinuclear weapons activists do not have the kind of constituency that was available to civil rights leaders in the 1960s—people who felt the weight of burdensome conditions on a daily basis and who were willing to assume significant risks to demonstrate that they found the situation intolerable.

This is particularly true of the effort to develop local opposition to the arms race. In a city such as Richmond, for example, citizens do not feel as immediately oppressed by nuclear weapons as black southerners did by the existence of legal segregation in their communities. In places where nuclear weapons are manufactured and have relatively high visibility, the presence of these facilities is usually perceived positively. Pacifists in the 1950s failed dismally in their efforts to convince the population of New London, Connecticut, that they ought to oppose the production of Polaris submarines built in a nearby shipyard. Prospects for this kind of action have not changed very much in the ensuing thirty years. In a recent book, A. J. Mojtabai describes how the men and women in Amarillo, Texas, where the Pantex plant is located, refer to the economic benefits that the industry provides for the city. She indicates that some citizens embrace religious beliefs which hold, as one woman observed, that "there's a possibility of nuclear war, but if it comes, it's because God allowed it." At Richland High School, near the Hanford Nuclear Reservation in Washington, a movement to change the school symbol, a mushroom cloud, has resulted "in a deluge of telephone calls from parents and alumni" protesting the recommendation.[9]

To point out the practical difficulties which peace activists have in translating their statements of personal conscience into public influence is not to suggest that these activities are devoid of value. On a small scale, the Plowshares action of Tim Lietzke, the establishment of the Community of the Servant, and the continued existence of tax resistance help to shape the identity of and provide reference points for other peace activists in Richmond. It is not uncommon to hear people who disagree with Tim Lietzke mention how they have been inspired in their own way by his example or how the Community of the Servant made them think more seriously about the connections between peacemaking and lifestyle issues. The willingness of people such as Elaine Shurie and Steve Hodges to risk personal injury in order to remain faithful serves as a treasury from which members of the broader peace community can draw energy and inspiration when they find themselves becoming lethargic and disenchanted.

Besides serving as an example to others, personalist experiments with civil disobedience may have a long-term impact that is not visible today. The attempts of social movements to use unconventional actions as a method of public persuasion is subject to a trial-and-error process. The movements may experience many failures before discovering the most appropriate tactical form. Though civil disobedience has yet to do for the antinuclear activists what it accomplished for the participants in the civil rights struggles, it may be a prerequisite for developing more appealing and successful campaigns. We should recall that the labor movement struggled for decades before it discovered the effectiveness of the sit-down strike.

Yet even if these efforts are not entirely successful, they may be worthwhile for other reasons. It is not unlikely that there will be as much to learn from the various Christian experiments with communal life as there was from some of the more celebrated countercultural locales of years past, if only because of the personal discipline of people such as Diantha Hodges, Steve Hodges, and Elaine Shurie. Moreover, the existence of these communities aids others who lead a middle-class lifestyle to think of ways in which they can incorporate a communal orientation into their own lives. The personalist insistence that works of mercy remain a visible part of a commitment to social activism has something important to teach others interested in social change about how to temper the ruthlessness and arrogance that frequently accompany radical commitment. These are not earthshaking outcomes, but they are necessary elements of any attempt to develop an alternative politics that combines global concern with local action.

7

Keeping the Faith:
Fulfillment,
Disappointment, and the
Future of the Peace
Community

IN A FAMOUS ESSAY, "Politics as a Vocation," Max Weber distinguished an "ethics of responsibility" from an "ethics of ultimate ends." Weber believed that although extraordinary individuals might render the two ethics compatible, they normally made different kinds of demands on people. An ethics of responsibility required that persons be concerned primarily with the consequences of their actions. Translated into the political realm, this meant that leaders had to recognize that "the attainment of 'good ends' is bound to the fact that one must be willing to pay the price of using morally dubious means or at least dangerous ones." Weber contended that an ethic of ultimate ends, embodied in the Sermon on the Mount, was not primarily focused on the consequences of action, but operated on the maxim that "the Christian does rightly and leaves the results with the Lord." He believed that this ethic was largely irrelevant to the task of governance because "he who seeks the salvation of the soul, of his own and of others should not seek it along the avenue of politics, for the quite different tasks of politics can only be solved by violence." Weber argued that a person who exhibited a genuine calling for politics must simultaneously confront "the diabolic forces lurking in all violence" and retain a commitment to noble ends.[1]

The personalist approach to politics described in this book obviously differs considerably from the perspective that Weber enunciated. Personalists would raise, I think, two major objections to Weber's argument. First, they would contend that it has become of paramount importance to reduce the level of violence in the world and minimize the threat of ultimate catastrophe posed by nuclear weapons. They would argue that political realism, however well-intentioned, has moved the world close to collective extinction and that our ways of conducting politics need to be tempered by the values and manners of those who should, according to Weber, "content themselves with cultivating plain brotherliness in personal relations." Second, personalists would maintain that the casual resort to violence in the political realm, the sense of powerlessless and alienation bred by modern bureaucracies, and the pervasive selfishness and greed in our culture demonstrate how our interpersonal relations have been infected by the values that dominate the political world. In this sense, they believe that the development of secure personal identities and the cultivation of brotherliness in social relations have themselves become political issues and need to be addressed by reform movements.

Personalists are thus committed to a politics that encourages self-development, the building of communities, and the attainment of concrete political goals. Indeed, their attempt to construct a social movement that operates on all these levels is a defining feature of their outlook. Yet such a commitment does not permit them to evade the questions that political realists typically raise. They have to ask themselves where they have succeeded and where they have failed. And they have to define what they plan to do in the future in order to make their efforts both more rewarding and more successful.

This chapter examines the assessment that the people to whom I spoke made of their own efforts from 1981 to 1986. It explains what their attempt to act faithfully has meant to their self-identity and spiritual development. In almost all instance, activists speak positively about the personal growth that their participation has promoted, even if it has required them to make unsettling personal choices. They are less sanguine, however, in evaluating the political effects of their undertakings. They do believe that the community they have created and the support they have generated in the area are significant accomplishments, but their sense of achievemet is tempered by disappointment with their difficulties in reaching large numbers of people. Confident that their own community will persevere, the activists are uncertain about the possibility of reforming society along the lines they believe are necessary and desirable. Many now think that the future success of the movement depends on building stronger alliances with the black community, connecting peace issues with broader questions of American foreign policy, and developing a more vigorous campaign of direct action and civil disobedience. These proposals represent an interesting extension of the movement's personalist base, but they also illuminate the obstacles it confronts in becoming significantly more influential.

Faithful Action and Personal Identity

The reelection of Ronald Reagan in 1984 compelled the national nuclear freeze campaign to assess its performance over the past three years and to design plans for becoming more effective in the future. The leadership of the freeze maintained that it had succeeded in making arms limitation a national issue and in changing the orientation of the Democratic party. It pointed to the reluctance of Congress to fund major new weapons systems and to the dramatic change in the Reagan administration's rhetoric about arms control as signs of influence for which the campaign could take credit.[2] Nonetheless, the results of the 1984 election clearly demonstrated that public approval for the freeze had not been translated into electoral clout. The majority of the population either believed that economic issues were more important than arms control or that President Reagan's military buildup was a prerequisite for effective negotiations with the Soviets. Successful in raising public consciousness about the potential danger of a nuclear war, the freeze campaign had not become a political force that candidates for national office across the country were compelled to fear.

1984 was also a time of reflection for local peace movements. A presidential election almost inevitably becomes the primary focus for the political life of the entire nation. Local groups make decisions about which (if any) candidate to support and how much energy they will invest in various campaigns. They call upon the networks they have developed and try to mobilize their supporters. After the election is held, thousands of postmortems are conducted as activists evaluate their success in constructing a political base and plan strategies for the future. In 1984, much of the energy of the Richmond peace community was directed at electing freeze delegates to the state convention of the Democratic party. The movement hoped to demonstrate that it could be a visible force in a conservative political culture. Most of those involved believed that their effort was surprisingly productive, as more than 20 percent of the delegates from Richmond were drawn from the peace community. Yet the outcome of the general election, both nationally and in the state, was thoroughly disheartening. The activists were painfully reminded that voters in the area were solidly behind President Reagan and Senator John Warner, men who had never supported the movement's postitions.

In Richmond, the process of self-examination instigated by the election was rendered more critical by the resignation of Steve Hodges as coordinator of the peace education center. The driving force behind its creation and the peace community's principal leader for three years, Steve had become increasingly disenchanted with the administrative load of directing the center. He wanted to spend more time with the SPAN group and other organizations around the state developing plans for direct action and civil disobedience regarding the nuclear arms issue and the potential escalation of the American presence in Central America. Steve had informed the center's board of directors of his intention to resign early in the year and, in the fall, made it clear that the decision was irrevocable. In response, the board embarked on a search for a new coordinator. Steve's decision prompted many others in the peace community to reflect on what had transpired during his directorship of the center. Activists thought about their accomplishments, failures, and the directions they ought to pursue in the future.

The men and women of the Richmond peace community felt that their personal experiences from 1981 to 1986 had been positive. No one that I interviewed in the early days of the study regretted participating in the movement four years later. None of the central figures had come to believe that they had misjudged the significance of the issue or the quality of the people with whom they had chosen to work. In fact, it was much more common for the activists to maintain that their commitment had been strengthened as a consequence of their involvement. They did, to be sure, acknowledge disappointments and infrequent moments of despair. They also noted the tensions that arose from trying to balance their political commitments with family obligations and recreational interests. The breakup of the marriage of Elaine Shurie and Tim Lietzke served as a prominent reminder of this. Yet these tensions were never presented as reasons for regretting the decision to participate.

Most of the activists have found their involvement to be personally satisfying. This has been particularly true, I think, for some of the older participants in the movement. In recent years, the psychology of adult life has become a popular topic of investigation. Much attention has been paid to the issues that become critically important to men and women as they advance in age. Most of the intelligent writing on this matter underscores that sustaining a sense of integrity is crucial to the establishment of a meaningful adulthood. People who are unable to do so often find it difficult to experience the satisfactions and ward off the terrors of late adulthood. It is probably not stretching it too far to suggest that one of the reasons why the antinuclear movement is so appealing to people of middle and advanced age is that its rhetoric and internal mode of operation (emphasizing personal responsibility, nurturance, cooperation, and community) are compatible with the psychological needs generated in contemporary American culture.[3]

Jerry Gorman explains his reasons for remaining active: "I enjoy what I'm doing. It challenges me and it has helped me to find out what my real interests and convictions are. I have a clearer idea today about who I am. I don't talk about this too much, but I'm fifty-three years old. Most of life is over. It's very important that I be committed to that which I really believe." Phyllis Conklin, who is sixty-three, speaks in very similar terms. "I've raised three children and think that I have done a good job with them. They're wonderful kids who have grown up to be fine persons. I think that the peace movement is a kind of parenting too, because it builds on the same vision we have for our children. The involvement is really challenging and I feel that it helps to keep me alive. It has brought wonderful people into my life who know how to laugh and to act responsibly at the same time. I think that their commitment is one of the things that make it worthwhile to be around them. At that level, it doesn't really matter how successful it is, because just the doing is good."

The centrality of religious motivation to many of the activists influences the manner in which they evaluate their experience. Since most of those involved see themselves not just as political activists but as sojourners on a spiritual odyssey, they frequently refer to their "inward journey" when speaking about their recent experiences. They mention that their "faith has been strengthened" and their "spirituality deepened" by participation in the peace movement. "I've gained a tremendous amount of personal maturity and spiritual depth in the last few years," states Steve Hodges. "I've learned what it means to stand up before a group of people that often does not agree with your point of view and I've also learned about the need for doing more than talking to people. I've benefited from having to struggle with what it means to develop a spiritual base for peacemaking and I'm still struggling to understand what a spiritual commitment to nonviolence means when the violence I see is both physical and structural. I'm not sure of the answers here, but these are really substantial questions that will affect my life for a long time."

Members of the peace community also noted how their spiritual orientation had been altered by their involvement in the movement. While their faith may have been deepened by their participation, the commitment to the institutional structures of religion actually declined among some of the activists. Says Wendy Northup, "I still see myself as a Catholic, but I don't think that anyone can tell me what this means any longer. I like the Catholic emphasis on community and its structure of celebration and faith. I also understand that it's often impossible to act without institutions, so I don't get terribly upset by their compromises and lack of purity. But if I found something better, I don't think that it would be too traumatic at all for me to move out." Jerry Gorman's commentary touches on a related theme. "Donna and I are still spiritual people, but we're not the kind of orthodox Catholics we once were. We've gone through a fantastic spiritual ferment and we're more concerned today with how we should be acting than with institutional structures. For example, we had an exchange of letters with the bishop after he publicly volunteered to be an official witness at the Briley execution. Well, we don't believe in capital punishment and we told him that he shouldn't do it, unless he was planning a dramatic Plowshares-type action, like going in and dismantling the electric chair. Some people said that it hurt the bishop that people in the peace community weren't giving him their full support. Yet I don't mind telling the bishop or the pope for that matter if I feel that they're doing something wrong."

The decline in commitment to institutional religion is probably most evident in the activists' evaluation of the churches' position on women's issues. Having gained experience as organizers, coordinators, and public spokespersons, fewer and fewer women are comfortable with the official pronouncements of church hierarchies. This is most noticeable with women who are members of the Catholic church. Wendy Northup remarks, "I am a much more ardent and adamant feminist than I was three years ago. I see the very male and the very hierarchical structure of the Church decaying and I think that this is good." Donna Gorman has begun to organize protests at ordination ceremonies for priests in the Catholic diocese. She maintains that "the Church is a great patriarchical institution. It tells us what to do, what to say, and how to stay in the state of grace. The internal working of the Church is extremely unfair. Most of the time they don't even ask women how we feel about a particular issue before they vote our position down. Until the patriarchy issue is cleaned up, I don't think that men as a class should be telling us what to do. I feel that I can have a say as a member of the Church, but I don't want to be preached to by men. I want them to join me in action on behalf of women."

What is interesting about the disenchantment with organized religion is that it has occurred despite strong support for the peace movement from the local Catholic clergy. Bishop Sullivan is not only an outspoken advocate for the cause, but has made significant contributions to maintaining it in Richmond. While Jerry Gorman feels free to disagree with him, neither he nor anyone else is unappreciative of the role that the bishop has played. The Catholic diocese donates space for the offices of the Richmond Peace Education Center. It also takes a very serious approach to its Office of Justice and Peace, maintaining a larger staff than is common across the nation. Pax Christi has numerous nuns and priests among its membership. And the Richmond clergy are about as progressive as one could possibly expect on the role of women in the Church. Thus it has not been a consistently unsympathetic hierarchy that has caused the activists to become less dependent on the institutional church, but their actual experience during the past four years. The movement itself functions as a school for democracy, placing a variety of individuals in positions of responsibility. As religious activists design liturgies for Pax Christi meetings, plan worship services for the SPAN group, participate in the Community of the Servant, and organize Hiroshima Day memorials, they begin to develop a democratic orientation toward the organization of faith itself. They feel less of a need to adhere to inherited definitions of spirituality, both individual and collective. If in 1981 and 1982 participants brought their religious perspective to bear on the political world, today they would utilize their political experiences to evaluate their religious institutions.

The notion of life as a spiritual odyssey has also begun to influence some of the activists' career goals. More of them are thinking of developing second careers or of using their vocational skills in a manner directly related to their faith. This has been increasingly the case with people working in middle-class jobs in the corporate sector. Steve Northup, for instance, decided in 1984 to complement his law practice by working on the appeals of prisoners who had received the death penalty, because he was certain that the punishment could not be justified on religious grounds. John Gallini began to think of ways to employ his expertise as a chemical engineer to benefit others more visibly. He started to examine the possibility of a second career as a college teacher and talked about eventually investigating what kind of chemical applications would be relevant to the use of appropriate technology in the Third World. Elaine Shurie gave up her job and possible career in a bank in order to work with the homeless and the hungry and then to become coordinator of the Richmond Peace Education Center.[4]

The positive assessment that the activists make of their own experience is not surprising, especially because their personalist approach is more attentive to participants' feelings than is a politics solely focused on winning elections or other pragmatic tasks. The reflections of the activists also indicate how certain forms of public activity can be important, in our era, for developing feelings of self-worth and secure personal identities. But the activists might be better served if the dilemmas and tensions that participation can generate were also highlighted. More attention to these matters might help them to understand why people in their audiences may agree with their assessment of issues, but are reluctant to devote significant amounts of time to the movement.

Faithful Action and Political Results

Activists in the peace community try to present a balanced assessment of their political effectiveness. They speak proudly about what they consider to be their principal accomplishments, but they also cite the failures and limitations of their efforts. On a more positive note, they frequently mention the very survival of the peace network as a substantial achievement. They cite their own relative inexperience, the conservatism of the culture, and the historical difficulty of building alternative movements as factors that militated against their continued existence. As John Gallini sees it, "We have survived and this is not a trivial accomplishment, given the media which presents a serious distortion of reality." He notes that while the sheer excitement of the movement has expired, people have recognized that attaining their goals requires a long-term commitment. Steve Hodges echoes these sentiments. "I think that just establishing the Richmond Peace Education Center and developing a movement has been a tremendous accomplishment. We've survived and this is something which we can be proud of because so many organizations and action groups dissolve after the initial enthusiasm is gone."

Many activists pointed to the functioning of the peace education center as an example of the dedication of the peace community. The center had become recognized by more people in the area and relevant groups throughout the state were aware of its work. Perhaps more important, financial contributions had not slackened, despite the blow administered to the movement on the national level. Throughout the mid-1980s, the center collected more than twenty thousand dollars from persons in the community and the churches supportive of its work. It did so without employing sophisticated solicitation techniques, relying primarily on contributions sent in twice a year from newsletter mailings. Whenever the board of directors worried about decreased support, it was able to easily generate funds through phone campaigns. The center has also received donations of office equipment, including files, bookshelves, typewriters, a photocopying machine, and a computer. Contributions of both money and equipment remained at a level that permitted the coordinators to plan and develop more programs.

The initial transition from Steve Hodges to the new coordinators for the peace education center also proceeded more smoothly and with more enthusiasm than some members of the peace community thought possible. When Steve's decision to resign was finalized, there was concern that the visibility and effectiveness of the center might be seriously reduced. But this fear was allayed when Wendy Northup and Elaine Shurie, central figures in the local movement, applied for the position jointly and agreed to take on its responsibilities when it was offered. The capacity to replace a coordinator of Steve Hodges' commitment and talent with activists as dedicated as Wendy and Elaine alleviated any anxiety that did exist about the center's continued functioning as the locus for peace activity in central Virginia. Although it is not yet possible to judge how different the center will be with its new coordinators, it was clearly able to undergo a change of leadership without disrupting what had been set in motion, a process critical to the creation of a permanent local movement.[5]

Besides the continued existence of the movement's organizational base, the expansion of peace activity in the area is mentioned as evidence of the progress that has been made since its inception. Steve Hodges observes that "the proliferation of peace groups over the last four years has been phenomenal. Most denominations in town have peace-making groups and task forces which focus on the issue." Phyllis Conklin, one of the few activists whose commitment antedates the seventies and the Vietnam involvement, remarks that it is the nature of the participants' commitment that impresses her most strongly. "The most exciting and hopeful thing that has come out of the movement is the rise of the churches, particularly the Catholics. I think that those people are incredible. In some ways, the put the old-time peace people to shame. There is a tremendous amount of dedication and discipline in that group." Wendy Northup tries to specify precisely what this discipline is. "The peace groups have touched their own memberships with the sense of 'long-termness' of this kind of effort. They have exhibited a willingness to keep at it when things aren't always sexy and fun and they volunteer to do the kind of boring things that have to be performed if the positive results are going to be obtained."

Many of the people in the peace community also believe that they have exercised a measure of political influence. Jerry Gorman notes that "the movement has shown a certain tough persistence and gained a lot of experience that it didn't have three years ago." Wendy Northup maintains, "I can't believe that the freeze wasn't successful at all. I see Reagan moving to the more moderate people in his own cabinet and the fact that he may pursue arms control is a hopeful sign. At a minimum, the freeze has been an important conscience prick in American society." Locally, the activists take credit for the mobilization of nuclear freeze supporters in the area for the Democratic party's mass meetings and state convention in 1984. John Gallini observes that they "did a remarkably good job in getting people involved in the Democratic convention. By and large, that group of people tends to be skeptical of the political process and it was a legitimate success of the peace movement in central Virginia to be able to convince its folk to participate in this process on the grounds that it was important for the movement."

The activists acknowledge, however, that there have been definite limits to their political influence and accomplishments. The results of the 1984 election and the shallowness of support for the freeze are the most visible pieces of evidence cited about the weaknesses of the movement. To advocates of the freeze, the election signified their inability to mobilize large numbers of people who would place their concerns about arms control at the top of their political priorities. John Gallini comments that "at one level, the nuclear freeze movement attracted a great deal more support than anyone had a right to hope for in 1981. But the fact remains that it has not led to a significant shift in American policy and a good deal of support that was expressed for it did not show up in the election. We got a lot of people connected to the issue, but they obviously did not relate to it in a very deep way. By expressing new interest in negotiating with the Soviet Union, Reagan was able to defuse any worry which people had about his arms control policy and military buildup."[6]

The national failings of the movement had parallels on the local level. In 1981 and 1982, activists were surprised at how willing people were to sign their petitions. Yet when they went back to these lists in 1984, they discovered that many of these ostensible freeze supporters did not believe that arms control was the most critical political issue. Activists came to see that the qualitative cultural change that they had been promoting was not occurring and that President Reagan's politics of self-interest had tapped the national pulse more accurately. As Phyllis Conklin views it, "We spent a lot of time getting signatures on petitions and this ultimately did not have much meaning. A lot of the work that was done turned out not to make that much of a difference. People can easily support the freeze without changing their attitudes and the way they live. The religious movement has obviously been doing very good work in this regard because it has a deeper impact than the petition drive. Unfortunately, this is a very slow process and it hasn't become widespread yet."

The failure of the movement to mobilize large numbers of people led to reflections on the difficulties that the movement had experienced in gaining the attention of the local citizenry. Members of the peace community realized that a significant portion of the population had yet to be affected one way or another by the debate over arms control. In the spring and summer of 1984, activists embarked on a campaign of door-to-door canvassing to raise funds, identify supporters, and fashion a larger political network. The canvassers discovered that many citizens were not especially well informed about the freeze. Some had yet to hear of it and were unfamiliar with the controversies that had energized the activists during the previous three years. Said John Gallini, "There is a substantial group of people for whom we are a genuine annoyance and who may believe that we are a radical political group. I suspect, however, that the majority of the people in the area don't really know of our existence and what we are trying to accomplish."

Along with their inability to influence large numbers of people in a profound manner, activists mentioned their failure to forge a solid coalition with other progressive groups as one of their principal shortcomings. They pointed most often to relations with the black community. Acutely aware of the white middle-class nature of the peace movement, they had hoped to broaden its base by 1985. As I have mentioned above, efforts were undertaken on this front. Activists believe that the programs which they have sponsored during Martin Luther King, Jr., Community Learning Week were a small step in this direction. They also think that participation in the coalition surrounding the Twentieth Anniversary March on Washington was a positive event. Still, no one suggests that they have done anything more than take first steps. Nobody claims that a genuinely interracial coalition has been formed on an agenda dealing with local, national, and global issues. In fact, a few participants are even more negative about the lack of accomplishment. Phyllis Conklin, for example, maintains that while the peace education center has "established itself firmly in the consciousness of many churches in the area, it has bombed in the black churches and has had almost no impact in the black community."

Faith and the Maintenance of Hope

Thinking about the particular areas where they had succeeded and failed led a number of activists to consider a broader question. Could the antinuclear weapons movement develop a larger following or was it destined to remain on the fringe of American political life, periodically introducing a measure of moral concern into the debate about the nation's strategic policy? "Is [it] really possible to move large numbers of people or is the kind of vision we possess always a minority vision?" wonders Wendy Northup. "Will we be just a strong voice on the Left that labors to keep the consensus in society from moving even further to the Right or is it possible to motivate the public to live in a non-nuclear world? I'm not sure. I guess that we should follow the latter strategy and work to convert the world, but understand that we may not be successful in doing it." Many of the people to whom I spoke in 1985 and 1986 were skeptical about the short-term prospects for converting a majority of the American population. John Gallini put this in its most pronounced form. "Let's face reality. Right now our ideas are too countercultural to be highly popular. The basic message of the peace movement is countercultural. Though it tries to reach large numbers of people, it isn't a reasonable expectation to think that this will happen quickly. At best, we can gradually build public acceptance and if we have proper leadership and if people continue to ask questions, perhaps we will get more popular."

Maintaining commitment in the face of defeat and outcomes that are not decisive victories is a recurring problem for social movements. It is an especially difficult challenge to meet because these rarely possess the human and financial resources to be able to compete equally with the institutions they are striving to reform or eliminate. Even in good times, opposition movements are always in danger of having their ranks depleted by fatigue. Sustaining commitment over the long haul when outcomes may not be favorable is a formidable task. It thus becomes critically important for a movement to develop an outlook on the world that justifies continued activity for its membership and leads them to perform the work that might bring more people to their side. Without such a mobilizing ideology, activists may either lose their dedication or adopt a cynical attitude that insulates them from disappointment but also isolates them from the rest of the population.[7]

To some degree, the men and women of the Richmond peace community were well served by the measure of skepticism they had exhibited during the salad days of the freeze movement in 1982. I described in chapter 4 how a number of the activists were reluctant to become too enthusiastic about the popular support for the freeze because they felt that the cultural foundations for a deep commitment to peace had not been solidly formed. In 1986, they were able to use this skepticism to justify their continued involvement in the movement. Having never believed that political salvation was at hand, they were not thoroughly immobilized by the results of the election. As Jerry Gorman remarked, "I think that the world is malleable, but a lot of people expect change too quickly. I'm skeptical of quick results and really don't believe in massive turnarounds of public opinion."

Yet by itself skepticism is rarely sufficient to sustain long-term political commitment. Something more is needed. Previous chapters have shown how the faith of people in the peace community prompted them to participate in a movement that appeared unlikely to have much effect on American politics. This faith was again employed in 1986, this time to sustain commitment in a period when peace activism had become less prominent. Religious faith provided a justification for perseverance that a purely secular assessment of the costs and benefits of involvement may not have. It also emphasized that despair was not a proper Christian response to wordly setbacks. Steve Hodges phrased it in the following manner: "I couldn't keep up peacemaking if I based my involvement only on hopes of achieving political goals. These are few and far between and even the victories can be somewhat unsatisfying. I continue to be involved because I have a feeling that this is what I was put on this earth to do and this is a feeling that has been enhanced over the past few years."

The faith of the peace activists serves to do more than reinforce their commitment to the cause. Indeed, it is central to their analysis of the movement's history and their estimation of its possible future. The people whom I interviewed interpreted their own experiences and the ups and downs of the nationwide movement in a way that emphasized its elements of emergent possibility. They felt that though ultimate success was still far beyond their grasp, a potential for change did exist that they were obligated to develop as fully as possible. The amount of hope and the level of confidence this faith brought varied, or course, from person to person. Some believed that a new rebirth of the Spirit was taking place in the United States, one that would be increasingly visible in the years to come. Others were more sober in their predictions, content to mention the faithfulness of small communities as reason enough for retaining modest hopes. They noted the changes that had occurred in their own lives and in the community that they had helped to form as instances of faithful action which might be harbingers of a better world.

The activists occasionally referred to changes that followed the life of Christ as justification for their hope in the future. Elaine Shurie, for example, suggested that it is the biblical story of the Resurrection that permits her to remain optimistic. "My basic hope comes out of the Resurrection. There is no guarantee, of course, but the Resurrection appears to be an incredibly life-changing event. If the accounts are true, God really vindicates Jesus and his effort to be fully human and faithful to God. My hope is that more people will understand this lesson and figure out what is really real and know that only the spirit of God can fulfill us." Tim Lietzke implies that what is important about Christ's life is that the persecution of civil authorities did not, in the long run, diminish the effectiveness of his witness. Writing from prison, Tim compares the government's prosecution of the Plowshares activists and its possible long-term outcome to the persecution of Christ who "stood out, the faithful one, a thorn in the side of the principalities and powers until they struck him down, then his spirit was reborn in a thousand human lives."[8]

The importance that the men and women in the peace community attribute to their own spiritual odyssey actually helps to maintain their sense of hope about others. In a number of meetings that I observed, activists described their own "journeys toward peace," frequently explaining how attitudes supportive of American policy were transformed by the influence of other people and significant events. These stories resemble the traditional religious-conversion narrative, in which those who have been saved tell of their lives prior to repentance and the process by which they have been saved. Activists regularly refer to their own personal transformation, to how they came "to see things differently" and "understand what my faith required." Since these stories are accorded a central place in the movement's activities, the possibility of transformation is constantly reiterated. Moreover, this potential is not merely an abstract concept understood intellectually, but one that resonates deeply with the personal experiences of the participants. Says Jerry Gorman, "Our long-term prospects are good because so many of us came out of middle America."

Activists point to the proliferation of church groups in the area as not only an indicator of their influence but a sign of ongoing transformation. They were especially apt to mention that the peace culture had spread to the mainstream churches and was no longer confined to faiths that were historically pacifist. Many of the activists believe that the movement here will continue to flourish. At a minimum, they are convinced that they constitute a significant minority within the church community. Phil Bauman, youth coordinator for the Richmond Peace Education Center and a member of the Community of the Servant, comments, "I see hope in many places, both here in Richmond and around the world. I think that it is noteworthy that peacemaking in the religious community is becoming more significant. We are coming to understand that peacemaking is the religious calling and, more and more, we want to bring wholeness to a broken world. I don't think that this is a development that is weakening but [that] it is really getting more powerful."

A number of the activists mentioned their own community in Richmond as a reason for maintaining hope about the future of the movement. Jerry Gorman noted, "Historically, there is some reason not to be pessimistic. Of course, this is a faith answer, but I am hopeful. The hope I see is in our interaction with each other and recruitment into the community." John Gallini also pointed to the Richmond community as a manifestation of hope in troubled times. "I am basically a hopeful person, though I am not oblivious to how things are actually proceeding. My hope comes out of my religious faith and not necessarily the politics of the time. If President Reagan continues to be successful with his plans, I wouldn't be surprised if the hands on the *Bulletin of the Atomic Scientists* clock . . . move even closer to midnight. Yet there is a certain probability that we will get by and survive. My hope is that communities can persevere and be faithful and I believe that there is a good reason to think that here in Richmond, we will be able to give proper witness."

Reflections such as these help to corroborate the argument made in chapter 4 about the relationship between the development of community and sustaining political commitment: while there is an inherent tension between the two goals, fostering communal development does not entail neglecting political objectives. In fact, I suggested that pursuing the former might be necessary for groups that want to sustain commitment to social reconstruction. If we take seriously Weber's statement that "politics is the slow boring of hard boards," certain features of the activities in Richmond—the effort to develop a sustaining community, the skepticism voiced about the possibility of rapid change, the disavowal of revolutionary rhetoric, and the willingness to adopt a long-term approach—might be instructive for any group that wishes to retain commitment in hard times. This does not necessarily mean that the activists' long-term political strategy will be successful (indeed, personalists are often weak in this regard) but that they are creating the conditions that make discussion of such a strategy more than an exercise in wishful thinking.

Future Directions

The reassessment that peace community members made of their strategy and goals in 1986 did not lead to a dramatic redefinition of the movement. Most believed that many of its specific emphases ought to be retained. More generally, activists continued to suggest that peace groups should function both as instruments of social change and as exemplars of countercultural community. Still, almost everyone maintained that changes should be made in the manner in which these functions were pursued. A variety of recommendations were put forth for how the movement could better meet some of the goals it professed to have but had not succeeded in achieving. Many of these proposals would require activists to develop more fully the experimental and radical side that the movement had always possessed to some degree.

The desire to retain continuity was evident in the emphasis that people wished to place on further enhancing their own communal ties. In fact, some members of the peace community saw their failure to reach large numbers of people as providing even more reason for attending to this element. They suggested that the spiritual nurturance that the groups provided was integral to their capacity to weather hard times and that the movement would be terminally damaged if the bonds which held them together were dissolved. Remarked John Gallini, "One of the things which we have done is to set up a small group in which we engage in faith sharing. We realize that we have to come together periodically to talk about what our faith means. This is not something which is new, but we need to be certain that not all our activity is aimed at the more casual participants in the movement. This is especially true these days when the level of enthusiasm is not as high as it previously was."

The board of directors of the Richmond Peace Education Center echoed this concern with the internal life of the organization when it decided to include community building as an important goal for 1985 and 1986. Believing that it was important for people who shared a basic outlook on peace issues to know one another better, the board developed plans to hold regular gatherings at people's homes. The membership was encouraged to host potlucks and parties that would help to sustain the supporters' commitment and increase the interpersonal satisfactions of people in the movement. The board hoped that people would put their musical, literary, and photographic skills to use by sponsoring evenings that would appeal to a cross-section of the movement's supporters.

Many of the activists also hoped that the movement would continue to furnish nonpartisan education about the threat of nuclear war to the church community in the area. Although they acknowledged the limitations of this strategy more readily in 1986, the activists generally believed that there was a legitimate niche for presentations like "The Facts of the Arms Race" and for films such as *The Last Epidemic*. They felt that these remained useful ways of introducing their concerns to those who had not thought deeply about the issue of nuclear war. Harold Houghton, for example, said, "I have always felt that one of our basic strengths is that we offer some very good factual peace education to the church community." Activists who supported these efforts noted that even in 1986 the peace education center was still receiving requests to provide basic information and speakers about the arms race. They also mentioned that the supporters of the center still felt that this was one of its primary tasks.

Many, though not all, of the activists believed that the effort to influence the Democratic party should persist. They argued that it is imperative for the movement to obtain influence in the circles where political decisions are actually made in the state. They claimed that at least some activists must commit a significant amount of energy to the task and that others must be willing to support them at the polls. Ultimately, advocates of this position hoped to open up the rules of the state Democratic party and mount a serious challenge to the Republican incumbent who represents the district in the House. No one, however, asserted that the substantive goals of the movement could be realized through the party process. Even the most determined advocates of the strategy considered it but one feature of a multifaceted approach.[9]

The principal changes endorsed by the members of the peace community involved, for the most part, placing heavier emphasis on features of the movement that they felt have been inadequately pursued or given less prominence than they deserved. The concern raised most often in this regard was the relationship of peace activists to the black community. This issue was mentioned numerous times in our interviews and drew the attention of the board of directors of the peace education center during 1984 and 1985 when they assigned high priority to hiring a black staff member in the near future. Various ideas about how to improve the relationship were offered, though a widely agreed-upon strategy for doing so had yet to crystallize. Some spoke about trying to "work more closely with the black community on the justice side of our beliefs" and drawing the connection between peace issues and the problems of the American political economy. Others, such as Jerry Gorman, recommended that the movement adopt a more specific agenda, one that would endorse local and state issues as well as national and global stances. "I think that unless we hone in on local issues, we will have to be reactive, responding to Reagan and world events. I think there is a possibility that we can sit down with black people and hammer out an agenda. I personally give high priority to the death penalty, to the corrections issue, and to uranium mining in the state."

Steve Hodges was one of the people who felt that the local movement's worst failing was its inability to relate to and incorporate the perspective of the black community. He was particularly disturbed that his own fellowship, the Community of the Servant, despite having very worthy goals, did not deal successfully with the issue of interracial conflict and fellowship. "We ourselves didn't include people of color and the community was not sufficiently influenced by their perspective." He believes that this can be accomplished only if "white people go to places where black people are gathered and look at ways they can join a group which from the beginning has had black leadership." Steve and a few of his companions from the Community of the Servant moved into a black neighborhood where he attended church and worked for community revitalization. He also became a central figure in the Richmond version of Jesse Jackson's Rainbow Coalition.

The Richmond Peace Education Center attempted to give institutional support to the beliefs articulated by Steve Hodges. The center embarked on a serious effort to implement its intention of hiring a staff person to work with and in the black community. It received a number of grants from national organizations (such as the Peace Development Fund and the A. J. Muste Institute) to help fund the position, and it matched these grants with vigorous fund raising in the Richmond area. In addition, the center also began to utilize its conflict-resolution programs to focus on matters of interest to members of the black community. It sponsored a conference on violence that brought community leaders and activists together to discuss how the schools and social service agencies could develop programs in conflict resolution that might make a long-term impact on reducing the level of violence in Richmond. The center was also invited to make a number of presentations about conflict resolution to agencies that worked primarily in the black community.

A second recommendation for change was to make the connection between antinuclear weapons agitation and other issues in American foreign policy more explicit. By 1986, most of the core activists believed that the movement should be broadened to focus on foreign policy matters other than the arms race. This idea has always been present to some extent because of the concern that the churches have exhibited about events in Central America and the Catholic interest in base communities and liberation theology. But the tendency became more pronounced in Richmond in 1984 when Steve Hodges and Wendy Northup visited Nicaragua. On returning, the maintained that the Reagan administration had falsified the reality of that nation in order to justify American military involvement. Steve Hodges was so influenced by his visit that he considered moving to Nicaragua for a time in order to organize the Witness for Peace more effectively. By 1986, activists were speaking about the "deadly connections" in American foreign policy between the arms race and Third World interventions, criticizing the Reagan administration's policy in Central America, South Africa, and the Pacific. Groups such as Pax Christi and individuals like Steve Hodges became important actors in promoting the Pledge of Resistance in the city and organizing groups committed to protest against further escalation of U.S. involvement in Central America.

Efforts to publicize the Pledge of Resistance were related to a third area of proposed change—the heavier emphasis that some activists wanted to place on civil disobedience. The core members of the peace community were always favorably disposed toward civil disobedience because of their skepticism about the moral commitment of mainstream politicians. By 1986, more of them were beginning to think that civil disobedience and direct action might be a possible answer to the shallowness of support for the movement. While still believing in nonpartisan education, they were more adamant in insisting that it not be the only or even the primary form of political persuasion used by the movement. Supporters of more vigorous campaigns of civil disobedience maintained that exemplary action of this sort affected people at a deeper level and contained possibilities for mobilization that nonpartisan education did not. In Steve Hodges' opinion, "More people are affected by seeing the actions of other people than by hearing persuasive arguments. Personal change often comes about through action and not by argument on an academic level. It is when people see their friends vigiling outside their congressman's office that they really begin to change. What if twenty people in Richmond from a variety of backgrounds and occupations get thrown in jail? I think that this would move people to consider their own lives and beliefs more deeply than they do now. Action gets into people's hearts in a way that leafletting and educational campaigns do not." The board of directors of the peace education center gave implicit approval to this emphasis when it agreed to keep Steve on as a consultant after his resignation, aware of the direction in which he was moving.

Future Prospects, Future Tensions

To speak about the future of peace activism in Richmond necessarily entails a degree of speculation, for this requires an assessment of both motivation and political strategy. How seriously will the members of the peace community pursue the goals they wish to achieve? What consequences are likely to follow the adoption of the strategies which they advocate? The first question is probably easier to answer. Given the importance that these men and women attach to acting on their beliefs, it seems reasonable to assume that they will pursue at least some of their stated objectives in a determined manner. Participation in the peace movement has contributed to the spiritual well-being of the activists. Almost all of them find the peace community to be a nurturing environment, even if it can be unsettling and demanding as well, and their faith provides them with sufficient motivation for undertaking the unpleasant chores that can discourage individuals from becoming socially involved. It is thus hard to imagine circumstances which would lead the core activists of the local organization to discontinue their efforts, for this would require a substantial redefinition of their personal identities.

The political consequences of their future activities are less predictable. Determination, tenacity, and good intentions do not guarantee success. There is reason, I think, to view some of the recommendations that have been presented as imaginative extensions of the movement's personalist orientation. The peace community's desire to use civil disobedience as an instrument of political education, the determination to forge an interracial coalition, and the interest in relating global concerns to a specific local agenda indicate a continued willingness to explore the full implications of the movement's underlying beliefs. Clearly, these activists remain interested in learning what it means to participate in a form of politics in which people "think globally and act locally." But these new emphases may also aggravate the dilemmas that have historically enervated peace activism by releasing tensions that work to immobilize the movement.

The possible outcome of a more vigorous civil disobedience campaign illustrates the movement's uncertain future. On a positive note, it should be mentioned that this strategy is not being advocated impulsively. Steve Hodges has been working for years laying the groundwork for its use. In 1982, he organized the first seminars on nonviolent action and later expanded their availability throughout the peace community. He has written numerous articles for the peace center's newsletter explaining his views on forms of action appropriate for Richmond. Steve insists that it is very important for acts of civil disobedience to be "performed carefully so that you show respect for those whose attitudes you want to change." He has labored to persuade people in the movement that the cause is best served by various forms of political action and public witness. It is not inconceivable that such extensive preparation and scrupulous reflection may result in the development of innovative forms of action that will bring even more citizens to take the issues which Steve has raised more seriously.

Yet, to the extent that civil disobedience replaces nonpartisan education and conventional political activity as the defining characteristic of local activism, the movement in Richmond runs the risk of polarization. Historically, peace activists have frequently quarreled over the methods of persuasion the movement should employ.[10] The advocates of a rationalistic, nonpartisan, nonthreatening approach have clashed with others who maintain that only dramatic acts of conscience gain people's attention in a compelling manner. By 1986, this dispute had yet to surface in an especially serious or divisive manner in Richmond, though a greater readiness to employ civil disobedience made this outcome a distinct possibility. To be sure, the core group of activists who had spent considerable time reflecting on the matter were generally supportive of relying more heavily on civil disobedience. But the reaction of the people on the periphery of the movement who contributed time and money could not be predicted.

The intention of the peace community to forge a better relationship with the black populace also brings with it heightened opportunity. If such a coalition could ever be realized, it would introduce a new element into the politics of the Richmond area. The symbolic import of success in this effort would be of great magnitude. For the peace movement in general, it would represent a significant addition to its constituency and an indication of its capacity to overcome a prominent historical limitation. Such an alliance would also indicate the possibility that activists in neighborhoods and cities could overcome class divisions and work on a mutually supportive progressive agenda. This is the reason, I think, that national organizations have been so willing to help fund the effort.

But forging this coalition will be infinitely more difficult than talking about it. Researchers who have written about social movements have noted that one of the most difficult alliances to form is that between groups motivated by a "moral" concern and those who struggle for material parity in an unequal society. It is not only that their demands are likely to be different, but that these groups are likely to have different agendas, organizational styles, methods of persuasion, and ideas about how to challenge the existing order and when to cooperate with its leaders.[11] The alliances that are made are likely to be temporary in duration and ineffective in promoting policy changes.

   Black activists who have been involved with the peace community are
quick to note the difficulty of reaching the majority of black citizens. Willie
Dell, a two-term city councilwoman who has served on the peace education
center's board of directors, does not entirely agree with Phyllis Conklin's
statement that the movement has completely "bombed" in the black community. "Our efforts to make contact with leadership, particularly in churches,
have been productive," she claims. "We have also conducted a number of
workshops that have convinced them of the connections between peace and
justice issues." Yet Willie Dell also maintains that neither the movement nor
the church leaders have been effective in transmitting the information to the
rank and file in a convincing way. "We really do not have too many teachers
addressing the issue or many of the student activists very concerned. I think
that many of our people see the issue as too distant from their concerns and
we haven't done a very good job in showing how their daily worries are
related to peace issues."
   Let me offer one illustration of this difficulty. Jerry Gorman mentioned
that he sees opposition to the death penalty as one important component
of a joint agenda. It is true, of course, that surveys show that black Americans oppose the death penalty in greater percentages than white Americans. When Linwood Briley, a notorious mass murderer, was executed in
Richmond in 1984, a remarkable display of racist imagery and sloganeering
took place outside the penitentiary. Supporters of the death penalty carried
signs saying Kill the Negro and tightened ropes into nooses for the television cameras. Such an occurrence could not but antagonize the black
population and give a measure of credence to Jerry Gorman's position. Yet
I wonder if most black citizens find the discriminatory application of the
death penalty to be as critical an issue as do the members of the peace
community who oppose it on moral grounds. Indeed, I would suggest that
a higher level of intensity exists about preventing crime in the black community than exists in regard to the punishment meted out to criminals.
And this is a matter to which people in the peace community are only
beginning to turn their attention.
   One might even suggest that the desire to build a black-white coalition
represents a confession of failure about the movement's ability to reach
working-class whites. Despite the lack of interaction between middle-
class activists in the peace community and black citizens, these groups
already share a common perspective on most political issues. American
blacks do not need to be convinced that the Reagan administration's
budget unfairly penalizes the poor and diverts an excessive amount of
funds to the military for weapons procurement. Many peace activists do

not require more intimate contact with black citizens to understand that the Reagan administration's priorities are not congruent with their notions of fairness and good relations between nations. It is just possible, therefore, that the movement's energies would be better directed toward those people who do not share its outlook, especially the white southern males who voted for Ronald Reagan in overwhelming numbers. In this sense, the migration of the Community of the Servant out of Oregon Hill may be symbolic of a larger failure—the movement's incapacity to influence the very groups that will have to be reached if American culture is to be seriously modified.

Events that took place after the research for this book was completed in 1987 and 1988 are obviously relevant to the analysis of this chapter. President Reagan's summits with General Secretary Gorbachev and the signing of the INF treaty were generally viewed as positive steps by the peace community. These accomplishments were presented by the Reagan administration and the Bush campaign in 1988 as confirmation of the peace-through-strength position that it had adopted in 1980. The administration argued that it was the placement of missiles in Europe, the willingness of the United States to increase its defense budget, and the prospects of the Strategic Defense Initiative that brought the Soviets to the bargaining table. They maintained that their success in negotiating with the Soviets invalidated the recommendations that freeze proponents had made throughout the 1980s. Indeed, the Bush campaign suggested that the modernization of nuclear weaponry had to be continued. The vice-president suggested that modernization was important, not only for its practical benefits but for the pressure it exerted on the Soviet Union.

Members of the peace community in Richmond obviously did not agree with this perspective. They believed that internal developments in the Soviet Union and Gorbachev's desire to reorient its domestic economy accounted for the Soviet willingness to negotiate. In addition, members of the peace community felt that it was the antinuclear weapons movements in the United States and Europe that produced the climate of opinion that prompted President Reagan to change his mind about the possibility of serious deliberations with the Soviet Union. Activists believed that the pressure exercised by the movement made the advice offered by people such as Nancy Reagan and George Shultz take precedence over that of hard-line conservatives who wanted to talk about violations of previous treaties before entering into new negotiations. Despite President Reagan's continuing harsh words about them, activists felt that they had helped to set the agenda that made the treaties possible.

But even if this were true, the case for the movement's influence is indirect and complicated. The administration surely succeeded in persuading many Americans that its approach was successful and it effectively removed the movement as a major actor in the national debate over foreign policy. It is still an open question how much the public believes that we ought to continue to spend in order to demonstrate political will and whether a portion of the military budget ought to be redirected to the civilian economy. This may provide an opening for the peace community's argument that excessively high military spending damages our capacity to address domestic problems. But in 1988 there was no galvanizing proposal that mobilized this sentiment in the political arena. Local activists like the ones in Richmond were obviously on their own, struggling to maintain the commitment of their own community and to redefine their purposes in light of the altered conditions.

In a poem titled "Candles in Babylon,"[12] Denise Levertov characterizes the work that people such as the Richmond peace activists perform as an effort to bring light to where darkness rules.

> Through the Midnight streets of Babylon
> between the steel towers of their arsenals
> between the torture castles with no windows,
> we race by barefoot, holding tight
> our candles, trying to shield
> the shivering flames, crying
> "Sleepers Awake!"

The men and women of the peace community would not be entirely uncomfortable with this characterization of their efforts. They would even be likely to persevere just on the hope that they might contribute to a rebirth of moral responsibility. Still, they clearly want to accomplish more than just shielding a flickering flame. They would hope that the ultimate outcome of their efforts is best captured by another poet, the Chilean Pablo Neruda, who spoke of people with a "burning patience" who eventually imbue the world with decency and justice. The activists' faith, determination, and willingness to confront tasks that have historically enervated peace movements suggest that they may, in the long run, be more significant than their modest achievements to date indicate. But the very difficulty of the tasks they confront and the formidable resources of the mainstream culture could mean that Levertov's characterization is also a description of personalism's practical limits.

8

Personalist Politics and Political Reform

A BOOK THAT is largely a case study necessarily raises the issue of representativeness. Are the activists that I have interviewed in Richmond typical of people who have become involved in the movement elsewhere? Are their strategies illustrative of the efforts that have occurred in other cities and towns across the country? Are their reactions to the successes and defeats of the movement consistent with those exhibited in other parts of the nation? These are but a few of the questions likely to be asked by people who are interested in the wider meaning of the activities described in the past six chapters.

The Richmond activists are not, of course, representative of the American peace movement in a strict statistical sense. I have made no effort to discover the various social, economic, political, and religious characteristics of movement participants nationwide and then look for individuals in a specific location who possessed these traits. Nor did I assume that the men and women to whom I have spoken mirrored these characteristics in any way that would satisfy the requirements of an accurate statistical representation. From all that I have read and observed about the national movement, I presume that many participants share the traits of the people described here. Nonetheless, the worth of the book does not rest on this sort of claim to representativeness.

In addition, the political sentiments voiced by the men and women in Richmond are not precisely the same as would be spoken by all participants in the movement. The desire to limit nuclear arms and their attendant dangers is shared by a significant portion of the population and is by no means limited to those who have such a highly critical view of American culture as the people described in this study. Moreover, there has always been a highly visible element of the movement that has focused on achieving legislative goals and has therefore concentrated on maintaining a "responsible" presence in Washington, D.C. Persons with this orientation have frequently been wary of those who suggest that civil disobedience is necessary to the disarmament struggle. To some extent, therefore, this study underrepresents the activists who have stressed legislative goals and worked to exclude other emphases.

But there are, I think, some important ways in which the activities and the people described in this book are "representative." In the first place, the questions and dilemmas faced by the men and women in Richmond are likely to be shared by most other groups interested in changing the attitudes and behavior of their fellow citizens with respect to nuclear weapons policy. Can activists use the political arena to promote their goals and still retain their moral integrity? Is it possible to reconcile the pursuit of social change with the development of a tighly knit community? What kind of civil disobedience might adequately express one's personal beliefs and be a convincing demonstration to others of the need to change policy? How far should people go in embodying their political beliefs in their personal lives and what form should this take?

My second claim is that the activists in Richmond are representative of a point of view that has been emerging for the past fifteen years in many church circles. Chapter 1 described how the leadership of numerous denominations in this country and authors who write for a religious audience have come to view the nuclear arms race as an imminent threat to survival and as a metaphor for other problems that they believe are embedded in the culture. They have utilized themes and imagery drawn from the Bible to illuminate our present condition and evaluate public policies. In addition, they have called for Christians to respond publicly to the threat of extinction and the other problems raised by the existence of nuclear weapons. The efforts by the men and women in Richmond to assume a measure of personal responsibility, bring their worries to the wider community, and enter the political realm are perfectly consistent with the emerging emphases in this antinuclear political theology. While the particulars of this involvement will differ from city to city, the essence of what has been described here should be familiar to anyone knowledgeable about the movement.

A third claim concerns the representativeness of what I have called the personalist approach to political issues. To some degree, I think that the personalist features of the movement account for its appeal to a broad spectrum of individuals. Personalist ideas about individual responsibility, the problems of modern culture, and the desirability of cooperation are widely accepted, even if all the political implications that the Richmond activists draw from these notions are not. In addition, I believe not only that personalism is an emerging and increasingly significant feature of peace activism in the United States, but also that its basic elements can be discerned in other movements for political reform that have developed in the country during the past twenty years. These similarities can be most easily seen in two primarily middle-class movements, environmentalism and feminism. Each of these endeavors has a personalist strain that stresses the importance of individual change, the development of community, and the necessity of imbuing politics with values normally associated with the household. These elements coexist—sometimes without friction and sometimes uneasily—with a traditional reformist component that stresses legislative lobbying, electoral contests, and bureaucratic maneuvering.

I also want to suggest that a number of the features of what I have labeled the personalist approach are not confined to left-of-center political movements. To the extent that personalists exhibit mixed feelings about the direction of modern life, maintain that responsible individuals are obliged to help purify a corrupt system, and want to make household values politically relevant, they are not limited to any one position on the ideological spectrum. We can see these beliefs in the politics of Christian conservatives as well as in the religious Left and the environmental movement. To be sure, the complaints about modernity, the evaluation of American life, the interpretation of biblical signs, and the content of responsible action differ considerably in the recommendations of these groups. Tim LaHaye and the Reverend Jerry Falwell often do not seem to live in the same world as Daniel Berrigan, Wendy Northup, and John Gallini. Nonetheless, the general form of their arguments possesses commonalities that are deserving of our attention.

This chapter attempts to substantiate these claims about personalism's presence in the wider culture. It begins by discussing and assessing its contribution to environmentalism and feminism. I suggest that authors and activists in these movements have used personalist themes to illuminate the connections between individual life and social policies in an interesting manner. At the same time, their own political actions are frequently marked by vagueness and an incapacity to motivate large numbers of people, problems common among the antinuclear weapons activists. The second part examines personalist features of contemporary Christian conservatism. I show how these activists have embraced viewpoints on American history, contemporary American culture, and the responsibility of citizens that, in general terms, resemble the criticisms voiced by the antinuclear activists. The third section explains some of the key differences in the use of personalist themes by Christian conservatives and the religious activists in the antinuclear weapons movement. I note how their contrasting views regarding the ordering principles of private life result in divergent political outlooks and hold different implications for their relations with the powers that have dominated government in the 1980s. The conclusion maintains that even though personalist approaches are unlikely to be ultimately successful, they will remain prominent in political reform movements for the foreseeable future, largely because they tap important sentiments about the direction of contemporary American culture.

Personalist Themes in Environmentalism and Feminism

During the past twenty years, environmental organizations have proliferated across the nation. Their analyses tend to focus on the "neighborhood effects" of industrial pollution, the health dangers posed by toxic waste, and the disruption precipitated by certain forms of growth. These organizations rely heavily on friendly scientific experts to frame issues and outline possible responses. Their conception of politics seems to be modeled on the style developed by Ralph Nader and the public-interest movement of the late 1960s and early 1970s, in which mainstream political institutions were ingeniously utilized to achieve reformist ends. Committed activists are hired to lobby in Washington and the state capitals, pressuring officials to acknowledge the legitimacy of environmental claims. The politics of the major power companies are challenged in hearings of state regulatory commissions and in the courtroom. Corporations whose practices are believed to be especially deleterious to the environment have their transgressions publicized in the media. Citizens are recruited as members through direct-mail campaigns and are exhorted to be vigilant in exposing ecological abuses in their own community. This element of the environmental movement has achieved notable legislative success and has raised citizen awareness about the need for ecological sensitivity.

Environmental politics does not, however, always fit so neatly within the parameters of liberal reformism. Much of the movement's literature, for example, not only criticizes the ecological consequences of corporate capitalism and bureaucratic socialism, but explicitly endorses the personalist tenet that individuals have to assume responsibility for problems in the world. Its supporters not only pressure governments to change policies, but work to persuade individuals that they ought to live an ecologically harmonious life. They maintain that despoilation of the environment is symptomatic of a wider social problem, that of being unable to impart meaning to our lives and to act decently toward others. Individuals are thus frequently enjoined to exchange the supposedly unfulfilling pleasures of consumerism for simple living and high thinking.

The work of Wendell Berry furnishes one of the best examples of the personalist component contained in this variant of environmentalism. A novelist, poet, professor, and farmer, Berry criticizes the ecological and human consequences of large-scale corporate agriculture. His major book, *The Unsettling of America: Culture and Agriculture,* details his indictment of current agricultural practices and uses the treatment of the land as a metaphor for the erosion of human relationships and our personal capacity to grasp what is truly important in life. Berry argues that the modern agricultural ideal has actually effaced the values intrinsic to the practice of farming—care, nurturance, the recognition of interdependence, and the acknowledgment of limits. It is a process that he believes can be discerned in all areas of the culture, from the formulation of an agricultural policy that views food as a weapon to the casual sundering of relationships in society at large.

For Berry, the ecological problems of the age derive from an adherence to misguided values that prompt the liberation of those elements of human nature that ought to be restrained while permitting the atrophy of the inclinations that make worthwhile lives possible. He characterizes this process by describing two paradigmatic orientations toward life that he believes have always been in conflict in American culture: nurturing and exploiting. "The exploiter is a specialist, an expert, the nurturer is not. The standard of the exploiter is efficiency; the standard of the nurturer is not. The exploiter's goal is money, profit, the nurturer's is health—his land's health, his own, his family's, his community's, his country's. The exploiter thinks in terms of numbers, quantities, 'hard facts.' The nurturer in terms of character, quality and kind."[1] Although Berry believes that the exploitative tendency has been present to an untoward degree in American life, he does not think that it has always been unchallengeably supreme. He contends, however, that in the contemporary era the ethos of the exploiter has supplanted the values of the nurturer.

Berry suggests that the first step in changing current practices is for individuals to opt out of the system and begin to construct a life of integrity. Much of his poetry is an autobiographical account of his own efforts to do this, describing why he left a teaching position in New York City to return to Kentucky, why he is trying to reclaim land that has been farmed neglectfully, and what this effort has meant for the development of his character and the quality of his family life. The autobiographical content of his work is presented with a didactic purpose, for he is providing practical instruction in the art of living in opposition to the dominant values of American society. The moral to be drawn is that other people can do the same. They can move beyond rhetorical attacks on problems and shallow political solutions to take a stand on character, to take what were described in chapter 6 as "complete actions," steps by which individuals incorporate their beliefs into their daily lives. Eventually, these individuals may help to make household values, particularly those of the nurturer, relevant to public policy.

The practice of environmentalism frequently reflects this personalist component. It is not uncommon for people who embrace an ethic of ecological responsibility to make changes in their own manner of living. At times, this can entail an almost complete rejection of industrial society, symbolized by those who leave what they consider to be unhealthy urban environments for the nurturance that comes from working on the land. On other occasions, it simply means becoming more attentive to the ecological components of everyday activities. Recycling, reduced consumption of resources, and changes in eating habits and vacation practices may go along with an expressed commitment to stewardship. This perspective is brought to the public in the form of educational programs, descriptions of ecological dangers, and political campaigns designed to show the problems inherent in unfettered growth. Environmentalists try not only to speak about sacrifice, but to phrase their beliefs in terms of quality of life, appealing to the notion that a genuine standard of living cannot be measured by the acquisition of material wealth.

Ecologists who embrace personalist themes often exhibit the ambivalence about politics that I observed among the activists in Richmond. They frequently seem to have an innate distaste for the politics of power, of compromise, of interest-group bargaining. Indeed, they are continually tempted to opt out of the public world altogether, because they believe that it often embodies the ethos of the exploiter. Berry remarks in one of his poems that he would rather be picking red berries than going to any public place. But environmentalists also realize that political activity is necessary to achieve their goals. Gary Snyder, ecologist and poet, expresses this sentiment by noting that "no one can afford to be innocent, or indulge himself in ignorance of the nature of contemporary governments, politics and social orders."[2] He recommends developing a community-based politics and forming local resistance to irresponsible development, living up to the Wobbly slogan of "building the new society within the shell of the old." In Snyder's words, the task is to "find your place on the planet, dig-in and take responsibility from there—the tiresome but tangible work of school boards, county supervisors, local foresters, local politics."[3]

The feminist movement in the United States during the last twenty years has exhibited interesting parallels with environmental and antinuclear weapons activity. To some degree, its philosophy and practice fit comfortably within the framework of liberal reformism. Feminists have frequently used the rhetoric of individual rights and civil liberties to promote their causes, calling for an end to discrimination based on sex in the economic and political arenas. The right-to-privacy argument that has been so prominent in the abortion controversy is one of the best examples of the influence exercised by liberal philosophical concepts on feminist discourse. In political terms, persons in the movement have lobbied actively on issues related to the position of women in the banking and credit systems. They sought to pass an Equal Rights Amendment. In 1984, the National Organization for Women was certainly instrumental in the selection of Geraldine Ferraro as the Democratic vice-presidential candidate.

But as with environmentalism and the antinuclear movement, feminism cannot be fully contained by traditional liberal categories. Indeed, feminist theory and practice are difficult to categorize because they have ranged over so many issues and been expressed from a variety of theoretical angles. Writers such as Alison Jaggar and Jean Bethke Elshtain, who have attempted to analyze the forms of feminist theory, suggest that an adequate description will recognize radical, socialist, and psychoanalytical versions as well as the liberal variant. Within academia, there is an ongoing debate about which approach is most essentially feminist and what the intellectual stakes are in adopting any particular outlook.

I do not plan to enter this debate here. What I want to argue is simply that feminist theorizing and political practice have recognizable personalist components. In general terms, feminist perspectives on contemporary society typically claim to illuminate its operation in a manner that will resonate with the personal experiences of individual women (and men). Feminism uncovers connections between the social structure and personal conditions that were previously veiled; it furnishes specific names and genealogies for anxieties and problems once thought to be caused by personal maladjustment; and it demonstrates to women and men how their view of the world and their activity within it has been distorted by an unexamined adherence to ideologies based on a form of male domination. It also frequently points to solutions, in part personal and in part political, that might alter existing conditions by dissolving the patterns of exploitation. As with antinuclear weapons activity and environmentalism, the capacity of feminism to connect with individual experience is vividly apparent in the powerful role that autobiographical writings have occupied in the dissemination of its perspectives.

The practice of feminism in academic circles is illustrative of its tendency to include liberal approaches while still pushing beyond them. To some extent, feminist scholarship has reflected a liberal, reformist approach to the accepted intellectual canon. In so doing, it has prompted an extensive rewriting of history, political theory, and sociology to include women in the body of scholarship and to accord them full rights as actors and victims in the construction of culture and scholarship. In a more radical sense, however, feminism has begun to challenge the very categories of scholarly analysis and intellectual judgment. Feminists have argued that the essence of the scholarly endeavor has been shaped and distorted by assumptions derived from the political dominance of males in the academy. Thus Evelyn Fox Keller maintains that the practice of science would have been vastly different if the concerns of women had been fully acknowledged and explored. Alison Jaggar suggests that the concept of equality would have to be revised if the meaning and implications of gender were adequately understood. Carol Gilligan argues that ideas about moral development should be altered in light of information about how women go about making ethical judgments.[4]

The relevance of household values to the public realm is frequently an important, albeit controversial, feature of this mode of feminist thinking. Feminists who adopt this viewpoint believe that the reformation of the culture needs to explicitly incorporate the experiences traditionally associated with women and removed from the political realm by men. Jean Bethke Elshtain states this argument in the following manner: "If it is the case that women have a distinct moral language, as Carol Gilligan has argued, one which emphasizes concern for others, responsibility, care, and obligation, hence a moral language profoundly at odds with formal, abstract models of morality defined in terms of absolute principles, then we must take care to preserve the sphere that makes such a morality of responsibility possible and extend its imperatives to men as well. . . . One moral and political imperative that would unite rather than divide women, that would tap what is already there but go on to redeem and transform it, would be a feminist commitment to a mode of public discourse embedded within the values and ways of seeing what Sarah Ruddick has called 'maternal thinking.' "[5]

The politics that emerges from this outlook takes two major directions. First, it calls for local activity and community building around issues concerning which women organize to provide services for themselves that have either been denied altogether or furnished in an inappropriate manner. This takes the form of support and consciousness-raising groups, women's health-care centers, women's artistic cooperatives, and caucuses within professional organizations. Second, it is often suggested that feminists have something distinctive to bring to movements for peace, ecological responsibility, and reform of the economy. The implication is that a feminist perspective can be fruitful in developing styles of political action that serve—as do the ecumenical communities of antinuclear activities—as intimations of the world that can be chosen and constructed.

The progress of environmentalism and feminism has, in some important ways, paralleled that of the antinuclear weapons movement. At one level, both movements have elicited widespread support for some of their goals. Most Americans believe, for example, that the environment ought to be protected and that the government has to assume responsibility for this. They also believe that women should not be discriminated against by the banking industry and should receive equal pay if they perform the same job that a man is doing. At another level, however, these movements have not been successful in persuading large numbers of Americans to embrace their personalist tenets. People may agree that we ought to be more sensitive to environmental needs, but they are not willing to take the steps that people like Wendell Berry might endorse to embody this belief in their daily lives. In addition, the prescriptions put forward by feminists and environmentalists with a personalist orientation may be found to be excessively vague. People may, for instance, agree with Evelyn Fox Keller that the activity of science might have been different if it had been informed by feminist issues, but may still wonder what a feminist science or public discourse imbued with the values of "maternal thinking" would be like.

Personalist Themes and Christian Conservatism

Some conservative intellectuals have written critically about the feminist, environmental, and antinuclear weapons movements, especially the latter two. One line of attack denounces these movements as romantic protests against modernity. According to this argument, the antinuclear weapons movement, for example, represents a maladaptive response of contemporary youth to their identity crisis. As James Foley puts it, participants "find great psychological satisfaction in belonging to the peace movement, for it allows them to project their alienation onto external objects that they have chosen to demonize—to wit, the threat of nuclear war, the Pentagon, the military industrial complex and related Satanic works and pomps. This deft psychological strategem is really a manner of self-deception, a means of escaping responsibility for facing the spiritual Angst, which is an unavoidable condition of living in the modern world."[6] Conservatives such as Foley argue that the movement cannot simply be dismissed as a passing fancy of the young because it has influenced mainstream discourse and thus has the potential to undermine the defense and security of the West.

A second line of attack from conservative intellectuals views these movements as the attempt by an emerging "new class" to gain control of the political apparatus in postindustrial societies. This argument posits that participants in these social movements are typically highly educated, upper-middle-class men and women who compose a nascent knowledge elite. While they claim to be offering an impartial moral critique of existing policies grounded in their religious traditions, their activities can be analyzed most adequately by ignoring their professed intentions. In an article about left-wing evangelicals, James Davison Hunter argues that their real social function is to provide a "sacred canopy over a world view that lacks one," namely, secular humanism. Looking at the disputes between Left-oriented evangelicals and their conservative counterparts, Hunter observes that "the stakes are once again power and privilege: the power to define and interpret the symbolic environment and the economic and social privileges that accompany it."[7]

My own feeling is that neither of these approaches are entirely helpful in understanding what is actually going on. The romantic-protest theory is correct in emphasizing the unease that participants exhibit about certain features of the modern world and in highlighting their desire to create a form of politics that provides communal support for the individual psyche. Moreover, such an outlook could be potentially useful in directing attention to some of the personality characteristics (courage, stubbornness, tenacity, etc.) that may distinguish activists from others who choose not to become involved. But the romantic-protest theory is almost willfully blind to elements of the movement that do not fit neatly within its framework. It completely misses the ambivalence that the participants feel about modernity and how their criticism of contemporary life is combined with a deep attachment to some of its principles. More important, the romantic-protest theory cannot acknowledge that any of the problems observed and mentioned by the activists might possibly be real. It implicitly assumes that the only genuine threat is that posed by the military expansion of the Soviet Union and that any analysis which runs to the contrary is a manifestation of alienation and angst. One is tempted to suggest that such reductionism is the intellectual equivalent of the Soviet practice of incarcerating dissidents by defining them as psychologically ill.

The new-class argument correctly draws attention to the social origins of most, though not all, activists in these movements. It also validly demonstrates the distance that often exists between the beliefs of the participants and rank-and-file Americans on many issues. By emphasizing the ongoing battle over social goods, the new-class argument has the virtue of not describing the activists as psychologically impaired by definition. But it too is seriously flawed. In the first place, it is premised on pinched and narrow assumptions. The new-class argument is itself reductionist because it refuses to take seriously the historical background and theoretical underpinnings of the movement, believing that it can be fully explained merely by placing it in the context of an old-fashioned power struggle. In addition, new-class theorists also fail to ask whether the problems addressed by these movements are genuine. Like the proponents of the romantic-protest theory, they believe that exposing the "real motivation" of the participants—namely, their sociological position—is sufficient to explain and discredit the cause for which they act.

A curious feature of the conservative arguments about progressive social activism is that these tend to ignore the similarities between the movements that they are criticizing and the causes which they support. My own feeling is that the conditions that have inspired left-wing activism may not be, in general form, all that different from those which have given rise, for example, to a religiously based political conservatism. That modern society has gone awry, that the American promise has been betrayed, that politicians have placed expedience before principle, and that individuals need to exercise responsibility for their activities are not ideas confined to nostalgic left-wing intellectuals or an emergent knowledge elite. It is certainly not only Dan Berrigan, Wendy Northup, and John Gallini who feel this way, but also Jesse Helms, Phyllis Schlafly, and Jerry Falwell.

To some degree, I think that it is possible to analyze the leadership of the religious Right in terms similar to the cynical position that conservative intellectuals have advanced about progressive activists. The sex scandals that rocked the PTL organization and Jimmy Swaggart's ministry, the cozying-up to dictators by Jerry Falwell, and the extortionist manipulations of faith by Oral Roberts all cast doubt on the moral intentions of those who are in the forefront of the movement. Moreover, the political utility of conservative evangelicals was certainly recognized and consciously promoted by people in the Republican party who were more concerned about the economic interests of corporate America than a presumed decline in the nation's moral fiber.

If these elements are viewed as the essence of religious conservatism, one might look at it simply as a vehicle by which charismatic ministers manipulate the faithful so they might obtain sex, money, and power, and as a tool adeptly employed by contemporary Republicans. But theories of manipulation can only be taken so far, because we eventually have to account for the appeal of these religious figures to a portion of the population. And to do this, we have to look beyond charismatic abilities and political intentions to the actual message that is being delivered. Why have people been receptive? There must be something in the ideas conveyed which resonates with the needs, interests, and experiences of the people watching and listening (and giving).

When attention is turned to the content of the messages and to the testimony of the people who find them persuasive, personalist themes repeatedly appear. Individuals are continually urged to assume personal responsibility for the decline in the moral standards of the nation. At times, such an injunction serves only as a clever fund-raising tool by suggesting that individuals can discharge their moral obligation by contributing to the work of the particular ministry. But it is also something more. The preachers of the Right invest individual life with meaning by suggesting that it is the focus of a historical drama, a battlefield on which the struggle between the love of God and the enticements of the devil are being played out. The audience learns that its own intrapsychic struggles and its own feelings about what is going wrong with the country are connected to developments in the unfolding of eternity, notwithstanding the impersonal and bureaucratic nature of the society in which this is occurring.

Liberal critics have sometimes charged that the religious Right is a collection of single-interest groups. This is mistaken because there is a complete world view undergirding the concern with an issue such as abortion. The religious Right often connects its position on abortion to an analysis of feminism, to the problems of the public school system, to the dilemmas of American foreign policy, and to the breakdown of the family in contemporary American society. Religious conservatives do not use the term "holistic" to describe their mode of analysis, but there is certainly a sense in which their arguments can be defined in this manner. Critics may accurately point out inconsistencies in the picture, such as the support for capital punishment that exists side by side with a professed pro-life perspective, but this does not mean that a relatively encompassing worldview is absent.

The attempt by Christian conservatives to create and nurture a culture of their own is further corroboration that they offer a holistic analysis of American society. Besides the omnipresent television evangelists, there are numerous indications of the religious Right's effort to redirect American culture. In the 1970s, for example, there has been a tremendous increase in the number of fundamentalist schools. These were intended to counter the influence of secular humanism that they believed was being propagated in public education and to imbue children with basic Christian values. At the same time, the Christian publishing industry became more prominent and more aggressive in its outreach. Polemics about the state of the country, guidebooks for spiritual growth, and practical lessons for everyday life all reached extensive audiences. Many of the industry's leading authors, unknown to many literate Americans, had sales far in excess of the authors who made the best-seller list of the *New York Times* and the shelves of the franchise outlets in the suburban malls.

The ambivalence about political activity that was exhibited by the antinuclear weapons activists is also manifested by the religious Right. On the one hand, activists speak about corruption and betrayal, proclaiming the takeover of American life by interests opposed to the basic values of the nation. States one person interviewed by Kristin Luker, "I think we all sort of took a lot of things for granted and one of them was that our government would follow itself, wouldn't start deviating from its original purpose, and this (*Roe v. Wade*) was such a strong deviation that it was kind of appalling to me. And it was the sort of a beginning of a lot of deviations in various areas."[8] On the other hand, despite the apparent corruption of the political realm, the religious Right encourages the practice of "Christian citizenship" as a purifying force and a method of restoring the original values of the nation. Despite the temptation to avoid politics and opt out altogether, they must attempt to invest the public world with the values in which they believe.

While the Christian Right professes to be interested in restoring traditional values and criticizes anything associated with progressive politics, it too contains an unarticulated ambivalence about modernity. It calls for a return to the good old ways, but uses the techniques of direct-mail solicitation and the technology of television to promote this restoration. Its view of the family, as we have seen, is decidedly patriarchal and antifeminist. But even here a hint of ambivalence can be observed. Tim and Beverly

LaHaye, for instance, ultimately suggest in their writings on family life that Christians have better sex lives than the unconverted. Carol Flake reports on a young man who tells LaHaye, "Pastor, I never dreamed that when I accepted Christ . . . He would invade our sex life, but we had never been able to make my wife's bells ring until after we were converted. Now she has a climax most of the time."[9]

A similar development can be seen in the emerging response of Christian conservatism to rock and roll. Since the days of Elvis Presley, some ministers have denounced rock and roll as the devil's music. The last twenty years have been no exception. Ministers have sponsored record burnings in their youth groups and have called for outright censorship of certain new-wave and heavy-metal bands. Jimmy Swaggart has devoted an entire television program to condemning the pornographic, incestuous, and politically subversive leanings of contemporary rock. But not all Christian conservatives have joined the campaign. In fact, one of the few major sources of growth in the music industry has been in the category of Christian rock. Numerous singers and bands have used rock music to express their Christian beliefs, combining traditional values with contemporary American teen culture. One of the most popular examples of this trend is Amy Grant. But what is perhaps more striking is the emergence of heavy-metal bands who sing for Christ while resembling Mötley Crüe, Alice Cooper, and Ozzy Osbourne in outward appearance.

Private Values and Public Policy

There are, of course, obvious differences in the manner in which Christian conservatives and the religious Left utilize personalist themes. To a large extent, these differences are the result of divergent beliefs about the values that undergird private life. Both groups want to inform public policy with themes drawn from the household, but they do not agree on the principles that characterize this level of existence. Consider their respective positions on the family. The religious Right tends to emphasize moral authority and role complementarity as the informing principles of family life. In a well-functioning family, the father will perform his biblically appointed role of providing overall guidance and the mother will be the spiritual exemplar so that the children can learn order, discipline, and commitment. At times, parents will be compelled to use what Augustine called "benevolent severity" to teach children the importance of restraining their impulses for their own good and for the welfare of their community.

The religious Left points most frequently to the egalitarian, cooperative, and sacrificial elements of family life as its distinguishing characteristics. Its adherents believe that families are places where human beings learn to treat one another with equal respect, to share resources, and to sacrifice immediate self-interest for the well-being of the larger community. They do agree with Christian conservatives that family life should teach children to place limits on their impulses for the benefit of others. But they suggest that biblical references to authority and role complementarity should be subordinated to the more egalitarian outlook on human relationships that they discern in the life of Jesus. Members of the religious Left want to draw attention to the trust, nurturing, and caring that takes place in families. They acknowledge that reality does not often approach these ideals. But they see the emotional disputes that arise as opportunities for learning the skills of nonviolent conflict resolution.

Beliefs about the family and the role of parents are related to the underlying psychology of the two movements. It is frequently said that religious conservatives promote a pinched and repressed view of human life. This is not entirely accurate because it ignores the elements of their outlook that highlight the ecstatic nature of religious experience and the heightened sense of life this provides individuals. This criticism also does not acknowledge the accommodation that religious conservatives have made to modern values in regard to issues such as sexuality. Yet it is important to note that the terms on which religious ecstasy and sexual satisfaction are experienced are not divorced from beliefs about authority and role complementarity. It is not through the natural unfolding of one's inner personality that these benefits are obtained, but from accepting proper guidance and instruction. Tim LaHaye, for example, does not believe that the sexual satisfaction of Christian women has anything to do with the ideology of feminism, because this only poses a threat to the male ego. Instead, he suggests that fulfillment is rooted in a "woman's surrender of her rebellious and infantile attitudes."[10]

The psychology of the religious Left shares the assumption of Christian conservatives that certain impulses need to be restrained and that individuals ought to be responsible members of a community. Observing the lives of these activists, one gets very little sense of the "do your own thing" hedonism that was present on the Left in the 1960s. Nonetheless, their psychological assumptions do hold that a self which unfolds along its own line of development may well be quite healthy. As I mentioned in the chapter on parenting and childhood education, they view the self as an entity to be nourished and want emotions to be fully explored. Participants in the religious Left tend to use metaphors about discoveries and journeys to describe the stages of religious experience. And their communities tend to support individuals who claim that the demands of their conscience require them to commit civil disobedience. It is not always clear how the religious Left will reconcile its support for individual conscience with its emphasis on communalism, but the attempt to do so is a central feature of its activity and ideology.

The political analyses of the religious Right reflect its concern with the erosion of authority and settled roles in the family. This is most visible in the conservatives' promotion of a "profamily" agenda that includes censoring pornography, eliminating sex education, teaching creationism and chastity education in the schools, criminalizing abortion, and reintroducing prayer in school. Yet distress about the problem of authority pervades their entire outlook on American society, for they believe that its breakdown in private life is paralleled by developments in the culture at large. To put private values at the heart of public policy would mean, for the religious conservatives, a more general attack on permissiveness. In practical terms, this would signify a more stringent criminal justice system, less adversarial media, and, in all likelihood, a more disciplined labor force.

The political relevance of household values carries far different implications for participants in the religious Left than it does for Christian conservatives. They are not primarily concerned about the breakdown of authority, but are more interested in bringing trust and caring to the political arena. Rather than affirming the claims of authority, they want those who hold power to utilize it for different ends—ends that would transform society. The Catholic bishops, for example, criticize contemporary American capitalism for its heartlessness and lack of compassion for the poor, and they call for the development of an economy that would give the poor a "preferential option." In the international arena, the Christian Left suggests that nonviolent conflict resolution in the family can be applicable to political disputes, at least insofar as it leads us to search for alternatives to war.

The conflicting views that the Christian Right and the Christian Left voice about the nature of the self, the lessons to be drawn from family life, and the central political issues facing the nation demonstrate that while both groups are ambivalent about modernity, the structure of this ambivalence is considerably different. At the risk of oversimplification, it can be argued that the Christian Right tends to believe that contemporary egalitarian ideologies—which they label secular humanism—have precipitated the breakdown of moral fiber and the corruption of society. For Christian conservatives, restoration of traditional values requires a direct attack on these ideologies and the political leaders who presumably embody them. The religious Left, however, sees no inherent conflict between contemporary egalitarianism and biblical teachings. What concerns its supporters is how some of these teachings—for example, that we are all God's children—have not been adequately embodied in American domestic and foreign policy. For members of the Christian Left, it is political realism, politics as usual, that has corrupted our society and endangered much of what we once cherished.

The manner in which Christian conservatives and the religious Left have fleshed out their personalist orientation has thus led to unequal access and influence in the corridors of power. Despite the rhetoric about the emerging power of the "new class," it has been the religious Right that has become most closely aligned with those controlling government in the 1980s. In the 1970s, the right wing of the Republican party decided to make recruitment of formerly apolitical Christian conservatives a priority. Incorporating these men and women into the Republican party was intended to serve two important purposes. First, it was designed to reduce the influence of the pragmatists within the party who supported the welfare state and endorsed detente. Second, it would help the party shed its image as the mouthpiece of corporate America and reshape it as a populist organization that was concerned about issues of interest to ordinary people.

The combination of a theology that frequently emphasized moral authority and the professed commitment of prominent Republicans to the agenda of Christian conservatism blunted, in some important ways, the potentially critical edge of the religious Right's personalist features. This development is probably most evident in its analysis of American foreign policy. The stinging criticism that the religious Right applies to popular culture and domestic policy is rarely extended to international affairs, unless it is to criticize human rights policies and American support for the United Nations. In fact, conservative spokespersons have almost fully endorsed the least critical versions of American civil religion in their foreign policy outlook. The nation whose abortion policy demands that it owes "Sodom and Gomorrah an apology" is transformed into a paragon of Christian morality on the world stage. It is now a shining city on a hill, a beacon to all humanity, an exemplar to the rest of the world. The domestic problems that are apparently so distressing pale before the barbarism of our international rivals.

The acquiescent nature of Christian conservatism can also be observed in its truncated criticisms of American capitalism. To some degree, the ideology and practices of the religious Right have been critical of the free-enterprise system and the greed that surfaces in its operation. Spokespersons like Dale Rogers are distressed by an ethos that she labels "gimme, gimme, gimme." The Christian Right has also exhibited a willingness to demand governmental restrictions on free enterprise in the name of community norms and to organize boycotts of companies that they believe are in violation of their principles. This is particularly true of the pornography issue. But the limits of their criticisms of capitalism are readily apparent. Christian conservatives have made little effort to hold corporations responsible for job creation or for long-term commitments to the communities in which they are located. They have said little about the duplicitous business practices of people who use proclamations of Christian virtue to mask their self-interest (indeed, their leaders themselves have not been exemplary role models on this issue). And for every jeremiad preached about the evils of greed, there is a paean to capitalism and an effort to discover biblical justifications for the accumulation of wealth.

Attention must also be paid to the role that television has played in the dissemination of Christian conservatism. It is well known that the more sophisticated evangelists have adopted the format of popular television shows as a way of promoting their message. As one commentator has noted, the "700 Club" resembles a cross between "Good Morning America," "60 Minutes," and "That's Incredible."[11] The reliance by many conservatives leaders on this medium reveals a tension at the heart of the movement's self-definition. The Christian Right calls individuals to a biblical faith that can, if taken literally, put them in opposition to many secular trends; yet its criticism of contemporary culture is mitigated by its presentation of faith as a consumer product in which piety is exhibited by switching on your favorite preacher and calling in your pledge via Mastercard to a toll-free number.

The ideas of the religious Left have fit to some measure within contemporary culture and politics. I have mentioned, for instance, how its distrust of formal authority and its fear of nuclear war are consistent with sentiments that can be seen throughout the culture. Moreover, these beliefs have found spokespersons within the political order. The Democrats in the House of Representatives were moved by the popular agitation of 1982 to vote favorably for a mutual and verifiable freeze on the production and deployment of nuclear weapons. Since that time, they have endorsed spending cuts in the defense budget and a host of measures, such as the comprehensive test ban, that have indicated support for the commitment of the religious Left to limit the arms race. In addition, the Jackson campaigns of 1984 and 1988 have embraced an economic vision in keeping with the ideas of the Catholic bishops.

Some features of the Christian Left have rendered it vulnerable to co-optation by the politically powerful, though it is manifested differently than with Christian conservatives. My feeling is that the political inexperience of its members and its communalist idealism have made it, at times, insufficiently critical of the governments that the United States is opposing. On occasion, it is difficult to see the critical intelligence that is applied to U.S. policy in the Christian Left's assessments, for example, of the Sandinista regime in Nicaragua. Many participants in the movement, I think, tend to accept the statements of good intentions voiced by Sandinista leaders and minimize any evidence that belies the proclaimed intentions—a reaction that would never be exhibited in response to the speeches of Ronald Reagan. In Richmond, this was evidenced in some of the statements by spokespersons for the peace community in their efforts to oppose U.S. intervention in Central America.

But it is also the case, I think, that the religious Left has been less vulnerable to co-optation by the powerful than the Christian conservatives. This can be explained by its own ideology and internal procedures. Its egalitarianism, emphasis on local activity, and commitment to democratic norms have made it more difficult for the movement to be so heavily identified with particular leaders. Despite the influence that the Catholic bishops have exercised on its internal debate, no individuals within the group have gained the publicity accorded Falwell or Robertson as "spokespersons" for their supporters. Nevertheless, a significant branch of the Democratic party has been attempting to distance itself from the ideas expressed by the religious Left. Concerned about being seen as weak on defense and beholden to special interests, many Democrats are simply not addressing questions of intervention abroad, the rising costs of defense, and the decline in services for the poor and the homeless. This is true not only of conservative Democrats in the South, but of some neoliberals who spent the 1980s developing a "winnable" ideology for the post-Reagan years.

Personalism's Appeal

The development of social movements with a personalist orientation has not been a chance occurrence. It is related to specific events and particular circumstances that have recently arisen in American politics. One could, for instance, trace the growth of the right-to-life movement to the mobilization generated in response to the *Roe* v. *Wade* decision by the Supreme Court in 1973. The recent antinuclear weapons agitation in this country is connected to the rearmament plans of the late 1970s and the frightening rhetoric about prevailing in a nuclear war that was voiced in the early days of the Reagan administration. Yet these particular events are probably best seen as catalyzing incidents rather than causes of personalist social movements. My own feeling is that their development has its origins in long-term structural changes in American life. These include the increasing bureaucratization of society, the reach of technology into areas where it previously did not intrude, the felt difficulty of having democracy function as it ought, and the sense of powerlessness experienced by individuals in a nation where the reigning ideology trumpets the importance of personal choice.[12]

These broader changes in the society have prepared the ground for the appeal of personalist movements. Beliefs about the destruction of traditional values and the improper use of medical science would eventually have to find an outlet in our society, even if the Supreme Court had never made the *Roe* v. *Wade* decision. Similarly, concern about the destructive potential of nuclear weapons and the lack of popular control over life-and-death decisions would have eventually generated popular protests, even if the feelings of the Reagan administration had never been publicly voiced. Personalist movements appeal to ambivalent feelings about modern life that have become part of our common experience. The emotions generated by this ambivalence can be very powerful because they connect the larger social and political world to intimate questions about survival, personal integrity, and the values imparted to our children. The social theorist Jürgen Habermas has described the origins of what I have labeled personalist movements as a reaction to the increasing "colonization of the life world." This description helps us, I think, to understand the moral fervor that is often expressed by the participants.

Originating outside the official party structure, personalist movements raise questions about the drift of mainstream politics rarely asked by its practitioners. These movements draw attention to the underside of progress, asking what is valuable and what has been discarded or forgotten in our embrace of modernity. They wonder about the meaning of democracy in the modern world and question whether the rhetoric of popular control over government has much relevance to the conditions present in large nation-states today. They probe the meaning of community and work to see if its practice can be restored in a viable way in modern America. They ask demanding questions about individual responsibility in the modern world, challenging us to assume obligations to the wider society and act upon professed moral principles. In all these ways, personalist movements have begun to politicize some of the most important questions that have been raised about modern culture.

This does not mean that personalist movements have always acted wisely and competently. To say that they will endure is not to claim that they will necessarily be successful in achieving their goals and reorienting American culture and politics. Some of their difficulties are related to their ideas, practices, and personalities. Personalists are often fuzzy about the political implications of their beliefs and the strategies that should be pursued: the Richmond activists support a restructuring of the American economy, but are vague about what this means in specific terms. Personalist movements also have to continually overcome the temptation to retreat from politics. This will be a recurring dilemma for any social movement that intends to bring household values to the political realm; it will be an even weightier problem when activists are motivated by religious beliefs that contain an ingrained skepticism about political action. The same idealism that animates their involvement can lead to a disenchantment with the compromise and bargaining that are business as usual in mainstream politics. Personalists may remain publicly engaged, but only through a politics of symbolic witness. Moreover, the participants' lack of political experience may prevent them from making the best use of their opportunities. They may form too close an alliance with the existing powers, as in the case of the religious conservatives. Or they may be blind to the opportunities that circumstances hold for building public support, translating their beliefs into legislation, and ultimately transforming the political world.

We also have to recognize the forces in our culture that work to lessen the appeal of these movements. Personalists may wish to reorient a consumer culture, but there are institutions and popular sentiments that function to stifle the possibility. One way they accomplish this is by linking our desire for personal fulfillment to the acquisition of consumer goods. Anyone who gets excited about the development of community organizations and the entrance of previously inactive people into the political arena should recognize that for every organization formed, there are probably five to ten new shopping malls under construction. The fastest-growing state in the Union, Florida, is not a testimony to a renewed sense of community and citizen involvement, but to the traditional American dream of making it through individual initiative. Personalist efforts are also blunted by a pervasive sense of cynicism and a belief that political action and public witness cannot really change what is wrong with society. Millions of Americans have rejected the promises of advertising and do not really think that genuine freedom can be equated with a wide range of consumer choice, but they also do not believe that anyone can do much to change this. Instead, they use the opportunities available in society to make their individual lives as palatable as possible and raise their children according to the values that they deem important.

Erik Erikson once noted that a culture may be best explained by noting the contradictions that are characteristic of it. One way, then, of understanding American politics is to observe the tension that arises between our pragmatic inclinations and our moral commitments. For more than two centuries, visitors to this country and students of American culture have stressed that Americans are a pragmatic, nonphilosophical people. But we also want to believe that our activities are infused with a special moral purpose. Much of Ronald Reagan's appeal, at least before the Iranamok scandal, rested on his capacity to persuade Americans that he was a leader who was both moral and efficient. This combination of pragmatism and righteousness can be dangerous, particularly when militaristic adventurism is garbed in the ideology of moral purity. But it also serves as an enduring reservoir for protest movements against the government. It should not be all that surprising that in times such as ours, movements desiring to bring a sense of morality to the political world should become a prominent part of the landscape. It should not be surprising, either, that there are people like Jerry Gorman, who describes his and his wife Donna's commitment to remain active by saying, "Woody Allen says 50 percent of success in life is just showing up. Well, Donna and I plan to continue showing up and standing up for what we believe."

NOTES

SELECTED BIBLIOGRAPHY

INDEX

Notes

Prologue

1   George Kennan, *The Nuclear Delusion: Soviet-American Relations in the Atomic Age* (New York: Pantheon Books, 1983), 201.

2   James J. Kilpatrick, "But the Right Should Speak Out," *The Philadelphia-Inquirer*, 22 March 1982, 9.

3   R. William Rauch, Jr., *Politics and Belief in Contemporary France: Emmanuel Mounier and Christian Democracy, 1932-1950* (The Hague, Netherlands: Martinus Nijhoff, 1972), 89. A complex, ambivalent, and even contradictory figure, Mounier exhibited a tension about political engagement with which contemporary personalists grapple. On the one hand, he thought it imperative to participate in efforts to reform society. On the other hand, he understood that such participation could weaken or perhaps destroy the spiritual impulse that motivated participation in the first place. In addition, the positions staked out by Mounier at various points in his life generated diverse criticisms, all of which can still be heard in reaction to the kind of politics that personalists endorse today. His effort in the years following World War II to generate a communist-Christian dialogue was criticized by conservatives for permitting Christianity to become unduly influenced by left-wing ideologies. His early reluctance to criticize the Vichy regime in France and the rhetorical embrace of certain personalist themes by the leaders of that regime led to Mounier's efforts after the Liberation to condemn the distortions and "perversions" of personalism. But his actions are also evidence for the liberal argument that a cultural and communitarian politics is not sufficiently attentive to individual rights and can be supportive of authoritarian politics. Finally, Mounier's reluctance to outline a political strategy has produced the charge that personalist notions are inherently escapist. The scholarly effort to interpret Mounier and the controversy that it has engendered can be seen in Rauch, *Politics and Belief in Contemporary France,* and in John Hellmen, *Emmanuel Mounier and the New Catholic Left, 1930-1950* (Toronto: University of Toronto Press, 1981).

4   I do not go so far as to claim that what has taken place in Richmond is a

microcosm of the movement at a national level. Local manifestations of antinuclear activity are, of course, related to the personalities and interests of the participants, as well as to the cultural and political environment in which they reside. But central features of peace activity in Richmond are representative of what has occurred across the entire nation in the past five years. Events in localities are related to theological and structural developments in the churches, to the materials for public persuasion that are used nationwide, and to the national communications network of the electronic age. Moreover, many of the Richmond activists are themselves active participants in these national undertakings. Cathy Rowan sits on the Congress of Pax Christi International; Steve Hodges is chair of the Nuclear Weapons Freeze Direct Action Task Force; and Tim Lietzke participated in one of the first Plowshares actions of Direct Disarmament.

In recent years, some observers have begun to recognize the significance of local studies placed under a broader framework. For comments on the paucity of work in this regard, see Chadwick Alger and Saul Mendlovitz, "Grass-Roots Activism in the United States; Global Implications," *Alternatives* 9, no. 4 (Spring 1984): 447–74. Works which contain material relevant to my focus include Harry Boyte's *Community is Possible: Repairing American Roots* (New York: Harper and Row, 1986), especially chap. 3, and his article "The Secular Left: Religion and the American Commonwealth," *Christianity and Crisis* 43, no. 8 (May 1983): 183–86. See also B. Welling Hall, "The Antinuclear Peace Movement: Toward an Evaluation of Effectiveness," *Alternatives* 9, no. 4 (Spring 1984): 475–517. The most relevant book is Paul R. Loeb, *Hope in Hard Times* (Washington, D.C.: Lexington Books, 1986). The two journalists who have been most attentive to these aspects of the movement are William Grieder of *Rolling Stone* and Colman McCarthy of the *Washington Post*.

Chapter 1. Antinuclear Political Theology

1   "The Use of the Atomic Bomb," *Fellowship* 11, no. 12 (September 1945):161.
2   See Alice Kimball Smith, *A Peril and a Hope: The Scientists' Movement in America, 1945–47* (Cambridge: MIT Press, 1970), and Robert Jungk, *Brighter Than a Thousand Suns* (New York: Harcourt Brace Jovanovich, 1958).
3   A. J. Muste, "Pacifism and Perfectionism," in Nat Hentoff, ed., *The Essays of A. J. Muste* (New York: Simon and Schuster, 1967), 308–21.
4   See A. J. Muste, *Not By Might* (New York: Harper and Brothers, 1947; Garland Publishing Company, 1971), 43, and "Of Holy Disobedience," in Hentoff, *Essays of A. J. Muste*, 376–77.
5   See Dorothy Day, *The Long Loneliness* (New York: Harper and Row, 1952; San Francisco: Harper and Row, 1981). See also William Lee Miller, *A Harsh and Dreadful Love: Dorothy Day and the Catholic Worker Movement* (New York: Liveright, 1973), and Mel Piehl, *Breaking Bread: The Catholic Worker and the*

Origin of Catholic Radicalism in America (Philadelphia: Temple University Press, 1982).

6   Muste, *Not By Might*, 21–22.

7   More extensive analyses of pacifist resistance can be found in Lawrence Wittner, *Rebels Against War* (New York: Columbia University Press, 1969); in Charles DeBenedetti, *The Peace Reform in American History* (Bloomington: Indiana University Press, 1980); and in Milton S. Katz and Neil H. Katz, "Pragmatists and Visionaries in the Post World War II American Peace Movment: SANE and CNVA," in Solomon Wank, ed., *Doves and Diplomats: Foreign Offices and Peace Movements in Europe and America in the Twentieth Century* (Westport, Conn.: Greenwood Press, 1981), 265–85.

8   Timothy Smith, *Revivalism and Social Reform: American Protestantism on the Eve of the Civil War* (Baltimore: Johns Hopkins University Press, 1980), 8. See also Ronald Walters, *American Reformers, 1815–1860* (New York: Hill and Wang, 1978); Robert Abzug, *Passionate Liberator: Theodore Dwight Weld and the Dilemma of Reform* (New York: Oxford University Press, 1980); and Lawrence J. Friedman, *Gregarious Saints: Self and Community in American Abolitionism, 1830–1878* (Cambridge: Cambridge University Press, 1982).

9   See Michael Lienesch, "The Paradoxical Politics of the Religious Right," *Soundings* 66, no. 1 (Spring, 1983):70–99, and "Right Wing Religion: Christian Conservatism as a Political Movement," *Political Science Quarterly* 97, no. 3 (Fall 1982):403–25.

10 Jim Wallis, "Biblical Politics," *The Post-American* 3, no. 3 (April 1974): 3. For similar descriptions of the Fall and contemporary politics, see William Stringfellow, *An Ethic for Christians and Other Aliens in a Strange Land* (Waco, Tex.: World Books, 1973); Jim Wallis, *Agenda for Biblical People* (New York: Harper and Row, 1976); and John Howard Yoder, *The Politics of Jesus* (Grand Rapids, Mich.: Eerdmans Publishing Company, 1972).

11 Wallis, "Biblical Politics," 3.

12 Peter Hebblethwaite, "The Popes and Politics: Shifting Patterns in Catholic Social Doctrine," *Daedalus* 3 (Winter 1982):87.

13 Ibid.

14 "Pastoral Constitution of the Church in the Modern World (Gaudium et Spes)" in Walter M. Abbott, ed., *The Documents of Vatican II* (New York: The America Press, 1966), 294.

15 Ibid., 295.

16 One indication of this international concern was the attention paid by Catholic magazines to the struggles of religious communities in Latin America and to the beginnings of U.S. military involvement in Central America.

17 David J. O'Brien, *The Renewal of American Catholicism* (New York: Oxford University Press, 1972), 209.

18 "The Challenge of Peace: God's Promise and Our Response," in Jim Castelli, ed., *The Bishops and the Bomb: Waging Peace in a Nuclear Age* (Garden City, N.Y.: Image Books, 1983), 208.

19   Ibid., 210.
20   Ibid., 232.
21   Ibid., 231.
22   Among the numerous good commentaries on the pastoral, a thoughtful discussion of this point and the inconsistencies regarding the bishops' approval of deterrence can be found in Susan M. Okin, "Taking the Bishops Seriously," *World Politics* 36, no. 4 (July 1984):527–54. I tend to agree with Okin's perspective on the pastoral, though I have a different outlook on the politics involved in its composition and the ultimate implications of its message.
23   "The Challenge of Peace," 235–44.
24   Ibid., 214.
25   Ibid.
26   Ibid., 225.
27   Ibid., 264.
28   *Sojourners* magazine routinely provides a clear and forceful exposition of this perspective. Some of the book-length treatments of contemporary issues which are generally compatible with this viewpoint are Dale Aukerman, *Darkening Valley: A Biblical Perspective on Nuclear War* (New York: Seabury Press, 1981); Ronald J. Sider and Richard K. Taylor, *Nuclear Holocaust and Christian Hope* (Downers Grove, Ill.: Intervarsity Press, 1982); Donald Kraybill, *Facing Nuclear War* (Scottdale, Pa.: Herald Press, 1982); Mary Lou Kownacki, *Peace is Our Calling: Contemporary Monasticism and the Peace Movement* (Erie, Pa.: Bennet Press, 1981); and Jim Wallis, ed., *Waging Peace: A Handbook for the Struggle to Abolish Nuclear Weapons* (San Francisco: Harper and Row, 1982).
29   Aukerman, *Darkening Valley,* 58.
30   Jim Wallis, "A Hope for Revival," *Sojourners* 13, no. 3 (March 1984):3.
31   Tim Lietzke, "The National Religion," *Resistance in Hope* no. 4 (July–August 1984): 4; idem, "Demolishing the Idols: Violence or Non-Violence," ibid., no. 2 (March 1984): 3.
32   Aukerman, *Darkening Valley,* 8.
33   For Bonhoeffer's original essays, see "Costly Grace" and "The Cost of Discipleship" in Dietrich Bonhoeffer, *The Cost of Discipleship* (London: SCM Press, 1959; New York: Macmillan, 1963), 43–87. See also Helen Woodson, "Reflections on Imprisonment," *The Nuclear Resister,* no. 24 (March 1984): 5. Woodson provides an interesting application of these ideas to the current civil disobedience practices of the antinuclear weapons movement, speaking of the need to assume willingly the costs associated with faithful action, even if this requires going to prison.
34   Besides *Sojourners,* there are a number of local and quasi-national newsletters that inform people of resistance activities that have occurred, tell of some that are planned, and publish reflections by activists who have been participants. Three of these are *Harvest of Justice* in Milwaukee, Wisconsin; *Resistance in Hope* in Richmond, Virginia; and *The Nuclear Resister* in Tempe, Arizona.
35   Aukerman, *Darkening Valley,* 202.

36 Ibid., 172–219. For discussions of the theological, historical, and practical justifications of this emphasis on community, see Clark Pinnock, "The Radical Reformation," *The Post-American* no. 5 (Fall 1972): 4–5; Wes Michaelson, "What Nurtures Us," *Sojourners* 7, no. 5 (May 1978): 16–19; and Bob Sabath, "A Community of Communities," *Sojourners* 9, no. 1 (January 1980): 17–19.

37 A good collection of autobiographical sketches of antinuclear activists is contained in Jim Wallis, ed., *Peacemakers: Christian Voices from the New Abolitionist Movement* (New York: Harper and Row, 1983).

Chapter 2. Portraits of Commitment

1 David Brion Davis, *The Problem of Slavery in the Age of Revolution, 1770–1823* (Ithaca, N.Y.: Cornell University Press, 1975), 13.

2 Erik H. Erikson explains his ideas about leadership in *Gandhi's Truth: On the Origins of Militant Nonviolence* (New York: W. W. Norton, 1969); in *Life History and the Historical Moment* (New York: W. W. Norton, 1975); and in *Young Man Luther* (New York: W. W. Norton, 1962). An explanation of how Erikson's concepts of leadership ought to be applied to the democratic struggles of ordinary citizens is contained in Robert D. Holsworth, "The Politics of Development: The Social Psychology of Erik H. Erikson," *The Georgia Review* 36, no. 2 (Summer 1982): 384–403.

3 See Blanche Glassman Hersh, "Am I Not a Woman and a Sister: Abolitionist Beginnings of Nineteenth-Century Feminism," in Lewis Perry and Michael Fellman, eds., *Antislavery Reconsidered: New Perspectives on the Abolitionists* (Baton Rouge: Louisiana State Press, 1979), 263.

4 William Allen, a noted nineteenth-century Quaker philanthropist, maintained that the "pursuits of science, properly conducted, tend to enlarge our views, to banish narrow prejudices, to increase our love of truth and order, and give tone and vigour to the mind." See Davis, *Problem of Slavery*, 245. In the late nineteenth century, Peter Kropotkin explicitly developed a cooperative interpretation of Darwin. As James Joll tells us, "According to Kropotkin, the law of nature was a law of cooperation, of mutual aid rather than of struggle. Within each species mutual support is the rule, and for each example of rivalry, a counterexample of reciprocal assistance can be produced. . . . Again and again in his writings Kropotkin comes back to Darwin's example of the blind pelican whom his comrades kept supplied with fish" (*The Anarchists* [Cambridge: Harvard University Press, 1980], 136).

Chapter 3. Fear and Loving in the Nuclear Age

1 Sheldon Wolin, *democracy* 2, no. 3 (July 1982): 2.

2 Ibid.

3 I do not mean to suggest here that there are no similarities between the two movements. Indeed, to the extent that activists in the peace movement rely on

fear as a motivating influence, their rhetorical strategy mirrors the thinking made popular by the direct-mail moguls of the New Right who frighten their constituents by conjuring visions of an America ruled by Jane Fonda and Ted Kennedy. Yet there remains a clear sense in which their conceptions of politics are distinct from the tactics of mass persuasion so popular today. One might even suggest, as I do in the final chapter, that many religious conversatives are also attempting to build a grass-roots culture that embodies their criticism of contemporary American society in a way that bears some important resemblances to the personalist approach of the antinuclear weapons activists.

4 The success of the campaign was probably best indicated by the fact that in 1985 the freeze organization was courted by district organizers of candidates for the Democratic gubernatorial nomination because of its visibility in turning out its supporters during the presidential years.

5 For a more extensive analysis of civil disobedience and the activists' feelings about it, see chap. 6.

6 There is, of course, ample evidence that this trend is beginning to be reversed during the Reagan years and that the level of trust in government has increased. Nonetheless, cynicism about government had become so pervasive that plenty of distrust remained for political movements to tap.

7 Hal Lindsey and C. C. Carlson, *The Late Great Planet Earth* (New York: Bantam, 1980). Other books by Hal Lindsey include *The Nineteen Eighties Countdown to Armageddon* (New York: Bantam, 1981); *The Rapture: Truth or Consequences* (New York: Bantam, 1983); and *The Terminal Generation* (New York: Bantam, 1977).

8 It is important to note that appealing to the populace's fear of nuclear war is often unconnected to any proposal to reduce its potential or even to a genuine commitment to avoid war. Only a few months before his provocative commercial was aired, Lyndon Johnson was busy pushing the Gulf of Tonkin resolution through Congress so that he might justify his conduct of the Vietnam War, knowing all the while that the so-called North Vietnamese attack remained unproven. In 1980, Jimmy Carter dutifully related to the nation his daughter Amy's worries about the end of the world right after he himself had proposed that the country embark on a massive military buildup. The counterproductivity of relying on fear is described in Paul Boyer's *By the Bomb's Early Light: American Thought and Culture at the Dawn of the Atomic Age* (New York: Pantheon, 1985), 65–75.

9 George Will, *The Pursuit of Happiness and Other Sobering Thoughts* (New York: Harper and Row, 1978), 186.

10 Lawrence Goodwyn, for example, speaks of contemporary American society as characterized by a sophisticated despair in which people recognize the injustice of their condition, but are unable to develop plans of collective action for rectifying it. See his book, *The Populist Moment: A Short History of the Agrarian Revolt* (New York: Oxford University Press, 1976), for an analysis of how a protest movement must develop a culture which enhances and sustains the self-respect of its participants.

Chapter 4. A World Worth Living In

1 Dwight D. Eisenhower, "Toward a Golden Age of Peace," in his *Peace with Justice: Selected Addresses* (New York: Columbia University Press, 1961), 37–38.

2 For a good collection of Eisenhower's statements on peace issues, see Eisenhower, *Peace With Justice: Selected Addresses.*

3 Samuel Huntington has argued that pointing out the discrepancy between the supposed ideals of American life and its actual performance is a characteristic feature of this nation's reform movements. See his *American Politics: The Promise of Disharmony* (Cambridge: Belknap Press, 1981).

4 Ronald Inglehart, *The Silent Revolution: Changing Values and Political Styles Among Western Publics* (Princeton: Princeton University Press, 1977).

5 Wini Breines, *The Great Refusal: Community and Organization in the New Left, 1962–1968* (New York: Praeger, 1982). See also Marshall Berman, "Sympathy for the Devil: Faust, the 60's and the Tragedy of Development," *American Review* 19 (1974): 23–75, and Jim Miller, *Democracy is in the Streets* (New York: Simon and Schuster, 1987).

6 Sennett makes his argument in an almost Nietzschean manner: "What kind of personality will be molded in the expectation, if not the experience, of trust, of warmth, of comfort? How can it be strong enough to move in a world founded on injustice? Is it truly humane to propose to human beings that their personalities 'develop,' that they become 'richer' emotionally to the extent that they learn to trust, to be open, to share, to eschew manipulation of others, to eschew aggressive challenges to social conditions or mining those conditions for personal gain? Is it humane to form soft selves in a hard world? As a result of the immense fear of public life which gripped the last century, there results today a weakened sense of human will. . . . Community is the celebration of the ghetto" (*The Fall of Public Man* [New York: Alfred A. Knopf, 1977], 260, 295).

7 A sampling of the more interesting writing on community includes George Will, *Statecraft as Soulcraft* (New York: Touchstone, 1983); Wendell Berry, *The Unsettling of America: Culture and Agriculture* (New York: Avon Books, 1977); Christopher Lasch, *The Culture of Narcissism: American Life in an Age of Diminishing Expectations* (New York: W. W. Norton, 1979); Theodore Roszak, *Person/Planet: The Creative Disintegration of Industrial Society* (New York: Anchor Press, 1979); Michael Sandel, *Liberalism and the Limits of Justice* (Cambridge: Cambridge University Press, 1982); and Clarke Cochran, *Character, Community and Politics* (University, Ala.: University of Alabama Press, 1982).

8 This attitude toward community is clearly related to the ambivalence about modernity that was mentioned earlier. It is not uncommon for men and women to lament the destruction and fragmentation of communal life even though they themselves struggled mightily to escape the bonds of their original community.

Chapter 5. Bringing the Message Home

1 See Richard Falk and Robert J. Lifton, *Indefensible Weapons* (New York: Basic Books, 1984), especially chaps. 1–3. The most extended argument from this perspective is found in Phyllis La Farge, *The Strangelove Legacy: Children, Parents and Teachers in the Nuclear Age* (New York: Harper and Row, 1987).

2 "Children Not Nearly as Afraid of 'The Bomb' as Popularly 'Believed, Psychiatrist Concludes," *The Chronicle of Higher Education*, 18 July 1984, 5.

3 Richard Barnet, "Teaching Peace," *Teachers College Record* 84, no. 1 (Fall 1982): 30.

4 Robert J. Lifton, "Beyond Psychic Numbing," *Teachers College Record* 84, no. 1 (Fall 1982): 15.

5 Skolnick is quoted in Christopher Lasch, *Haven in a Heartless World: The Family Besieged* (New York: Basic Books, 1979), 187–88.

6 See Shulamith Firestone, *The Dialectic of Sex: The Case for Feminist Revolution* (New York: Bantam, 1971), 189.

7 George Gilder, for instance, describes the process as one by which fathers of low-income families are "cuckolded by the compassionate state" (*Wealth and Poverty* [New York: Bantam, 1981], 139–40).

8 Jean Bethke Elshtain, "Feminism, Family and Community," *Dissent* 29, no. 4 (Fall 1982): 443.

9 Christopher Lasch, *The Culture of Narcissism: American Life in an Age of Diminishing Expectations* (New York: W. W. Norton, 1979), especially chap. 7, "The Socialization of Reproduction and the Collapse of Authority."

10 Elshtain, "Feminism, Family and Community," 447.

11 My argument should not be taken to mean that Elshtain would necessarily concur with all the political conclusions that the Richmond activists draw from their agreement with her on the position of the family in the contemporary United States.

12 A sampling of materials on childhood education, parenting, and the Christian lifestyle includes Kathleen McGinnis and James McGinnis, *Parenting for Peace and Justice* (Maryknoll, N.Y.: Orbis Books, 1981); Michael True, *Homemade Social Justice: Teaching Peace and Justice in the Home* (Chicago: Fides/Claretian Books, 1982); David S. Young, ed., *Study War No More* (Elgin, Ill.: Brethren Press, 1981); and Doris Lee Shettel, *Lifestyle Change for Children* (New York: United Presbyterian Program Agency, 1981).

13. Wendy Northup, "Parenting for Peace and Justice," *Richmond Peace Education Center Newsletter* 3, no. 5 (May 1982): 2.

14. See McGinnis and McGinnis, *Parenting for Peace and Justice,* and Kathleen McGinnis and James McGinnis, *Christian Parenting for Peace and Justice* (Nashville: Discipleship Resources, 1980).

15 The McGinnis' *Christian Parenting for Peace and Justice* includes an outline for a session titled "Celebrating Human Potential: The Roles of Men and Women." The biblical foundation for their ideas is explained in the following way. "All men and women were created in the image of God. We are all called to be as

much as we can be, to be the hands of the Creator here on earth. 'Yahweh called me, before I was born . . .' The call of Yahweh is for us to build a just world. We cannot afford to have men and women shackled in their attempt to build shalom" (52). In *Parenting for Peace and Justice* the McGinnises write that the "life of Jesus points very clearly to the importance of drawing out the fullest potential of each human being. Jesus treated other people, both men and women, as persons of special potential. He treated women in ways that were different from traditional patterns—Mary and Martha, Mary Magdalene, the women caught in adultery, and the Samaritan woman at the well. Jesus came to fulfill the prophecy of Isaiah—'to loose the fetter of injustice, to untie the knots of the yoke, to let the oppressed go free, and release those who have been crushed.' Fighting the oppression of women, lifting the yokes that fell on both men and women because of sexism was a way of liberating them. And to cooperate with Jesus in that same task today is a way of being part of his liberating mission" (77).

Chapter 6. When the Spirit Says Protest

1 A brief history of the various Plowshares actions can be found in Elaine Shurie, "The Plowshares/Direct Disarmament Movement, 1980–1984," *Resistance in Hope* 1, no. 6 (November–December 1984): 3–6.
2 Tim Lietzke, "Action for Disarmament: A Constitutional Right," *Resistance in Hope* 1, no. 4 (July–August 1984): 5.
3 War tax resistance as a witness against nuclear weapons policy has received a good bit of attention within various church communities since 1980. It has either been endorsed or mentioned as a potentially faithful act by a variety of synods, councils, and organizations with a religious affiliation. These include the Lutheran Peace Fellowship, the general synod of the United Church of Christ, the Methodist General Conference, the Unitarian Universalist Association, the New Call to Peacemaking, and the Philadelphia Yearly Meeting of the Religious Society of Friends. Perhaps the most widely publicized statement of an individual cleric was that of Archbishop Raymond G. Hunthausen of Seattle, who declared, "Form 1040 is the place where the Pentagon enters all of our lives and asks unthinking cooperation with the idol of nuclear destruction. I think that the teaching of Jesus tells us to render to a nuclear-armed Caesar what that Caesar deserves: tax resistance." Three publications that regularly report on the strategy of tax resistance, carrying personal testimony, legal advice, and outcomes of cases around the nation are *Center Peace: A News Journal for Alternative Living*, put out by the Center on Law and Pacifism; *Conscience and Military Tax Campaign—U.S. Newsletter*, published by the Conscience and Military Tax Campaign in Bellport, New York; and *God and Caesar: A Forum Newsletter for Sharing Information, Questions and Convictions on War Taxes*, published by the Commission on Home Ministries of the General Conference of the Mennonite Church.

4 Berry phrases the idea in this manner: "What, then, is a complete action? It is, I think, an action which one takes on one's own behalf, which is particular and complex, real not symbolic, which one can both accomplish on one's own and take full responsibility for" ("The Reactor and the Garden," in Wendell Berry, *The Gift of Good Land: Further Essays Cultural and Agricultural* [San Francisco: North Point Press, 1981], 167).

5 The problems of developing a racially integrated coalition in Richmond have existed for a long time. The failure of the Knights of Labor to construct this kind of alliance in Richmond is described in Leon Fink, *Workingmen's Democracy* (Urbana-Champaign: University of Illinois Press, 1983).

6 See Erik H. Erikson, *Gandhi's Truth: On the Origins of Militant Nonviolence* (New York: W. W. Norton, 1969).

7 This tension is also evident, I think, in the theological foundations of antinuclear political activity. While authors frequently point to the sacredness of the family, they also speak about the costly nature of discipleship. In this latter sense, it becomes clear that Jesus can be a stern taskmaster and that the "sword" that he brings can divide members of families from one another.

8 In fact, by 1984 the Internal Revenue Service had decided to crack down on what was a small yet growing number of tax resisters by imposing a five-hundred-dollar fine for a frivolous deduction. Articles in the movement journals which focused on tax resistance now spent much time addressing the question of how to respond if one received such a penalty and how groups could pressure Congress to alter the tax code so that statements of conscience would not be considered frivolous. The outcome of these efforts is currently uncertain, but the situation does reveal the considerable discretionary power of the government in general and the Internal Revenue Service in particular. I should also mention, however, that the IRS had occasionally resorted to heavy-handed reprisals such as the auctioning of homes, which, when publicized, probably work to the benefit of the movement.

9 The New London protest is described in Maurice Isserman's *If I Had a Hammer: The Death of the Old Left and the Birth of the New Left* (New York: Basic Books, 1987), 160–63. For more recent responses, see A. J. Mojtabai, *Blessed Assurance: At Home With the Bomb in Amarillo, Texas* (Boston: Houghton Mifflin, 1986), 95, and Timothy Egan, "Little Sentiment Here to Ban the Bomb," *New York Times,* 14 January 1988, A–14.

Chapter 7. Keeping the Faith

1 Max Weber, *Politics as a Vocation* (Philadelphia: Fortress Press, 1965), 46–55.
2 Randall Kehler, "Message From the National Coordinator," *The Freeze Focus* 4, no. 10 (December 1984): 3.
3 This point has been made with special forcefulness by Erik H. Erikson and Christopher Lasch. Erikson argues that integrity is possessed "only (by) he who in some way has taken care of things and people and has adapted himself

to the triumphs and disappointments of being." He suggests that one feature of integrity "is a sense of comradeship with men and women of distant times and of different pursuits who have created orders and objects and sayings conveying human dignity and love" (*Identity and the Life Cycle* [New York: W. W. Norton, 1980], 104). See also Christopher Lasch, *The Culture of Narcissism: American Life in an Age of Diminishing Expectations* (New York, W. W. Norton, 1979), especially chap. 9, "The Shattered Faith in the Regeneration of Life."

4   Frank Parkin's study of the British Campaign for Nuclear Disarmament in the mid-sixties devotes a chapter to the occupational location of what he labels middle-class radicals. As might be expected, he discovered that most of them worked in services related to what we often call today the helping professions. See Frank Parkin, *Middle-Class Radicalism: The Social Bases of the British Campaign for Nuclear Disarmament* (Manchester, England: University of Manchester Press, 1968). One interesting feature of the activism in Richmond is how it is prompting people who work in the private sector to devote part of their leisure to using their occupational skills in ways that resemble the vocational orientation of the helping professions.

5   Political scientists have been very attentive to the importance of the transition from a founding leader to a successor in the establishment of new states. This concern can be applied more broadly to most new political entities, and certainly is especially critical for local organizations that frequently depend so much on the character and skills of a particular individual to be able to survive and prosper in a period of leadership transition. Indeed, one function of leaders in democratic movements is to help others develop the skills that will make the movements themselves less dependent on any particular persons for their survival.

6   The interviews for this book were completed prior to 1987 and the signing of the INF treaty. President Reagan's decision to pursue this agreement with the Soviet Union and perhaps move to deep cuts in strategic weapons illustrates the difficulty in evaluating the effectiveness of the antinuclear weapons movement nationally. President Reagan, his political supporters, and some journalists believe that the treaty emerged because of the hard line that the president had taken with the Soviet Union and his commitment to pursue the Strategic Defense Initiative. At the same time, participants in the peace movement insist on taking some of the credit for themselves. They argue that they helped to create the climate of opinion that made the public desire a nuclear arms agreement and that led figures such as Nancy Reagan to be concerned with the historical reputation of Ronald Reagan. The problem, of course, is that though concepts such as a "climate of opinion" are valid, it is difficult to say with certainty if, when, and how they influence policy.

7   Some of the literature produced and used by the movement deals explicitly with this theme. See, for instance, Joanna Rogers Macy's discussion of "despair and empowerment work" in *Despair and Personal Power in the Nuclear Age* (Philadelphia: New Society Publishers, 1983).

8   Tim Lietzke, "Letter from Prison," *Resistance in Hope* 1, no. 6 (November–December 1984): 4.

9   People who oppose the infusion of energy into partisan politics tend to believe either that the peace community is best served by remaining officially nonpartisan or that the political order is so corrupt that attempts to reform it from within are inevitable failures.

10 In the 1940s and 1950s, the movement's unity was weakened because of arguments about the advisability of direct action. In 1984, this memory was again evoked when the convention of the National Freeze Campaign split on whether or not to accept the draft report of its Direct Action Task Force.

11 In social science parlance, this dilemma is often described as the problem of uniting "beneficiary constituents" and "conscience constituents." See John D. McCarthy and Mayer N. Zald, "Resource Mobilization and Social Movements: A Partial Theory," *American Journal of Sociology* 82, no. 6 (1977): 1212–41.

12 Excerpt from Denise Levertov, "Candles in Babylon," in her *Candles in Babylon* (New York: New Directions, 1982), p. ix.

Chapter 8. Personalist Politics and Political Reform

1   Wendell Berry, *The Unsettling of America: Culture and Agriculture* (New York: Avon Books, 1977), 7.

2   Gary Snyder, "Buddhism and the Coming Revolution," in *Earth Household* (San Francisco: New Directions, 1969), 91.

3   Gary Snyder, "Four Changes," in *Turtle Island* (San Francisco: New Directions, 1974), 101.

4   For a good summary of work on this subject, see Virginia Held, "Feminism and Epistemology: Recent Work on the Connection between Gender and Knowledge," *Philosophy and Public Affairs* 14, no. 3 (Summer 1985): 296–307.

5   Jean Bethke Elshtain, *Public Man, Private Woman: Women in Social and Political Thought* (Princeton: Princeton University Press, 1981), 335–36.

6   James Foley, "The Idea Base of the Protest Movement," in James E. Dougherty and Robert L. Pfaltzgraff, Jr., eds., *Shattering Europe's Defense Consensus* (Washington, D.C.: Pergamon-Brassey, 1985), 23.

7   James Davison Hunter, "The New Class and the Young Evangelists," *Review of Religious Research* 22, no. 10 (December 1980): 166.

8   Kristin Luker, *Abortion and the Politics of Motherhood* (Berkeley: University of California Press, 1984), 141.

9   Carol Flake, *Redemptorama: Culture, Politics and the New Evangelicalism* (New York: Penguin Books, 1984), 84.

10 Ibid.

11 Tim Luke, "From Fundamentalism to Televangelism." Paper presented at the American Political Science Association Annual Meetings, 1985.

12 In fact, scholars who examine what they label the "new social movements" speak of this development as a phenomenon in evidence throughout the indus-

trial democracies in the 1970s and 1980s. They typically point to these movements as responses to the changing nature of industrial capitalism, to the
danger posed to human life by environmental deterioration, and to the threat
of nuclear war posed by the continuation of the bloc system in international
relations. For a thoughtful analysis and critique of these movements, see Carl
Boggs, *Social Movements and Political Power* (Philadelphia: Temple University
Press, 1986). Although Boggs does not focus on antinuclear weapons politics
in the United States or mention its connection with religious belief, his argument about the strategic limitations of neopopulism is relevant to the viewpoint persented here.

Selected Bibliography

Abbot, Walter M., ed. *The Documents of Vatican II*. New York: America Press, 1966.

Abzug, Robert. *Passionate Liberator: Theodore Dwight Weld and the Dilemma of Reform*. New York: Oxford University Press, 1980.

Alger, Chadwick, and Mendlovitz, Saul. "Grass-roots Activism in the United States: Global Implications." *Alternatives* 9, no. 4 (Spring 1984): 447–74.

Aukerman, Dale. *Darkening Valley: A Biblical Perspective on Nuclear War*. New York: Seabury Press, 1981.

Berry, Wendell. *The Gift of Good Land: Further Essays Cultural and Agricultural*. San Francisco: North Point Press, 1981.

Berry, Wendell. *The Unsettling of America: Culture and Agriculture*. New York: Avon Books, 1977.

Bonhoeffer, Dietrich. *The Cost of Discipleship*. London: SCM Press, 1959; New York: Macmillan, 1963.

Boyer, Paul. *By the Bomb's Early Light: American Thought and Culture at the Dawn of the Atomic Age*. New York: Pantheon, 1985.

Boyte, Harry. *Community is Possible: Repairing America's Roots*. New York: Harper and Row, 1986.

Boyte, Harry. "The Secular Left: Religion and the American Commonwealth." *Christianity and Crisis* 43, no. 8 (May 1983): 183–86.

Castelli, Jim, ed. *The Bishops and the Bomb: Waging Peace in a Nuclear Age*. Garden City, N.Y.: Image Books, 1983.

Cochran, Clarke. *Character, Community and Politics*. University, Ala.: University of Alabama Press, 1982.

Davis, David Brion. *The Problem of Slavery in the Age of Revolution, 1770–1823*. Ithaca, N.Y.: Cornell University Press, 1975.

Day, Dorothy. *The Long Loneliness*. New York: Harper and Row, 1952; San Francisco: Harper and Row, 1981.

DeBenedetti, Charles. *The Peace Reform in American History*. Bloomington: Indiana University Press, 1980.

Egan, Timothy. "Little Sentiment Here to Ban the Bomb." *New York Times,* 14 January 1988, A–14.

Eisenhower, Dwight D. *Peace with Justice: Selected Addresses.* New York: Columbia University Press, 1961.

Elshtain, Jean Bethke. "Feminism, Family and Community." *Dissent* 29, no. 4 (Fall 1982): 442–49.

Erikson, Erik H. *Gandhi's Truth: On the Origins of Militant Nonviolence.* New York: W. W. Norton, 1969.

Erikson, Erik H. *Life History and the Historical Moment.* New York: W. W. Norton, 1975.

Erikson, Erik H. *Young Man Luther.* New York: W. W. Norton, 1962.

Falk, Richard, and Robert S. Lifton. *Indefensible Weapons.* New York: Basic Books, 1984.

Firestone, Shulamith. *The Dialectic of Sex: The Case for Feminist Revolution.* New York: Bantam, 1971.

Friedman, Lawrence J. *Gregarious Saints: Self and Community in American Abolitionism, 1830–1878.* Cambridge: Cambridge University Press, 1982.

Gilder, George. *Wealth and Poverty.* New York: Bantam, 1981.

Goodwyn, Lawrence. *The Populist Movement: A Short History of the Agrarian Revolt.* New York: Oxford University Press, 1976.

Hall, B. Welling. "The Antinuclear Peace Movement: Toward an Evaluation of Effectiveness." *Alternatives* 9, no. 4 (Spring 1984): 475–517.

Holsworth, Robert D. "The Politics of Development: The Social Psychology of Erik H. Erikson." *The Georgia Review* 36, no. 2 (Summer 1982): 384–403.

Huntington, Samuel. *American Politics: The Promise of Disharmony.* Cambridge: Belknap Press, 1981.

Isserman, Maurice. *If I Had a Hammer: The Death of the Old Left and the Birth of the New Left.* New York: Basic Books, 1987.

Jenkins, J. Craig. *The Politics of Insurgency: The Farm Worker Movement in the 1960's.* New York: Columbia University Press, 1985.

Joll, James. *The Anarchists.* Cambridge: Harvard University Press, 1980.

Jungk, Robert. *Brighter Than a Thousand Suns.* New York: Harcourt Brace Jovanovich, 1958.

Katz, Milton S. *Ban the Bomb.* Westport, Conn.: Greenwood Press, 1986.

Katz, Milton S., and Neil H. Katz. "Pragmatists and Visionaries in the Post World War II American Peace Movement: SANE and CNVA." In *Doves and Diplomats: Foreign Offices and Peace Movements in Europe and America in the Twentieth Century,* edited by Solomon Wank, 265–85. Westport, Conn.: Greenwood Press, 1981.

Kehler, Randall. "Message From the National Coordinator." *The Freeze Focus* 4, no. 10 (December 1984): 3.

Kennan, George. *The Nuclear Delusion: Soviet-American Relations in the Atomic Age.* New York: Pantheon Books, 1983.

Kilpatrick, James J. "But the Right Should Speak Out." *The Philadelphia Inquirer,* 22 March 1982, 9.

Klatch, Rebecca E. *Women of the New Right*. Philadelphia: Temple University Press, 1987.

Kownacki, Mary Lou. *Peace is Our Calling: Contemporary Monasticism and the Peace Movement*. Erie, Pa.: Bennet Press, 1981.

Kraybill, Donald. *Facing Nuclear War*. Scottdale, Pa: Herald Press, 1982.

Lasch, Christopher. *The Culture of Narcissism: American Life in an Age of Diminishing Expectations*. New York: W. W. Norton, 1979.

Lasch, Christopher. *Haven in a Heartless World: The Family Besieged*. New York: Basic Books, 1979.

Lens, Sidney. *The Day Before Doomsday*. New York: Doubleday, 1977.

Lienesch, Michael. "The Paradoxical Politics of the Religious Right." *Soundings* 66, no. 1 (Spring 1983): 70–99.

Lienesch, Michael. "Right Wing Religion: Christian Conservatism as a Political Movement." *Political Science Quarterly* 97, no. 3 (Fall 1982): 403–25.

Lietzke, Tim. "The National Religion." *Resistance in Hope* 1, no. 4 (July–August 1984): 4–5.

Lindsey, Hal. *The Nineteen Eighties Countdown to Armageddon*. New York: Bantam, 1981.

Lindsey, Hal. *The Rapture: Truth or Consequences*. New York: Bantam, 1983.

Lindsey, Hal. *The Terminal Generation*. New York: Bantam, 1977.

Lindsey, Hal, and C. C. Carlson. *The Late Great Planet Earth*. New York: Bantam, 1980.

Loeb, Paul R. *Hope in Hard Times*. Washington, D.C.: Lexington Books, 1986.

Macy, Joanna Rogers. *Despair and Personal Power in the Nuclear Age*. Philadelphia: New Society Publishers, 1983.

McCarthy, John D., and Mayer N. Zald. "Resource Mobilization and Social Movements: A Partial Theory." *American Journal of Sociology* 82, no. 6 (1977): 1212–41.

McGinnis, Kathleen, and James McGinnis. *Christian Parenting for Peace and Justice*. Nashville: Discipleship Resources, 1980.

McGinnis, Kathleen, and James McGinnis. *Parenting for Peace and Justice*. Maryknoll, N.Y.: Orbis Books, 1981.

Miller, William Lee. *A Harsh and Dreadful Love: Dorothy Day and the Catholic Worker Movement*. New York: Liveright, 1973.

Mojtabai, A. J. *Blessed Assurance: At Home with the Bomb in Amarillo, Texas*. Boston: Houghton Mifflin, 1986.

Muste, A. J. *Not By Might*. New York: Harper and Brothers, 1947; Garland Publishing, 1971.

Muste, A. J. "Of Holy Disobedience." In *The Essays of A. J. Muste,* edited by Nat Hentoff, 355–77. New York: Simon and Schuster, 1967.

Muste, A. J. "Pacifism and Perfectionism." In *The Essays of A. J. Muste,* edited by Nat Hentoff, 308–21. New York: Simon and Schuster, 1967.

O'Brien, David J. *The Renewal of American Catholicism*. New York: Oxford University Press, 1972.

Oki, Susan M. "Taking the Bishops Seriously." *World Politics* 36, no. 4 (July 1984): 527–54.

Parkin, Frank. *Middle-Class Radicalism: The Social Bases of the British Campaign for Nuclear Disarmament.* Manchester, England: University of Manchester Press, 1968.

Peshkin, Alan. *God's Choice.* Chicago: University of Chicago Press, 1986.

Piehl, Mel. *Breaking Bread: The Catholic Worker and the Origin of Catholic Radicalism in America.* Philadelphia: Temple University Press, 1982.

Pinnock, Clark. "The Radical Reformation." *The Post-American* 1, no. 5 (Fall 1972): 4–5.

Roszak, Theodore. *Person/Planet: The Creative Disintegration of Industrial Society.* New York: Anchor Press, 1979.

Sandel, Michael. *Liberalism and the Limits of Justice.* Cambridge: Cambridge University Press, 1982.

Sennett, Richard. *The Fall of Public Man.* New York: Alfred A. Knopf, 1977.

Shettel, Doris Lee. *Lifestyle Change for Children.* New York: United Presbyterian Program Agency, 1981.

Shurie, Elaine. "The Plowshares/Direct Disarmament Movement, 1980–84." *Resistance in Hope* 1, no. 6 (November–December 1984): 3–6.

Sider, Ronald J., and Richard K. Taylor. *Nuclear Holocaust and Christian Hope.* Downers Grove, Ill.: Intervarsity Press, 1982.

Smith, Alice Kimball. *A Peril and a Hope: The Scientists' Movement in America, 1945–47.* Cambridge: MIT Press, 1970.

Smith, Timothy. *Revivalism and Social Reform: American Protestantism on the Eve of the Civil War.* Baltimore: Johns Hopkins University Press, 1980.

Stein, Arthur S. *Seeds of the Seventies: Values, Work and Commitment in Post-Vietnam America.* Hanover: University Press of New England, 1985.

Stringfellow, William. *An Ethic for Christians and Other Aliens in a Strange Land.* Waco, Tex.: World Books, 1973.

True, Michael. *Homemade Social Justice: Teaching Peace and Justice in the Home.* Chicago: Fides/Claretian Books, 1982.

Wallis, Jim. *Agenda for Biblical People.* New York: Harper and Row, 1976.

Wallis, Jim. "A Hope for Revival." *Sojourners* 13, no. 3 (March 1984): 3.

Wallis, Jim. "Biblical Politics." *The Post American* 3, no. 3 (April 1974): 3.

Wallis, Jim, ed. *Peacemakers: Christian Voices from the New Abolitionist Movement.* New York: Harper and Row, 1983.

Wallis, Jim, ed. *Waging Peace: A Handbook for the Struggle to Abolish Nuclear Weapons.* San Francisco: Harper and Row, 1982.

Walters, Ronald. *American Reformers, 1815–1860.* New York: Hill and Wang, 1978.

Will, George. *The Pursuit of Happiness and Other Sobering Thoughts.* New York: Harper and Row, 1978.

Will, George. *Statecraft as Soulcraft.* New York: Touchstone, 1983.

Wittner, Lawrence. *Rebels Against War.* New York: Columbia University Press, 1969.

Yoder, John Howard. *The Politics of Jesus.* Grand Rapids, Mich.: Eerdmans Publishing, 1972.

Young, David S., ed. *Study War No More.* Elgin, Ill.: Brethren Press, 1981.

Index